# HYPNOTISM TODAY

BY **LESLIE M. LECRON, B.A.**
CONSULTING PSYCHOLOGIST AND PSYCHOTHERAPIST
AND
**JEAN BORDEAUX, B.A., M.A., Ph.D.**
CONSULTING PSYCHOLOGIST AND PSYCHOTHERAPIST

FOREWORD BY
MILTON H. ERICKSON, M.D.
DIRECTOR OF PSYCHIATRIC RESEARCH, WAYNE COUNTY HOSPITAL, ELOISE, MICHIGAN

**Published by**
Melvin Powers
WILSHIRE BOOK COMPANY
12015 Sherman Road
No. Hollywood, California 91605
*Telephone: (213) 875-1711 / 983-1105*

Wilshire Book Company edition
is published by special arrangement
with Grune & Stratton, Inc., N.Y.

*Printed by*

HAL LEIGHTON PRINTING COMPANY
P.O. Box 3952
North Hollywood, California 91605
Telephone: (213) 983-1105

Library of Congress Catalog Card No. MED 47-1654

Copyright 1947
by
LESLIE M. LeCRON
and
JEAN BORDEAUX

Printed in the United States of America

ISBN 0-87980-081-X

SINCE ITS earliest use by primitive people, hypnosis has been endowed by both friend and foe with supernatural attributes, magical values and miraculous significances that still cling tenaciously and deter the development of a general recognition of its scientific validity. The remarkable complexity of hypnosis as a psychological manifestation and the striking, even startling, character of its phenomena have made easy the acceptance of half-truths, misconceptions, and the promotion of wishful thinking instead of careful, laborious, scientific study. Additionally, and even more pertinently in explanation of the general attitude toward it, hypnosis constitutes a seriously disturbing challenge to any complacency and smug self-satisfaction in the continuance of accepted and traditional understandings of human behavior. This threat to comfortable contentment with time-established beliefs and explanations of human behavior arouses the same antagonisms and defensive attitudes that invariably oppose and delay and cause the neglect of every new far-reaching development in science, even those developments far removed from so sensitive a problem as that of the human personality, its capacities, potentialities, and the meaningfulness of its expressions. Hence, any adequate exposition or demonstration of hypnosis, its applications and values, makes disturbingly apparent for everyone, however well trained, the need to realize that present-day conceptions of what constitutes human behavior and what can be encompassed and achieved need revision and extension, and, above all, a recognition that present knowledge is most inadequate and that there is much to be learned that cannot be explained or even understood in terms of current knowledge.

As a consequence of these attitudes and reactions, hypnosis is peculiarly susceptible to unwarranted condemnation, misrepresentation, distortion, abuse and outright exploitation on the one hand and to overenthusiastic, uncritical support and uncontrolled wishful thinking on the other.

One need review only briefly the history of hypnosis to realize the extent of the condemnation, exploitation, wishful thinking and misrepresentation and the poverty of really sound, comprehensive, scientifically controlled studies and expositions that have marked the development of hypnosis since the days of Mesmer. In the literature published within the last ten years in scientific journals by persons otherwise of good repute, one can find declarations that hypnosis is a transient fraudulent form of behavior without meaning or validity, the emphatic assertion that a few moments of hypnosis can transform a decent citizen into a criminal, and the well-intentioned declaration that simple hypnotic suggestions can cure some chronic organic diseases for which medicine knows no cure.

In many instances, books on hypnosis written for the general public are a hodge-podge of ignorance, misconceptions, partial truths and assertions based on tradition and not on knowledge. Too often, they constitute a curious selection of scientific facts and the wares of the charlatan, compounded in the comfort of an armchair, free from the laborious toil of actual adequate personal endeavor and scientific study, and motivated by a desire for self-aggrandizement by becoming an author. As a consequence, hypnosis as a field of scientific inquiry is brought into disrepute and neglect, and oversight becomes its lot.

One other item needs to be mentioned before concluding this foreword. At the annual meeting of the American Psychiatric Association in Chicago, May, 1946, various outstanding members of the association expressed emphatically their strong conviction that hypnosis as a field of scientific inquiry and as a method of psychotherapy should be promoted and developed by everybody concerned with the science of human behavior. Secondly, they declared with equal emphasis the importance of recognizing and accepting and utilizing fully in programs of psychotherapy, rehabilitation and scientific inquiry into the nature of personality disorders the special skills, training and knowledge of the psychologist.

The authors of this book are two psychologists, earnestly and honestly interested in furthering a scientific knowledge of hypnosis. Their purpose is to present to the lay and professional public simply and adequately the available information on hypnosis and to portray their own use of hypnosis as a psychotherapeutic and investigative procedure as demonstrated by their own experience under medical supervision.

They have selected their material well, their exposition of it is excellent, and their presentation of their own studies is unassuming and straightforward.

This book is entirely worthy of full attention and study by everyone, and those who have worked extensively in hypnosis will feel grateful to the authors for offering a book to the public that presents hypnosis as a worthy, serious field of scientific endeavor.

MILTON H. ERICKSON

ELOISE, MICHIGAN

# CONTENTS

ALTHOUGH THE LITERATURE on hypnotism is extensive, most of the more comprehensive books on the subject were written a number of years ago, between 1890 and 1920. Because of increasing interest in the science, we believe the more modern aspects should be recorded, and this volume is offered to satisfy a growing popular demand for up-to-date knowledge of this fascinating science. It is intended to serve also as a text for students, psychologists, psychotherapists and physicians who seek detailed information on the scientific and therapeutic phases. With this in mind we have tried to keep the material in popular style but have included the results of the more important experimental work carried out in psychological laboratories during recent years.

The great practical value of hypnotism lies in the experimental study of human behavior and in the therapeutic field, particularly in psychotherapy, and we believe we have brought out in detail its possibilities and scope, both the old and the newer methods being thoroughly discussed.

The older literature on hypnotism was written mostly by physicians who were engaged in the general practice of medicine; more recently the authors have been psychologists from universities writing from the educational viewpoint and psychiatrists who have both medical and psychological training. The authors of this book are consulting psychologists engaged professionally in daily psychotherapeutic work. We have frequently lectured and demonstrated, usually before groups of physicians, and therefore are familiar with stage hypnotism and its methods. Our combined experience covers a period of many years. "Tricks of the trade" which are detailed herein are offered because they should prove of value to the student, and even to the educator or psychotherapist experienced in hypnotism. Heretofore, professional consultants have not invaded the literary field, and our approach is essentially from the consultant's viewpoint.

We proffer the results of various experiments, advance many new ideas, and suggest certain factors and phenomena which need further investigation, hoping other psychologists with laboratory facilities may wish to experiment along the lines indicated—for example, the induction of hypnosis.

Most known hypnotic phenomena were discovered before the turn of the present century and here we can add but little. The older literature makes many references to applications which have been ignored or neglected by modern practitioners and educators, and we point out some which deserve study and consideration. While the value of hypnosis in the treatment of functional disorders is now recognized, almost no attention has been paid recently to its possible uses in alleviating organic disease or to the new field of psychosomatic medicine. Skeptical by training and his scientific background, the physician is likely to dismiss such possibilities as absurd. However, there is considerable evidence to prove that organic diseases of many kinds may be benefited or relieved by means of suggestion. Christian Science, which is most unscientific, points to thousands of such cases remedied by faith and suggestion.

In recent years, some popular type books and a multitude of magazine articles have served greatly to debunk and remove the mysticism from hypnotism. The recent war has brought into prominence the advantageous use of hypnotic methods in the treatment of war neurosis—battle fatigue. As a result, the public is losing much of its misapprehension and fear of hypnotism and a great revival of interest is apparent, dormant previously for a quarter of a century. We wish to demonstrate here that hypnotism is a true branch of psychological science, and to aid in removing some of the last lingering traces of the esoteric which still cling to it.

# CHAPTER I

# Hypnotism Today

TO MOST PEOPLE the word "hypnotism" conveys a suggestion of the supernatural. It is tinged with occultism, shading towards necromancy, the mysterious and mystical. The mental image of a "hypnotist" brings visions of the fictional Svengali or the real-life Rasputin—tall, dark, gaunt and sinister, with glittering, piercing eye. The scientist, the educator, the business executive, the professional man, almost any well-educated intelligent person asked to become a hypnotic subject, shows alarm and hastily declines, fearful of damage to his mind or of finding himself in the power of the hypnotist.

If questioned, he probably would freely admit a complete lack of knowledge of the subject. Perhaps he has seen a stage performance where volunteers were summoned from the audience, placed in a hypnotic state and caused to perform various amusing antics. While under the hypnotist's control, strange hallucinations were created in the minds of these subjects who were made to play the clown before the audience. Such a performance may be interesting and diverting but it serves no other purpose. It probably was partly faked, partly genuine. The observer comes away with a feeling of having witnessed weird phenomena but with no inclination for closer personal experience with such a mysterious power. Strangely enough, there are always volunteers who go forward. Some are curious and some seek the spotlight, while others go to the stage in actual fear under a psychological compulsion, these last frequently making excellent subjects for hypnosis.

Certainly such shows have been largely responsible for the past and present bad reputation under which hypnotism has labored with the American public. Reflecting public opinion, the negative attitude of the medical profession also has contributed to this disfavor. Unfortunately, a science offering much of practical value has thereby been completely neglected. Reputable physicians in general practice, regardless of their personal opinions, today dare not use hypnotism lest they be charged with charlatanism or quackery, and, similarly, it is not practiced to any extent in state or national institutions through fear of adverse public opinion. For these reasons, many psychiatrists who recognize its advantages have hesitated to adopt it. Few medical schools even mention the subject in their courses of study, and most doctors have as little knowledge of the merits or possibilities of hypnotism as has the general public, viewing it with the same skepticism and apprehension.

But there are indications that the science is gaining recognition as a healing agent, at least for the lesser mental disturbances, since the recent war led psychiatrists in the armed services to employ hypnosis as a short-cut in overcoming battle fatigue, the former "shell shock" now more properly termed war neurosis. This occurred also during the first World War when other methods failed dismally in alleviating this condition. Hypnotism was adopted then by many psychiatrists and psychologists in war service, such as McDougall, Rivers, William Brown, Hadfield, and others, for the treatment of such mental cases. Its use might have won even greater general acceptance had not Freud and his disciples discouraged it, claiming that their new method of psychoanalysis was more suitable. Owing to the long time required for complete psychoanalysis, often running into hundreds of hours, this form of psychotherapy has been found quite impractical in treating the large numbers afflicted with war and other neuroses.

Meanwhile hypnotism continued in disfavor among psychiatrists and psychotherapists generally, although outstanding development work was performed by such courageous scientists as M. H. Erickson and his associates and students at Worcester State Hospital and later at Wayne County General Hospital at Eloise, Michigan. Extensive experiments were conducted at both these institutions and at the Medical School of Wayne University, where the application of hypnosis to psychotherapy is taught by Erickson in his classes in psychiatry. Although not published in book form, papers written by him for technical journals exceed in volume those of any other research worker and have contributed greatly to our knowledge of hypnotism, particularly as to advanced technique. Erickson's and other reports have made psychiatrists aware of the potential value of hypnotism, and many service psychiatrists (including some of Erickson's students) during World War II turned to its use as a short-cut in psychotherapy. Numerous popular magazine articles recited their results, bringing a better picture of hypnosis to many readers.

In 1939 the Menninger Clinic (psychiatric) at Topeka, Kansas, became interested in hypnotism. As a result, medical foundations granted the clinic funds now being devoted to extensive study of hypnotism in its application to functional cases. Reports of the excellent results have been published.[1]

Today, many patients ask their physicians if it is advisable to seek hypnotic aid for the treatment of nervous and mental conditions. The physicians also have read some of the popular or technical articles and many are now willing to and do recommend it. The practice of the writers comes entirely from medical men who prescribe hypnotherapy for patients suffering from functional ailments.

The early practitioners of hypnotism were mostly physicians, and much of our knowledge was derived from their study and experiences. Invariably those who became proficient in the practical application of the science were converted into its ardent devotees, even if they were thereby discredited, as sometimes happened. Others, like Freud, never gained a comprehensive understanding of the methodology of hypnosis and gave it up after failing to obtain results which could have been theirs with more knowledge of the subject. Freud [2] himself admitted in 1919 that if psychotherapy were ever to become widely available to the public, a return to hypnotism as a short-cut would be necessary, thereby proving to be an excellent prophet.

Liebeault, Bernheim, Forel, Braid, Moll, Wetterstrand, Bramwell, Pitzer and a host of others published books describing their successes. Hundreds of cures of various disorders and conditions were narrated and, it must be remembered, their patients usually came for treatment only as a last resort, in despair, given up as incurable by more orthodox medical men. These diseases were not only functional but organic as well, for the hypnotic practitioners took all comers. This fact has been completely overlooked in the present revival of interest. The case histories of these physicians tell of conditions almost miraculously alleviated, more remarkable because at that time so little was known of neuroses, phobias, obsessions, hysteria, and like conditions, nor was there any understanding of their causes. Failures, too, were admitted and noted by the early practitioners, for hypnosis is far from a cure-all. But despite the preponderant beneficial results, the new science earned little recognition as a therapeutic agent.

In Europe the situation today differs somewhat from that

in America. There, hypnotism has not received general acceptance but it is not in disrepute. Prior to World War II many physicians practiced it in the large cities of Russia, Germany and Austria. Even in smaller communities physicians could often be found who utilized hypnotherapy.

Much laboratory investigation of hypnotic phenomena has been carried out by educational psychologists in our universities and colleges, where there are proper equipment and facilities to carry on experiments. Some interested educators have been greatly handicapped because school authorities sometimes forbid experimentation, fearing parents might become alarmed at the exposure of their offspring to supposed occultism. Others have neglected hypnotism because of more interest in other branches of psychology.

Men like Brown, Cutten, McDougall, Prince, James, and P. C. Young, pioneers in psychology, performed many hypnotic experiments. Their students carried on the work of scientific study and investigation and became leaders in the field, Hull, Wells, Estabrooks, Rowland, Winn and many others of the present generation thus augmenting our knowledge. Among medical psychologists, leaders in hypnotic experiment today are Erickson, Wolberg, Kubie and Gill.

Most consultants who practice hypnotherapy, either psychologists or psychiatrists, lack time and facilities for experimental work and cannot use their paying clients for research. But every consultant does experiment in order to increase his knowledge and improve his technique.

The practicing hypnotic consultant frequently is amused by some of the technical articles appearing in psychological journals. Capable men of high repute write, and these magazines publish, papers on hypnotism and hypnotic experiment which display a grave lack of understanding of the subject, in many instances showing no indication of skill or technique.

The most comprehensive volume on experimental hypnosis in its scientific aspect is that written by Clark Hull of Yale [3] entitled *Hypnosis and Suggestibility*, but the methods described therein prove the operators veritable tyros, earnest yet inept investigators. Some were associates of Hull but most were graduate or undergraduate students working under his guidance. Had Hull's assistants been more experienced or had they been aided by a professional, many of the results and conclusions reported undoubtedly would have been completely reversed, as was pointed out by W. R. Wells.[4] Hull's book is of most value in showing the proper methods of conducting scientific laboratory experimentation in hypnosis and in indicating areas for investigation and the need for study, rather than for the conclusions it contains.

No slight is intended here to any educational psychologist. Some are highly proficient hypnotists. But an educator's approach differs entirely in viewpoint and interest from that of a professional consultant. The educator is concerned only with the phenomena produced; the practitioner is interested mainly from the practical and therapeutic standpoint. To the educator, hypnotism is merely a branch of psychology; it is the essential one to the consultant. The latter has far more opportunity, generally speaking, to gain a thorough knowledge of hypnosis by reason of daily practice, thus obtaining more proficiency than can ordinarily be acquired by university psychologists even though the latter may be well informed on theory. The consultant must show results to receive payment for his services and to build a reputation. By necessity he has to learn the laws and proper application of suggestion. Here the educator is weakest. Each category can and should learn from the other. In future experiments the educator ought to seek the cooperation of a reputable professional, and most would be eager to aid in experimental work.

Psychology is a science in which experimentation is difficult compared to fields such as physics or chemistry where the same formula always produces the same result. The science is still in its infancy. Actually we know little as to the workings of the conscious mind and the effects of emotions on the body, even less about the phase of the mind often termed the "subconscious" whose importance was unrecognized until Freud reported his studies of neuroses. Psychology deals with intangibles, hence its theories can seldom be definitely proved. This is particularly true of hypnotism where so much depends on the operator and even more on the subject and his personality, making accurate observation difficult no matter how close the control or how perfect the conditions.

Estabrooks [5] mentioned this in his book *Hypnotism*. To quote him, "The psychologist, in his determination to get standard conditions, may, in some cases, completely defeat his own ends and become a very unscientific scientist. Hypnotism supplies us with our most glaring examples and, for this reason, hypnotism is probably the most difficult of all subjects in psychology to investigate. The personality of the operator is of such great importance."

He goes on to give the example of highly eminent men in the field—Erickson [6] on the one hand, W. R. Wells, L. W. Rowland [7] and still others on the other hand—who completely disagree in their findings after testing the possibility of using hypnotism to cause the committing of criminal, harmful or antisocial acts. Wells and Rowland believe they show it can be done; Erickson demonstrates exactly the opposite. The Erickson experiments were very conclusive, but those who made opposite findings would never admit it.

There are just as many conflicting opinions on other types of hypnotic phenomena, among them the production of skin blisters, stigmata and the like; whether or not clairvoyance, telepathy and other extrasensory matters are possible under hypnosis; as to the practicability of hypnotizing a person against his will; the question of hypersensitivity; and other factors which have been debated pro and con with attempts by various advocates to prove their contentions. In all these, under scientifically controlled conditions where one experimenter secures positive results, a wrong technique on the part of another operator is indicated if he fails to get the same results; or perhaps he may have consciously or unconsciously communicated his personal views to the subject, or possibly he has worked under conditions which prevented attainment of the desired results. It must be remembered that a good subject invariably tries to do whatever is desired or expected of him by the operator. The subject under hypnosis displays uncanny ability to guess what is desired and responds to the most minimal cues even when no direct suggestion is given as to how he is supposed to act. This may be the basis for the oft-heard assertion that telepathy is present in certain cases. In tests, however, the operator too often seeks to substantiate his own theory or to disprove the findings of someone else. No matter how well concealed, his attitude or ideas are communicated to the subject, who promptly reacts as expected or desired by the operator.

Furthermore, a great deal depends on the subject himself. One who enters the deepest hypnosis may reject suggestions for some reason, often to the embarrassment of the hypnotist. In one of our experiments made to show the phenomenon of body temperature increase under hypnotic suggestion, a subject was used who had repeatedly been found amenable to all suggestions. A positive reaction was obtained experimentally and a few days later an attempt was made to duplicate the test with the same subject for the edification of a skeptical medical friend. For reasons unknown, the result was completely negative this time, no matter what suggestion was given. The previous test had been conducted before several witnesses with the thermometer carefully checked, temperatures taken by a registered nurse and the readings verified by all present. The body temperature had gone up two degrees within a short time, just as had been suggested. In the second attempt there was no change at all, even though the subject showed all the same signs of discomfort and fever. The explanation may lie in the point of view of the subject— "Why go to all the trouble necessary to elevate the temperature when it is so much easier merely to exhibit the outward signs?"

Bordeaux has a subject who is of moody temperament and fluctuates in receptivity to hypnotic suggestions. At intermittent intervals this subject enters the deepest state within only a few minutes. At other times hypnosis cannot be attained at all after two or three hours of persistent effort. The personality pattern of subjects is too often ignored by the operator, but it greatly affects responses.

Another great difficulty in hypnotic investigations is in obtaining good subjects. It is not enough to use those who reach only the lighter stages of hypnosis. For most tests they must be somnambulists able to enter the deep state, and time and patience are required to develop somnambulism. Experiments are inconclusive unless many subjects are tested, and even psychologists connected with large universities find it difficult to locate numerous suitable and willing subjects.

Although we have advanced in our knowledge of hypnotism in recent years, much remains to be observed and scientifically proved. As is pointed out herein, a great amount of investigation is still sorely needed.

# CHAPTER II

# The Background of Hypnotism

EVER SINCE MANKIND settled into tribal communities, hypnotism has played a part in human life. Practiced by witch doctors, medicine men, shamans, priests and religious leaders, though never admittedly as hypnotism, its phenomena were often described as miracles performed by the gods. Today it is seen in the rituals of many of the Oriental, African, Polynesian, American Indian and other races. The Hindu fakir on a bed of nails and South Pacific fire dancers probably make use of hypnotic anaesthesia to pain, as perhaps was done also by the early Christian martyrs. In ancient Egypt there were "sleep temples," and a papyrus of three thousand years ago sets forth the procedure for hypnosis much as it is performed today. In Greece, pilgrimages were regularly made to Epidaurus, where the temple of Aesculapius, God of Medicine, was located, and there were other temples devoted to healing. Here the sick were put into a hypnotic trance by priests and through suggestion saw visions of the gods, with resulting cure. The Grecian oracles and the sibyls probably prophesied while in self-induced hypnotic trance, as is probably the case with some modern spiritualistic mediums.

The priests of most ancient races, particularly in the Orient, were familiar with hypnotism. It is described in some of the mantras of India written in ancient Sanskrit and undoubtedly has reached its highest development among the Indian yogis of today, whose methods merit careful study. The Persian Magi, the Mongols, Tibetans and the Chinese all had knowledge of hypnosis. A detailed description of it is given in the *Kalevala,* great epic poem of the Finns.[8]

The more modern history of the science is usually said to begin with Franz Anton Mesmer,[9] a Viennese physician of the late eighteenth and early nineteenth century. Mesmer observed the faith cures of a Catholic priest known as Father Gassner who lived at Klosters in what is now the boundary of Switzerland. Discovering healing powers in himself, Gassner explained his work as a form of exorcism, in order to secure church approval. Hundreds of the afflicted, possessed by devils according to the belief of the day, came to be healed and the priest would appear before them, clad all in black and holding aloft a crucifix. One observant physician has described the treatment of a peasant woman. Gassner, after a theatrical entrance into the room, touched her with the crucifix and she promptly fell to the floor in a swoon. Speaking in Latin, he ordered her to move her left arm, which she did, although supposedly not familiar with that language, stopping at the command *"Cesset!"* He then ordered her heart to beat more slowly, and the physician found the pulse very slow. At a further command it increased to 120 beats per minute. Gassner then told the woman to lie dead on the floor, announcing he would restore her to life. Soon the physician pronounced her dead, for no pulse nor respiration was discernible. On command, she revived and rose completely "cured" of her disorder after the demon had been ordered to depart.

Mesmer watched a similar demonstration by Gassner in the year 1770 and was greatly impressed though he took little stock in the demonic possession hypothesis. He did realize that some unknown force was working and reasoned out a theory, conjecturing that the body had two poles like a magnet, with an invisible magnetic fluid being thrown off by the body. Disease was only an improper flow of this fluid, and illness could be cured by correcting the flow. Only certain people, Mesmer included, were gifted with the power to control the fluid and such persons could cause it to flow from them into the patient. This could even be done indirectly by "magnetizing" any object, perhaps a bottle of water which would then impart the fluid to anyone touching it.

Despite many successful demonstrations, Mesmer's ideas were not well received in Vienna. Too many patients were visiting him. After being warned by the authorities to discard such unorthodox methods, he became disgusted and removed to Paris. Here he began to practice in 1778 and quickly created among the French aristocracy a vogue for mesmeric treatment. Patients in a large hall gathered about an enormous tub from which projected a number of iron rods which they could touch. Water in the tub was "magnetized" by Mesmer or an assistant and the magnetic fluid reached the patient through one of the rods. From time to time, the great physician would appear in a long flowing robe, carrying an iron staff with which to tap the afflicted. When the sufferer had become sufficiently magnetized, a convulsive seizure termed a "crisis" would come on and he would at once be cured of his ailment. The crisis was considered a necessary adjunct to relief.

Many diseases were treated in this fashion, and Mesmer began reaping a fortune from the credulous nobility and society folk, much to the envy of fellow physicians. Eventually they persuaded the French government to order an official investigation, and a commission (which included Benjamin Franklin, United States ambassador to France) was appointed for the purpose. Mesmer's previous request for an investigation by the French Academy had been denied. He now indignantly refused to submit to an inquiry, and the commission was able to witness only such demonstrations as his pupils could provide. The official report most undeservedly branded Mesmer as a fraud in spite of successful results with hundreds of people. True, his spectacular methods smacked of charlatanism, but no open-minded researcher has ever questioned Mesmer's sincerity. One committee member filed a minority report urging further inquiry since some new phenomenon was undoubtedly involved, but the majority finding was made official.

The unfortunate and discredited physician finally left Paris and lived for a time under an assumed name in England, then returned to Austria to carry on his magnetic cures. He died in obscurity in 1815. Mesmer's memory has been marred by obloquy, but honest retrospection finds nothing discreditable in his actions. While he accepted large fees from the wealthy, Mesmer treated hundreds free, and certainly there is nothing illegitimate in receiving a financial return from a medical discovery, which seems to have been the only real charge proved against him. He was unorthodox and a showman, but numerous reputable physicians today do not disdain the use of "front." Many great discoveries in medicine have been accorded the same skepticism Mesmer received, and the nonorthodox medical man usually is an object of scorn, with professional ostracism his lot.

Followers and students, among whom was Lafayette, kept Mesmer's theories alive, and the name "mesmerism" and "animal magnetism" came to be applied to them. Developments and changes in theory naturally resulted as time passed. The Marquis de Puységur magnetized a shepherd boy who had never heard of the convulsive crisis supposed to occur spontaneously, and was surprised when the boy, Victor, went into a quiet trance condition which the Marquis labeled somnambulism. Subsequent to this trance there was complete forgetfulness or amnesia for the events of the trance. This happening was highly noteworthy as the first critical observation of a hypnotic subject. Soon other hypnotic phenomena had been noted by experimenters.

Although Mesmer did not use passes to induce a trance, his followers made it a practice to stare intently into the eyes of their subjects, concentrating and willing them to go to sleep, while making long passes with the hands along the subject's body from the head to the toes, thus supposedly passing magnetic fluid from the magnetizer into the person being mesmerized. Reversing the direction of the passes from the feet to the head caused awakening, they believed. Later, many hypnotists continued using passes in the suggestion method of induction, believing them of real value, while others employed passes only as stage dressing. To the uninformed, these gestures add mysticism and for this reason may assist in bringing on hypnosis, but they are quite unnecessary. Strangely enough, certain hypnotists even today are firmly convinced of the efficacy and power of such magic gestures.

A long controversy developed between Mesmer's followers and those adhering to the teachings of the so-called Nancy school made famous by Liebeault and Bernheim. The magnetists accepted Mesmer's original theory of a magnetic fluid but revised it somewhat. He had finally decided that the whole universe floated in a fluid resembling ether with one physical body influencing another through the vibrations of this fluid. His followers believed the magnetizer emitted a nervous fluid somewhat similar to the aura which modern spiritualists claim surrounds the human body. The later mesmerists were firmly convinced this fluid should be visible to a subject. Following the mental suggestion of the operator, some magnetized folk accordingly declared they could see a magnetic fluid streaming from the finger tips of the mesmerizer when the room was darkened, and numerous attempts were made to prove this contention.

Most mesmerists and many hypnotists of the Nancy school believed in the effect of magnets on the human body, especially under hypnosis. This is an old idea originating in the Orient, where the magnet was known long before Europeans learned of its properties.

One phenomenon attributed to the magnet was termed "polarization," a reversal of any functional state or condition. For instance, a magnet could be used to change the mental image of any color into its complementary color. A person under hypnosis who gazed at a blue object would see it as yellow whenever a magnet was placed near him.

If a sick person was seated back-to-back with a magnetized subject and a magnet placed between them, his symptoms would pass to the magnetized subject, thus effecting a cure. No doubt this would be a bit unpleasant for the subject, but perhaps he was supposed to throw off the symptoms when he awakened! If catalepsy was induced on only one side of the body of a magnetized person, the magnet could switch the catalepsy to the other side.

These and other actions supposedly brought about by the potent magnet were accepted as facts even by scientists, though all the phenomena of animal magnetism and the alleged influence of the magnet came as a direct result of suggestion. The subject did exactly as was expected of him. A careful study of the action of magnets on the human body was made by two extremely reputable psychologists, Binet and Féré;[10] the former's name is still famous for his work on mental age known as the Binet-Simon test. Extremely capable in the field of general psychology, these intelligent men were most gullible and unscientific when it came to hypnotic experimentation. The book reporting their studies is a mass of misinformation and misconceptions. Many other savants believed implicitly in these and other properties of the magnet—men like Charcot, Babinski, Luys, and Lombroso.

Animal magnetism created a stir throughout the scientific world, enlisting a host of followers in France, Germany, Austria, and eventually in the United States. There was continued experimentation, much discussion and many official inquiries, but science rejected it. However, popular belief in the strange force continued for generations. Even today the term "mesmerism" is frequently taken by educated people as being synonymous with hypnotism. As fact it is the same, but the theories are vastly different.

The English failed to become excited over the new "science," and magnetism gained little headway against British skepticism. James Braid, a Scotch physician practicing in Manchester, England, watched a touring French magnetizer demonstrate and became interested, aware that some unusual force was involved. Unwilling to accept the magnetic theory, he experimented and found that a trance-like state could be induced by holding any bright object above and in front of the subject's head so as to strain the eyes and quickly fatigue them. Braid eventually found the eyestrain detrimental and modified his procedure by placing the object some twelve inches from the eyes. This is one of the methods used today. It is in reality only a way of fixing attention and has nothing else to do with inducing hypnosis.

Braid noticed that the trance produced was similar to that of animal magnetism but at first thought it a different condition. Later he concluded the two were identical. Early in his work he believed that the fixation of the eyes on the bright object brought on a trance but, with more experience, concluded that suggestion was the real explanation. It was Braid who coined from the Greek word *hypnos,* meaning sleep, our words "hypnotism" and "hypnosis" to describe this new science and the trance condition produced. For many years Braid practiced in London, using suggestion therapy and performing operations by use of hypnotic anaesthesia. He published a book [11] and many papers about his findings.

According to Moll,[12] the first surgical operations on magnetized subjects were those performed by Récamier in 1821. Cloquet reported to the French Academy of Medicine in 1829 his use of such anaesthesia. In 1843 another British doctor, John Elliotson, wrote about his experiments with it, performed much earlier, Elliotson being also among the first in England to learn the use of the stethoscope. He probably made the earliest use of hypnotism in treating hysteria, at least intentionally, though Mesmer undoubtedly treated many hysterics but did so unwittingly. In America Dr. Albert Wheeler cut a polyp from the nose of a patient while the magnetizer Phineas Quimby served as anaesthetist—the first such use in this country.

A doctor named James Esdaile, an adherent of the magnetic school, performed operations in 1840 with mentally induced anaesthesia. Esdaile was in the employ of the British East India Company and three years later persuaded the British government to establish a hospital in Calcutta devoted to hypnotic healing. This was just prior to the discovery of chloroform and ether as anaesthetic agents. A surgical patient at that time customarily was strapped down and carved while he screamed and struggled. Esdaile [13] used hypnotic anaesthesia while performing thousands of operations, including more than three hundred major ones, nineteen limb amputations among them, together with the removal of tumors, and all without pain to the patients. One observer wrote of witnessing Esdaile remove a diseased eye from a patient while the other eye looked on unblinkingly. With pain the usual and expected accompaniment of surgery, Esdaile was distinctly popular with patients but anathema to competitors. Suffering a fate similar to Mesmer's, he finally was forced to close the hospital and returned in disgrace to England.

During the controversy over his unorthodox methods, one physician solemnly declared that the use of anaesthesia was sacrilegious, since God had doomed mankind to pain and suffering which ought to be borne with Christian fortitude. Another maintained that such anaesthesia was entirely faked, that patients only pretended to feel no pain when Esdaile sawed busily away at a leg. In his determination to discredit Esdaile, this cynic even paid the expenses to England from India of one of Esdaile's former patients, a Hindu, so he could testify to this effect. The plan backfired somewhat when the native naïvely mentioned the fat fee received for his testimony. However, the attacks were eventually successful and Esdaile was barred from practice by the British Medical Society, dying in relative obscurity.

In 1864 a French country doctor named Liebeault became interested in hypnotism after reading Braid's book. Moving to Nancy, he devoted his entire time to hypnotic healing. His theory, essentially Braid's, emphasized suggestion as the key to everything in hypnotism. Though Liebeault is often referred to as the father of hypnotism, Braid really merits the title. The Frenchman did contribute much to modern hypnotism, however. He published his new theories in 1866 but the book was completely ignored. Finally he interested the eminent doctor Hyppolite Bernheim,[14] one of the "greats" of French medicine and a man of flawless reputation. Bernheim at once realized that Liebeault had something. After intensive study with Liebeault, Bernheim began to employ hypnotic therapeutics exclusively and science took notice, for his reputation was well established. Giving Liebeault due credit, Bernheim perfected techniques still used for the induction of hypnosis, substantiated suggestion as the basis of the science and hypnotism emerged finally on a firm scientific foundation, albeit with some mud clinging to its sills. This marked the end of animal magnetism, around which controversy continued for a time. Even now someone occasionally comes forth with a "new" theory as to some occult power possessed by the hypnotist.

Another controversy soon developed. About this time the French neurologist and anatomist Charcot became interested in hypnotism, calling his theory "major hypnotism." As the Liebeault-Bernheim theory was called that of the Nancy school, Charcot's is termed the Salpetrière, after the hospital in Paris where he practiced and taught.

All Charcot's work was done with hystero-epileptics and was confined to experimentation with a few women patients. As a result, Charcot decided that hypnotism was an attribute of hysteria and theorized that the hypnotic state comprised three distinct stages which he termed lethargy, catalepsy and somnambulism. In the first the subject could not hear or speak and the eyes were closed. If the eyes were then opened, the cataleptic stage was entered and the limbs stayed in any position in which they might be placed, the ability to hear or speak still being lacking. The third or somnambulistic stage was induced by rubbing the top of the patient's head. It is difficult to understand how a scientist like Charcot could have formulated this theory, which is so completely at variance with fact, particularly the belief that subjects are deaf and dumb in the first and second stages.

Bernheim respected Charcot, under whom he had studied, but knew the latter's observations were ridiculous. He pointed out these errors and demonstrated the truth of his own contentions by reproducing Charcot's three stages through suggestion. The controversy between the two schools stirred up scientific circles for a time, much weight being given to Charcot's ideas because of his prominence in medicine. But Bernheim was too evidently right and eventually his hypothesis became generally accepted.

Now firmly established in Europe, hypnotism was widely taken up by physicians and psychologists. Donato, Hansen, and other showmen demonstrated it on the stage until its use for entertainment was prohibited in almost every European country. For a number of years interest continued to be great. Among the leading European practitioners were such prominent scientists as Forel in Switzerland, Krafft-Ebing and Breuer in Austria, Moll, Sperling, Dessoir, Kraepelin and Schrenck-Notzing in Germany, Pavlov in Russia, and Wetterstrand in Sweden. In Britain, however, there was much opposition and few accepted the science although a handful of physicians did adopt it. These included Felkin in Scotland, Bramwell, Lloyd, Hack Tuke and Lloyd Tuckey in England.

In America, Grimes had earlier tried to give magnetism a new slant by calling it "electrobiology." Beard became one of the leading hypnotic practitioners and even more famous was Phineas Quimby, who treated Mary Baker Eddy in 1862 for a neurotic condition. Although Quimby made no religious claims for his method and explained it as entirely suggestion, Mrs. Eddy, who studied under him, denied that suggestion had anything to do with it. She added a religious flavor, a dash of mysticism, a sprinkling of faith, and called the resulting brew Christian Science. One of the stock sermons of the sect is a warning against "malicious animal magnetism, hypnotism and suggestion"—the very forces responsible for the cures effected by "Science"!

The history of hypnotism shows several cyclic periods. Soon after Mesmer's discovery, interest soared and then sank following the investigation which discredited him. About thirty years later there was a great revival when animal magnetism reached "craze" proportions throughout Europe. Another lull followed until Bernheim's suggestion theory was promulgated and the controversy with Charcot developed. The subsequent period from about 1885 to 1910 probably marked the acme of interest, which gradually waned owing to the failure of the medical profession to grant consideration to hypnotism as a therapeutic agent. It again surged briefly with its application to the treatment of war neuroses after World War I, when interest was shown more by psychologists than by the public. The popularity of psychoanalysis and Freud's rejection of hypnotism caused its eclipse thereafter. A new cycle now seems to have begun. The subject has been largely debunked, and, with further badly needed scientific study, hypnotism should receive increasing respect as a legitimate branch of psychological science.

# CHAPTER III

# Inducing Hypnosis

AT THE HEIGHT of the animal magnetism vogue, when trance induction was accomplished with much hocus-pocus, a strange and mysterious wise man appeared out of the East, the Abbé Faria. He was a Portuguese who had spent many years in the Orient before going to Paris in 1814, and his travels probably had brought him into contact with hypnotism in India, since he was familiar with the basic facts of the science. Faria knew the value of showmanship, and he always appeared in a gorgeous robe and assumed an impressive mien, although he disdained the "hokum" of the magnetizers. According to his theory no unknown or mysterious force was involved. All was entirely objective, he maintained, a direct result of suggestion. His method was to secure relaxation in subjects, then command "SLEEP!" in a loud tone, repeating the word several times. The more susceptible promptly went into hynotic slumber.

Probably the Abbé should be considered the first of the modern hypnotists as distinguished from the magnetists; certainly he is the first who recognized suggestion as the motive force in hypnotism. He caused something of a sensation for a time, but enemies employed an actor to pretend to be hypnotized, then to cry "fake" at the opportune moment. Faria was discredited by this apparent exposé; his beliefs were disregarded and soon entirely forgotten.

While Braid in England eventually recognized the part played by suggestion in trance induction, it remained for Liebeault and Bernheim to perfect its application and, when only suggestion is employed, it is termed the "Nancy method." Bernheim scoffed at the magnetists. He definitely proved that the trance was brought on by suggestion alone, no matter what ceremonies or rituals were used. To secure fixation of attention, he had the subject gaze at the ends of his fore and middle fingers held drooping from the wrist at a point above the patient's head so the eyeballs would be turned up. Bernheim's method is the one in general use today, though attention may be fixed in many ways, such as looking into the eyes of the operator or by staring at a spot on the wall or ceiling. If a bright object of any kind is employed for fixation, it is termed "the Braid method." As a matter of fact, eye fixation is quite unnecessary and mere closing of the eyes is sufficient.

When hypnosis is to be induced in a subject for the first time, the attempt should always be preceded by an explanation which serves several purposes. Relaxation can be begun and the talk should be filled with suggestion. It is essential for the subject to know what is expected of him. He must be put at ease and his physical comfort assured by having him either lie on a couch or sit in an easy chair completely relaxed. A cushion for the head will allow the neck muscles to loosen and, if a chair is used, will prevent the head from rolling when sleep comes. Breathing is also easier when the head and neck are comfortable and the muscles of the neck are relaxed. When sitting in a chair, both feet should be on the floor with the legs extended, hands resting on the arms of the chair or in the person's lap. Since lying down is the normal position for sleep, the greatest relaxation is gained by having the subject supine on a couch, and we favor this posture.

Comfort, room temperature, lighting arrangements and

atmospheric conditions seem to influence matters greatly, as experience will demonstrate. A draft through the room, especially a cold one, may be enough to prevent hypnosis or may cause a hypnotized person to awaken. When Esdaile was performing operations in torrid India, he found that patients were often aroused if they were stripped for surgery, and thereafter he kept them covered as much as possible. Room temperature probably is best at 73 to 75 degrees, somewhat on the warm side. Best results come with the room slightly darkened, and no light should shine into the eyes of the subject. At night a single lamp may be placed behind the subject. Indirect lighting is always preferable.

When conditions are bad the hypnotizer sometimes may have difficulty securing the trance and may not be able to discover any valid reason for such failure. During a demonstration before friends, LeCron tried to hypnotize three different subjects who ordinarily went into a deep state almost immediately. With one he was unable to produce the slightest result; the others woke up repeatedly, and finally it was necessary to give up after trying various arrangements of the lights, the seating and other room conditions. The only explanation seemed to be the temperature and humidity of the air, which was unusually dry and hot. None of the subjects was able to offer any explanation but all said they were vaguely uncomfortable. Bordeaux has had similar experiences.

To fix the attention of the subject, almost anything bright may be used. A silver Christmas tree ornament is an excellent device for this, particularly if a lamp is placed on the floor behind and below so its rays will shine on the bottom of the ornament to produce a bright spot of light on which to focus. Such a ball should be hung by a thread to dangle about a foot above the center of the subject's forehead, so his eyes must be turned up to see it. For impromptu use a watch is an excellent substitute, but the operator's arm and hand become tired after holding it a few moments.

Fixation of the gaze on the eye of the operator offers some advantages and is a preferred method with us on healthy subjects, for we believe that quicker results follow. Hull agrees with this preference. Some suggestion is involved, for most subjects think the operator's fixed stare produces sleep. Personally we prefer to explain that it is only for attention.

With this system, the operator should bring his own eyes within eight inches of those of the subject. Winking should be avoided by the hypnotist as it tends to distract the subject. The subject should focus on one of the eyes of the hypnotist but, after a moment, is instructed to let the eyes go out of focus; this will tend to blur the vision, aiding in securing hypnosis. The operator should also let his eyes go unfocused, apparently looking right through the subject.

When required to look into the operator's eyes, some people become uneasy and turn the gaze away or move the eyeballs. In such cases it is better to have the subject gaze at a bright object or simply close his eyes. In the practice of hypnotic psychotherapy, looking into the hypnotist's eyes may cause psychic distress or discomfort, which should be avoided.

Still another scheme is the use of a machine which flashes a light intermittently into the subject's eyes. A French physician named Luys devised a system of rotating mirrors operated by clockwork to accomplish this, and we have adapted his idea, a small electric motor turning a half-circle disk in front of an electric light bulb to make an intermittent flash. This is enclosed in a black plastic box resembling a small radio cabinet. A hole at one end permits the subject to watch the flashing light, its amount and brilliance controlled by means of a camera-type iris which may be opened or closed as desired; a larger opening is best for daytime use, a small one at night. A sound device is activated by the rotating disk, each revolution producing a sound like the muffled beat of a drum synchronized with the flashing light. A metronome will serve the same purpose.

This device has proved excellent for inducing hypnosis, particularly at night. The monotonous rhythm of the flashing light is tiring to the eyes, and the added auditory stimulus is helpful, particularly when the subject concentrates his attention on the sound. Even when the fixed gaze method of induction is used, a metronomic sound effect assists in obtaining mind passivity and concentration of attention.

Sensory fatigue is always an aid in bringing on hypnosis. A tired person is far more susceptible than one who is wide awake, and fatiguing the eyes by concentrating the gaze is a definite part of induction methodology. Pitzer [15] advocated fatiguing the subject's eyes before beginning the sleep formula. He asked him to blink his eyes for four or five minutes to the beat of a metronome or by monotonously counting in a low voice.

One of the most effective methods of induction, rapid in effect and of advantage when dealing with a difficult subject, is to have the subject let his eyes and unfocused gaze follow the movement of the hypnotist's hand up and down, held about three inches in front of his eyes. After one or two moments of this he is told to close his eyes. The movement of the hand should be accompanied by continued repetition of the phrase "up and down, up and down" and suggestion that the eyes are growing tired and heavy.

Before attempting trance induction after the subject has been settled comfortably and before fixation of the eyes is requested, an explanatory talk should be made to put him at his ease mentally and emotionally, as well as physically. He undoubtedly will be nervous and apprehensive, wondering what

will happen and what his sensations will be, perhap
self-conscious if others are present. Many expect some
mental "click" to occur as they enter the trance and n
believe they have been hypnotized unless some such sensation
is experienced. Explanations are therefore in order and the
subject must be told to expect only the feelings of drowsiness,
of lassitude and perhaps of detachment.

In describing his impressions, the hypnotized person will
sometimes compare it to lying or floating on a cloud; perhaps
he will feel that he is sinking down into such a cloud, and we
often suggest this in our talk. However, such a feeling of floating or of detachment seems to be a definite phenomenon, as
many will feel it without its appearance being suggested. It
seems to come only with the deep stage of hypnosis, though
frequently it is not evidenced even then.

Since there is much variance in the reactions of individuals, it is always wise to ask each subject about his sensations
in the trance. Those experiences should be noted and brought
into the sleep formula during subsequent inductions.

The subject is now told that he will be perfectly comfortable throughout and will awaken refreshed and invigorated, just as easily as from a sound natural sleep. If not so ap-
prised, he frequently will inquire if there may not be difficulty
in awakening him, this being a point about which there is
usually some apprehension. By making this explanation, the
hypnotist is actually using indirect suggestion to induce easy
awakening.

It is further stressed that there will be no loss of consciousness, for the subject will know at all times what is happening. The operator should never induce hallucinations or
force actions from the subject to which he might object. Assurance of this is of value. Many people also fear that they
may be compelled to reveal or may volunteer "state secrets"

when hypnotized, and they should be reassured that no embarrassing questions will be asked.

If the person to be hypnotized is highly intelligent and especially if he is of the analytical type of mind, it is wise to say he will enter the hypnotic state entirely through his own efforts—or lack of effort, to be more exact—by following the instructions of the operator. He is told to give undivided attention and to try to accept statements without analyzing them, if best results are to be obtained. In other words, he will produce the result himself by cooperation and conforming to the directions given.

There may be some question as to the truth of this, for some contend that all suggestion is heterosuggestion (coming through another, from without), while others believe that all is autosuggestion (coming through oneself, from within).

Complete passivity of mind or concentrated attention is necessary for the induction of the hypnotic state. It is difficult to keep the mind fixed on one thought, particularly without long practice. Learning to attain mental passivity is one of the exercises of yoga, and the adept is able to hold the mind inert for hours. This is taught in Japan in connection with judo, and one of the requirements for a high judo degree is to be able to sit motionless for four hours without the slightest movement. Those who have acquired such passivity claim the hours pass quickly and seem to be only minutes.

Passivity of mind and concentration of attention are not the same thing. In the first, the mind becomes lethargic and organized mental activity is suspended, though consciousness is maintained and there is awareness. In concentration, the mind is focused intently on a thought or group of thoughts. Some hypnotists seek always for concentration and ask the subject to pay close attention to their words; others, by telling the subject not to listen consciously to their words, strive for complete passivity, believing that the mind is more receptive when inactive. Response is then subconscious.

We have found passivity the better mental state for the induction of hypnosis, but here again much depends on the individual's type of mind. It is easier to concentrate than it is to make the mind passive, and it may be preferable to call for attention, especially in early attempts at hypnosis. In stage demonstrations few subjects become mentally passive. Under normal conditions the use of a metronome or similar sound device during the sleep suggestions will help bring mind passivity after a short time. A skilled hypnotist must be versatile, using attention at one time and turning to passivity as necessary when hypnosis is not reached on the first attempt, suiting his methods to the individual subject.

The length of time required for induction of hypnosis is extremely variable with different individuals. Only a short time may be needed with a susceptible person even on the first attempt, sometimes only a moment, sometimes several minutes. With difficult subjects, as Erickson [16] has pointed out, a deep sleep may be gained only after two, three, or even four hours of continued suggestion of sleep. Somnambulism may thus be reached where no great depth would ever be gained otherwise. Such persistence would seldom be feasible for ordinary purposes, but in hypnotherapy, patience and effort are important to secure the relaxation and passivity necessary for the trance.

Sometimes an unusually good subject enters a deep trance almost instantly. In one of his earliest attempts at hypnosis, LeCron found a young lady subject of this type. To his surprise her eyes closed and her head fell to one side within five seconds and before one sentence was completed. Suspicious of a hoax, he studied the situation. Everything indicated deep hypnosis. Breathing was regular, she was in a cataleptic condition, and when told to open her eyes, they stared fixedly. Other tests indicated that there was no simulation. This subject subsequently, without suggestion to that effect, entered the trance state at the mere command to "SLEEP!"

One interesting modern development in the induction of hypnosis is the use of a phonograph record—certainly a prosaic and nonmysterious method. G. H. Estabrooks is credited with making the first attempt at induction with a recording. Such records can be purchased or easily made, and they are sometimes of value for use in controlled experiments where more than one subject is to be tested and exactly the same wording is desired in order to obtain a certain result. However, the suggestions made in inducing hypnosis meet with such varied individual responses that recordings seldom can be of much value to the professional hypnotherapist. As a rule, a recording would seldom induce hypnosis in a subject who has never been hypnotized.

During induction, both direction and suggestion are given the subject according to the signs of approaching hypnosis which he exhibits. For the benefit of students wishing to learn the detailed phrasing of a practical formula for suggesting sleep, here is a verbatim transcription of a phonograph record of our own. A detailed analysis of this talk is given in a later chapter. It must be remembered always that each subject requires suggestions fashioned to fit his personality traits. The induction of hypnosis is not a recital of a magical formula, nor is it a ritual, nor does it require any specific time period. It is imperative to use words which fit the occasion and the individual. The printed formula below does not reveal any voice intonations or vital personal qualities contained in spoken suggestions. This formula would be appropriate and effective with some subjects, but would fail entirely with others. However, it does serve as an example.

"Stretch out comfortably with your hands in your lap and your head tipped back a little so you are looking up. Look at the bright ball above you and keep your eyes focused on it. Do not move your eyeballs. Now take a deep breath and relax completely. Let your mind be as inactive as possible. Try to keep it as passive as you can make it. Pay no attention to anything but my voice. As you go to sleep, other sounds will become less and less important and you will pay less attention to them, for they mean nothing.

"You will probably feel a desire to blink your eyes. Wink whenever you wish, it doesn't matter. After you look at the ball for a few minutes, your eyes will tend to blur and the eyelids probably already have a slight feeling of heaviness. They will grow heavier and heavier, too heavy to hold open; they will soon be too heavy to hold open.

"You are now relaxed and comfortable. A pleasant feeling of drowsiness, a sleepy feeling, will begin to come over you soon. Your eyelids are growing heavier and heavier now, heavier and heavier every moment, heavier and heavier. Now you are beginning to realize that you are becoming sleepy, and you want to go to sleep. Your eyes gradually grow heavier and heavier. They are very heavy and you want to close them because they are so tired and heavy. They are so heavy now, let them close. Close them now, let them close.

"The dreamy, drowsy feeling will begin to deepen soon. You are getting drowsy and sleepy, drowsy and sleepy. The dreamy feeling is much as though you were lying on a cloud. It seems as though you were floating on the cloud, floating and sinking slowly down into the cloud. It is a pleasant feeling and you notice now that you are growing more drowsy and sleepy, sleepier and sleepier. Your hands will soon feel heavy, your legs and arms will begin to feel heavy; a feeling of numbness is creeping into your arms and legs as they grow heavier and heavier. Your whole body is feeling heavy. You are very drowsy now, drowsy and sleepy and comfortable. Relax! Let all your muscles relax. That's right, relax completely.

"You are drowsy, sleepy, so sleepy, soon you will not be able to stay awake any longer, you must sleep. You do not want to stay awake; it is so pleasant and comfortable to let yourself drift away into the cloud. Drowsy, sleepy, sleepy, getting sleepier with every breath you take. Breathe deeply with long, slow breaths. You will go a little deeper with every breath, deeper and deeper. Soon you will be sound asleep, fast asleep. Sleepy, sleepy and drowsy, going deep asleep. Drowsy, drowsy, you are almost asleep now, almost asleep. Deeper and deeper. You are sinking deep into sleep. Now you are asleep and as I count up to three you will sink deeper and deeper asleep, into a very deep sleep.

"ONE—you are asleep now and going still deeper asleep. It is so pleasant to go deep asleep. TWO—you are sound asleep, fast asleep, and going still deeper, deeper asleep. THREE— you are deep asleep now, deep asleep, perfectly conscious but sleeping deeply! Breathe slowly and deeply, sleep deeply.

"You will sleep now until I tell you to wake up. Nothing will disturb you. You are perfectly conscious but deep asleep and you feel too comfortable to move or even to think. You will not awaken until I tell you to. Sleep deeply. You are to pay attention to what I say and do exactly what I ask but I will ask nothing which you would be unwilling to do. When you awaken, you will feel refreshed, clear-headed and wide awake. When I tell you to awaken, you will be wide awake at once but until then, sleep deeply."

The suggestions used to awaken the subject should be along similar lines, brief but emphatic.

"I am going to awaken you now. You will feel rested, fresh and fit. I will count to three and you will be wide awake at the count of three, wide awake. ONE—you are about to wake up. TWO—almost awake. THREE—wake up! Wake up! You are wide awake now, wide awake!"

Snapping the fingers or clapping the hands together, but not too sharply, will assist in the awakening though it is quite unnecessary and may tend to startle the subject. A sleeper almost invariably opens his eyes with a slight start, one of the signs of hypnosis though it does not necessarily indicate more than a light trance. Sometimes the subject does not fully awaken at once and may be a little lethargic for a few moments, perhaps needing further encouragement to arouse. Until it has been established beyond doubt that he is awake, he should never be permitted to leave.

With almost everyone there is not the slightest difficulty in awakening, and the student hypnotist can dismiss any fear of encountering trouble. It is inducing hypnosis which is most difficult, not arousing the subject. Only in a few instances is there subsequent lassitude, and there rarely is actual perversity in awakening. But the student must be prepared to meet such a contingency even though it is unlikely to arise.

In lecturing, LeCron once hypnotized a volunteer subject who entered a deep trance at once, with some of the phenomena then demonstrated. When finally told to awaken, the man remained motionless with eyes closed. Insistence made little difference, and his head was bowed as though deep in sleep. After further commands, his head lifted, the eyes opened, only to close again while his head sagged limply to one side. The situation might have become embarrassing, but calling attention to the time of day and the necessity of returning to his office finally aroused him, though it was a good ten minutes before the man was wide awake.

Questioning brought out the probable cause. The subject had recently been discharged from the army, where he had received treatment for a nervous condition by use of sodium amytal, a hypnotic drug. This drug had sent him into a deep sleep, which narcosis he had associated with the present hypnosis since the states are similar. Therefore he had supposed he should go just as deeply asleep and be as difficult to arouse as it had been to awaken him from the drugged state.

If this case had proved more refractory, other methods were available to awaken him. Proper procedure would then have been to make direct inquiry of the subject as to why he refused to wake up, for he was fully conscious and able to reply. Such a subject can be asked what should be done to arouse him, and a reply may give the solution. Remonstrance, persuasion or commands may be employed, but threats should never be used. Such a subject who stays asleep always has a reason which is satisfactory to him. He may even be trying to punish the hypnotist, who perhaps has caused him to do something which he has resented.

There is absolutely no danger if awakening still proves impossible, for the hypnotic state always reverts to normal sleep when a recalcitrant subject is left alone, or else he will decide to awaken. Suggestion should then be made that a normal sleep will come within a few minutes. If this fails he will eventually awaken of his own accord, and there is no known record of anyone ever failing to waken within a few hours.

While occurrences of this nature are embarrassing to the hypnotizer, he must remain cool and never become excited, since there is no danger. When a subject is of hysterical nature and the operator manifests concern, he may have an unpleasant scene on his hands, hence the importance of keeping his wits. But such cases are extremely rare and are seldom encountered even in years of practice. Ordinarily it is as easy to awaken one from hypnotic sleep as it is from normal sleep.

Often there is a desire on the part of the subject to stay in hypnosis simply because he is comfortable and finds the condition pleasant. Frequently a person will ask to be allowed to continue in hypnosis or assert that he does not want to wake up, but there is ready compliance when firmly told to awaken.

In the example of sleep induction cited above, an attempt has been made to secure deep hypnosis without any interruption of the process. No tests have been made to ascertain or indicate the depth of trance reached. An experienced hypnotist knows the various signs of the hypnotic state and will watch continually for them.

As a result of suggestion, the eyes usually become heavy rather quickly. Often they will close of their own accord or will partially close. The trance may come even while the eyes are still wide open, but in most cases they will close first. After they have remained open long enough to become tired from fixation or if they begin to water, it is best to ask the subject to close them voluntarily. In a few instances a seeming inability to move the eyelids is felt and the eyes will remain open even after a definite request is made that they be closed. Then the operator should push them shut very gently with his fingers, saying, "You may close them now." This is better than a direct command to close them, overcoming any resistance.

While the eyes are still open and usually for a moment or two after they close, the lids frequently tremble and flutter, a definite indication of the beginning of hypnosis. It is the eyes which betray most of the signs and close attention must be given them throughout, with suggestion directed to observed signs which should be, emphasized. If the eyes narrow slightly or the lids are partially closed, they are feeling heavy,

41

which should at once be mentioned. Some comment should always be made immediately after the subject closes them. These indications and reactions are thus used to make the subject aware that he is becoming more amenable to suggestion, making it easier for subsequent signs to develop and the trance to arrive.

There are other eye factors for which to watch. Even if the lids are closed, movements of the eyeball can still be seen. Often the eyes will roll upward as the trance sets in or perhaps they will roll slowly in a circular motion, each independent of the other, all coordination lost. One may even move in a clockwise circle while the other wanders in a counterclockwise orbit. This eye movement is often seen in the subject who reaches a trance state with eyes open. It is interesting and curious to see the eyeballs start such a slow swimming action, usually accompanied by a glazed appearance. Sometimes only a fixed stare is assumed, difficult to describe but quite noticeable.

There are still other common signs, one being a complete relaxation of the face muscles. Another is a deepening of the breathing, a change as in natural sleep though not usually to the same extent and often not apparent at all. Frequently the pulse will be slower in hypnosis. There is some question as to both breathing and pulse being an actual hypnotic sign, for they may be simply a result of relaxation. Perhaps, too, the slow breathing is suggested because of its association with natural sleep. Another rather common sign is a twitching of the mouth muscles or of the whole lower jaw, manifested just as the trance is reached. However, movements of the jaw, and also smiling, may be indicators of resistance, and clinical experience is needed for correct interpretation of behavioral responses. When a subject changes position during the giving of sleep suggestions or moves any part of the body, it is almost a certainty that the hypnotic state has not yet developed. The suggestions should then be continued for some time.

There are certain tests which aid in determining the depth of hypnosis and an adept operator can employ them frequently. Until experience is gained, however, it is best to avoid these, for they are challenges. Should they fail (and they often do), that failure may be most detrimental to success or even prohibit obtaining the trance. The skilled hypnotist avoids this and will make no challenging tests unless reasonably sure they will succeed.

One of the tests most likely to be positive at an early stage is with the eyes. As has been noted, hypnosis seems to affect most quickly the eyes and eye muscles. When it is judged that the sleep formula has progressed long enough to have become partially effective, the hypnotist may say:

"Now your eyes are closed. Close them tightly and squeeze the lids together. Now the eyelids are locked together; they are glued tightly together. No matter how much you want to open them, they are glued shut and you cannot open them. You may try but they will not open. The harder you try, the tighter they will stick together. Now try to open them. Try, but you can't open them! Try hard, but you can't open them!"

This is one of the tests most often used in demonstrations in order to find good subjects from an audience. If twenty people are present and are challenged in the waking state with the above words, strangely enough four or five usually will fail to open their eyes. Others will succeed only after some effort. Some will not try, a sign in itself, due to lethargy. Those who show these results may be used for further tests as they indicate definite susceptibility to suggestion.

If this test is used while giving sleep suggestions, the operator must watch carefully, and at the slightest indication of the eyes coming open he should declare, "Now you can open them, now they will come open." This may prevent a failure, for it leaves the subject uncertain as to whether or not he might have succeeded in opening them.

Even in a light stage of hypnosis it is generally easy to inhibit muscular control. Smaller muscle groups such as those of the eyes are easier to influence than larger ones. Having made the eye test, we can proceed further.

"Now close your mouth tightly. Press the lips firmly together. Now you may try to open them but the jaws are locked. They will not open. Try, but you can't open them."

Of course this is a similar test but it involves different muscles. We can do the same with the muscles controlling speech and prevent the subject from speaking at all or from uttering designated words, such as his name. He will then find himself able to say anything else, but not the prohibited words. This test will succeed only if a trance of at least medium depth has been induced and would fail with a light trance.

Continuing the inhibition of muscular movements, a most effective test involving the hands and arms is often used by hypnotists. The subject is asked to clasp his hands together in front of him with fingers interlaced and told to squeeze them tightly together. Then a suggestion is given that they are locked together and cannot be unclasped. This test is particularly good because the fingers normally tend to lock when the hands are squeezed together and it is difficult to separate them until the muscles are relaxed. It is more effective if the hands are extended with the arms straight instead of with bent elbows.

The word "catalepsy" is frequently encountered in the literature, but it has never been well defined. When a limb is maintained in any position in which it is placed by the operator, it is said to be cataleptic. Many believe that catalepsy implies rigidity, yet rigidity is not necessarily involved. There has been some argument as to whether catalepsy is an actual hypnotic phenomenon or whether it results only from suggestion, either direct or indirect. If the definition considers only the maintenance of a limb in the position in which it is placed, the factor responsible perhaps *is* suggestion. But catalepsy should include much more. Hull rejected catalepsy as an actual phenomenon of hypnosis perhaps because of lack of clear definition of the term, but his experiments were quite inconclusive.

Erickson [17] believes that catalepsy is a function of incomplete responsiveness to stimuli or of intense absorption by the subject. Part and parcel of the condition are visual relaxation, loss of focus and glazing of the eyes, loss of psychomotor responses and change of muscular tonus such as is evidenced in changed handwriting by a hypnotized person.

Change in muscle tonus is also observed in the relaxation of the skeletal musculature, which develops sometimes to a degree impossible to reach voluntarily. When this is extreme, it is given the technical term *cerea flexibilitas*. Sometimes the lifted arm of a sleeper feels so limber that the bones seem to have turned to rubber. We lift the arm and let it fall. It flops down like a wet rag. We raise it again, hold it in one position for a moment and it will remain there, provided the subject receives the impression this is desired. Otherwise it may fall limply again. We direct the arm to remain rigid, stiff and boardlike, and it stiffens so we are unable to bend it. And we should remember to remove the suggestion, saying it is relaxed and normal once more.

Stroking the arm or moving the hand along it somewhat in the manner of the hypnotic passes of the magnetists will increase the rigidity. Moll noted this, and our experience confirms his observation. Not that there is any "magnetic" effect, but the touch or movement serves to center a subject's attention on the arm.

A further arm test involves the inhibition of muscular control. We raise the arm slightly and say it is now impossible for the hypnotized person to lift it further—he can lower it (requiring less muscular effort) but cannot raise it. The facial muscles may contort, the arm may twitch as though much effort were being exerted, but it does not move. It can even be suggested that the sleeper cannot arise from the chair or couch. Seemingly without strength, he is unable to bestir himself.

Even when successful, these tests do not necessarily indicate a complete and deep hypnosis. If attempted too soon the subject frequently will overcome the suggestions. Even in the early stages there is a general unwillingness to make any effort or to exert oneself, a feeling of lethargy having set in. When questioned, the person may claim he did not try to move and feels sure he could have, had he so desired, but the failure to try is itself a sign. Under subsequent hypnosis, he may be surprised to find himself quite unable to move.

Muscle action can not only be inhibited, it can be excited and made automatic. One of the best tests for this is to have the subject rotate the hands slowly around each other, describing circles in the air before his body. When the movement has been speeded up and the arms are going around and around each other, he is told he cannot stop no matter how he tries. No effort may be made to cease or the arms may slow up, hands bumping into each other, the muscles stiffening, but the hands continue to go around. If this is accomplished, a medium or deeper stage of hypnosis has probably been reached.

Still we may not have induced the state known as somnambulism. Tests for this include instructing the subject to talk, to rise and walk about and to open his eyes, but he must be told these actions will not cause awakening. Somnambulism undoubtedly has been reached if he does not awaken.

Other tests for somnambulism are the eliciting of hallucinations, carrying out of posthypnotic suggestions, the establishing of anaesthesia to pain, and other phenomena. One of the most important is amnesia, forgetfulness for or inability to recall the events of the trance on awakening. Anaesthesia and amnesia are excellent proofs of hypnosis to the subject, tending to settle doubts which are often entertained because of lack of definite sensations. To the operator, one of the best proofs is anaesthesia. Testing for pain or for the lack of sensibility to an electric shock will disclose any simulation or insufficiency of trance depth. These phenomena are discussed in detail in a later chapter.

Catalepsy is also an excellent test for hypnosis. When genuine, it includes all muscle groups, and a subject who is simulating will overemphasize or underemphasize certain of these, making directed movements always in terms of his comprehension or understanding and not in accord with the actual tactile stimuli. With this in mind, Erickson sometimes suggests to a subject, shortly after beginning his sleep suggestions, that the right arm lying extended on the couch, or perhaps in the subject's lap, will start to rise slowly into the air as he feels hypnosis developing. The arm is to continue to rise until it has been elevated about eighteen inches and will remain there until a deeper hypnosis is reached, when a movement in another plane or direction will commence. It is explained that these movements will be automatic and are to be neither assisted nor resisted, the only cooperation being to allow the arm to obey the impulse to move. He is told he will be interested in following all this in his mind. Such participation on the part of the subject has many advantages. Any simulation is easily detected and the operator is better able to observe the response to his induction suggestions as he proceeds.

Oskar Vogt, one of the old-timers, advanced a variation of the usual methods of trance induction. This involves procedure in slow degrees, step by step, making frequent tests and arousing the subject after each, then starting again and gradually leading him into the deeper stages. The hypnotizer is thus given an opportunity to question the subject and note his feelings and responses and reactions, which are then emphasized during subsequent talk. The method has advantages but is exceedingly slow, and the repeated interruptions tend to prevent hypnosis from becoming as deep as it could become in the same length of time if uninterrupted. Sometimes this type of induction is beneficial as a training device, particularly when a long time is being devoted to trance induction.

Resort has often been made to drugs as an aid for inducing hypnosis in difficult subjects. An increase of suggestibility through the use of some drugs such as alcohol has been noted, but the narcotic state produced by most is certainly not true hypnosis. Chloroform, ether, chloral hydrate, paraldehyde and a host of others have been tried.

During the recent war Grinker and Spiegel,[18] United States army psychiatrists, introduced the use of sodium pentothal, tests showing it to be the best of the barbiturate drugs for the purpose. The barbiturates produce a narcotic "hypnosis" differing from simple narcosis and apparently similar to verbally induced hypnosis. This is the conclusion reached by Brenman and Gill[19] in summarizing recent reports. All the usual hypnotic phenomena have been produced during narcotic hypnosis by Horsley,[20] and he regards the states as identical. On the other hand, Erickson, Grinker and Spiegel and many others disagree and consider the states only similar.

In our own clinical experience with pentothal we have noted differences. So far, barbiturate narcosis has had little laboratory investigation though it is receiving much employment in a practical way.

With pentothal it is possible to induce a narcohypnotic state in difficult subjects or those who resist hypnosis and in those who could not be hypnotized otherwise, such as psychotics, agitated or melancholic people and mutes. There is also a possibility of using it to obtain information from criminals.

Horsley, Schilder and Kauders,[21] Kubie,[22] and several others have reported verbal induction of hypnosis often readily accomplished subsequent to narcotic hypnosis if suggestion to that effect is given while a subject is narcotized.

One great advantage in using pentothal is that it requires only a moment or two to obtain a deep trance state, the subject requiring no conditioning by the repetition of monotonous verbal suggestions.

With his background of medicine, the psychiatrist may prefer to use drugs, but there are drawbacks to the barbiturates. Kubie and Margolin [23] cite possible bad reactions, sometimes violent ones, and the development of toxic poisoning. Since dosage varies greatly with individuals, it is difficult to control the depth of the narcotic hypnosis. Administration is intravenous and the intention is to give only enough to bring narcosis but not sufficient to produce loss of consciousness, in which case all rapport with the subject is lost. This frequently happens. With use of pentothal, it is undoubtedly best to dispense with the drug following the initial narcosis, employing hypnosis thereafter.

Some old-school hypnotists advocated the shock method of inducing a trance in stubborn subjects. Some seem to hover on the brink of hypnosis, finding it difficult to "let go," much affected but unable to sink into a trance. When a strong light is flashed suddenly into the eyes or a sharp noise is made or the loud command "SLEEP!" is given, it may startle such a subject into hypnosis. Only an experienced operator can use this technique successfully, for the subject frequently will be startled into wakefulness instead.

The monotonous ticking of a clock or metronome aids induction and offers many advantages. The authors have experimented with a phonograph record as a sound background which is still better. This records the monotonous beat of native drums accompanied by the swishing sound of Cuban maracas (gourds) and runs for about ten minutes. Our experience is not extensive enough to permit a definite report on its worth, but there can be little doubt of its merit. Drums have been used as a hypnotic aid from prehistoric times.

One manner of hypnotizing is worthy of attention because it is most unusual. A stage hypnotist, who was formerly a chiropractor with some knowledge of the nerves, in his act apparently throws volunteer subjects into an instantaneous trance. Seizing them by the back of the neck and the throat, pressure is exerted on certain nerve centers causing temporary paralysis (death could result from prolonged or too strong pressure). The Japanese system of judo or jujitsu presumably employs knowledge of this fact. The state produced seems similar to the tonic immobility or cataplexy seen in so-called animal hypnotism.

The subject is at least partially paralyzed for a few seconds by this method and appears to enter a trance immediately, for he responds to suggestions and all the usual hypnotic phenomena can be elicited. The technique is extremely spectacular and highly successful. Supposedly no suggestion is given, but it is whispered in the ear just as pressure is applied to the nerves, according to some who have been "hypnotized" in this fashion. They report having been told to go to sleep and complain of feeling dazed after being awakened, sometimes with a headache as accompaniment. Some fall to the floor unconscious when the pressure is applied, as though from a blow. Certainly this form of physical abuse is too dangerous even for a physician to use.

Relaxation, both mental and physical, is important in securing the trance. Nothing is more conducive to physical relaxation than massage, which loosens the muscles and stimulates a flow of blood through the manipulated parts. It is a common occurrence for a person to fall asleep under massage, and a gentle rub-down as an accompaniment to sleep suggestions should be helpful.

Few hypnotists are successful in hypnotizing members of their immediate family. One of our students tried unsuccessfully several times to induce hypnosis in his wife, but one night he performed the husbandly chore of massaging her back. Casually he began to give her sleep suggestions and was surprised to have her sink into a deep trance within a few moments. Certainly the massage was an influential if not the chief causative factor.

"Can anyone be hypnotized against his will?" Authorities have discussed this question pro and con. Most literature on hypnotism answers in the negative, but Wells and others have tried to demonstrate that previously hypnotized subjects can be placed in hypnosis involuntarily. The point can be considered still undecided, but the danger of an unscrupulous operator's hypnotizing a person against his will is most unlikely. Moreover, there would be no opportunity for gain even if the operator were successful, for it would be impossible to keep anyone in a trance without his willingness. Any susceptible subject may easily be safeguarded by means of a posthypnotic suggestion to the effect that no one will be able to hypnotize him without his written consent. Some conscientious hypnotists make it a point to give this suggestion to all whom they hypnotize, but this is unfair to the subject unless he is informed of the suggestion.

One way of inducing hypnosis without the subject's conscious consent is by changing normal sleep to hypnosis, which is easily done, though opportunity may be rare. When a subject proves unamenable to hypnosis, this method may succeed.

The operator should seat himself comfortably beside the sleeper and whisper softly, mouth close to his ear, "You hear me but you will not wake up" or a similar phrase which is repeated over and over with gradually increased tonal volume. After a moment or two, the question, "Do you hear me?" should be asked. When there is no answer, the phrase should be repeated with a gradual increase of the volume of the voice until normal tones are reached. If the sleeper continues to remain silent, one hand may be laid gently on his forehead, this serving to attract attention by touch as well as by voice. The gesture also may cause him to awaken instead of entering the hypnotic state.

If the subject is an adult he will often awaken when spoken to by the operator. If there is a reply and the eyes remain closed, then normal sleep presumably has changed to hypnosis. Should the subject carry out a test suggestion, then hypnotic rapport is definitely established.

It may be that the subject first awakens, then enters hypnosis as a result of the suggestion not to awaken. This is a possibility, but we have questioned two hypnotized subjects in whom the trance was thus induced and both stated they were sure they had gone directly from sleep into the trance. However, such statements cannot be regarded as proof.

When resumption of natural sleep is suggested, the patient will return to that state. If no such suggestion is made, he will return to normal sleep of his own accord after a short time.

The Swedish physician Wetterstrand [24] made use of this method with many difficult subjects who were his patients. He would ask a relative of the recalcitrant subject to follow this formula and, if successful, to implant the suggestion of being easily hypnotized whenever the doctor tried to induce hypnosis. This method is often effective with adults but is far easier with children. While it involves involuntary production of a trance, any subject who objected to hypnosis would of course awaken from the trance.

Discussion of induction methods thus far has considered only subjects undergoing a first hypnosis. Induction conforms to the rules of habit formation and the conditioned reflex, becoming easier with each successive session until a norm is reached. Usually only the light or medium state results at the first sitting, the trance becoming deeper with further attempts.

When the trance is fairly deep, the operator may save much time and breath by giving a posthypnotic suggestion as to future inductions, training the subject to enter hypnosis quickly. Some type of signal may be designated and the subject directed to go to sleep instantly whenever it is given. Similarly, a signal may also be used to awaken him. With these, the subject can repeatedly be put to sleep and awakened with only a few seconds intervening—quite a spectacular matter for onlookers.

Such a signal should be easily understood and recognized. It may be visual, auditory or tactile. For instance, we can say, "When I tap you on the right shoulder, you will go to sleep immediately; if on the left shoulder, you will promptly awaken," or "You will go to sleep at once when I pass my hand in front of your eyes, and wake up when I snap my fingers." These short-cuts are extremely helpful when hypnosis is to be repeated often.

When the trance is reached the subject to all appearances goes to sleep, but research has proved that the trance differs entirely from sleep. During the induction process, the thought of sleep, of drowsiness, and the suggestion of going to sleep are repeated over and over again. In the state which ensues, there will be no loss of consciousness, no feeling of sleep other than drowsiness and lassitude. Therefore it is not strange that some subjects fall into normal sleep while hypnotized, perhaps with accompanying snores. It is rather disconcerting when a psychotherapist is interrupted by a loud snort while talking earnestly to a patient, but this happens at times.

With all the suggestions of sleep, a perfect imitation of sleep should result, and ordinarily it does. After the trance has been reached, all lethargy and the appearance of sleep may be banished by suggestion and a natural manner and mien will be assumed. If this suggestion is given, even an expert finds it difficult to decide (other than by direct tests) whether or not the person is hypnotized. Careful study will disclose certain rigidities in the subject's movements, a difference in muscular reactions, and the eyes show pupillary dilation. A lag is detectable in speech, in gestures and in head movements.

Most hypnotists customarily allow their subjects to remain in a condition of apparent lethargy, though there is no need or advantage in doing so. Suggestion for alert mental and physical activity during hypnosis may be valuable.

Some hypnotized individuals, even with all our sleep suggestions, give little appearance of sleep except for closed eyelids. Breathing may be natural and the usual lassitude may not appear.

Bordeaux had one unusual case, the subject being a successful dentist. Somnambulism was very quickly produced. Then, when questioned while hypnotized, he sat up straight, opened his eyes and, to Bordeaux's astonishment, animatedly began to discuss his condition, expressing surprise at having been hypnotized despite skepticism. As it was of particular interest to one of his profession, anaesthesia was induced and he exclaimed when given an electric shock which was not felt. Throughout, he reasoned and asked logical questions as though wide awake, and at the conclusion of the trance was unable to recall anything after suggestion of amnesia. This dentist had never seen anyone hypnotized, and in the brief induction talk there had been no mention of sleep. Though it is rare, others sometimes talk or move of their own volition, but this case was extraordinary for the mental activity displayed.

As will be seen in the next chapter, we believe present methods of hypnotizing are not too efficient. Research is needed for others more adequate. In seeking these improvements there seems to be a lack of information as to the mode in favor in India, where adepts have practiced the science for thousands of years. Such knowledge could probably be had from yogis, the yoga trance seemingly being the same as hypnosis.

Behanon,[25] in *Yoga, A Scientific Evaluation,* seems to believe that the yoga trance and hypnosis are identical. So far as we know, little information is available as to trance induction in India, though one description tells of intense concentration, staring into the subject's eyes from a distance of three or four inches and at the same time blowing into his nostrils. An Occidental subject probably would not find this process enjoyable and we have never tried such blowing. Perhaps the mesmerists were right in their contentions about intense concentration on the part of the operator. In a personal communication to us, Dr. Erickson has mentioned that he worked for two years at Worcester State Hospital with some Hindu medical men who specialize in hypnosis in their home practice of psychiatry and medicine. Aside from cultural and prestige differences and attitudes, he reports that their technique and beliefs are similar to and in accordance with his own.

We have tested one yoga process, though not as a controlled experiment. On subjects previously found difficult to hypnotize, we have used a form of yoga rhythmic breathing prior to giving sleep suggestions. The subject was asked to breathe rapidly, taking thirty quick short breaths at the rate of two per second. This was followed by one long, deep breath inhaled through the left nostril (two seconds required) while the right was held closed by the thumb of the right hand, the palm over the mouth. The air was retained for eight seconds, then the left nostril closed by the forefinger of that hand and the air exhaled through the right nostril (four seconds needed). The process was then repeated until a sensation of light-headedness was felt. The subject then finished with four deep, long breaths as described: in through the left nostril, and out through the right.

Experience showed that this exercise had merit. In a number of cases where hypnosis had not been previously produced, a trance resulted, sometimes light but more often a fairly deep one. Of course there is always the possibility that the same state would have been reached without these breathing exercises but in previous attempts there had been no success. Certainly the method is worthy of experimentation under controlled conditions. One value of such a method is that the subject is actively participating and cooperating. Participation is of more effect than negativeness and having things done, which is an important consideration.

Mention should be made here of so-called "animal hypnotism." Oft demonstrated is the trick of holding a chicken's beak against the floor while a chalk line is drawn from the beak outward, the fowl remaining motionless in a "trance" for a few moments thereafter. Most animals, even some insects, can seemingly be thus immobilized for a short time by one means or another. The resulting state seems to be due to fear, resulting in a tonic immobility or cataplexy, but no direct relationship between this state and hypnosis has been demonstrated.

## STAGE HYPNOSIS

The professional hypnotic consultant selects an office where all is quiet, with conditions designed to prevent distraction of the clients' attention, and there is the same aim in laboratory hypnotism. Instead of the quiet and comfort provided by a consulting room, a stage hypnotist works under conditions exactly the opposite. There is audience noise, there are glaring lights and the subjects are usually seated in hard, straight-backed chairs. Some volunteers may even be hypnotized while standing before the stage hypnotist. Furthermore, the subject is in front of a crowd whose eyes are upon him and of course he is self-conscious, rather than relaxed mentally and physically, which is deemed essential in office practice. Yet the stage performer obtains good results, sometimes more quickly than does the consultant. Why is this?

It must be remembered that the stage hypnotist provides entertainment. Trickery and deceit are not barred. Much of the performance may be faked, but some is real. The stage demonstrator always has "stooges" planted in the audience, not merely to fool the audience but because they are trained subjects. They are used to start the movement of volunteers to the stage—bellwethers, as it were.

The stage operator must be able to pick good somnambulists from the volunteers. When several people have come to the stage, the hypnotist begins sizing them up, usually keeping some of the younger ones, especially teen-agers of both sexes, choosing a variety of types from among the others but accepting only those he feels will be good subjects. Then he requests all the remainder to return to their seats because he is unable to handle so many. While far from infallible, a professional stage performer learns to judge well and seldom fails to pick one or two somnambulists from the group, also selecting his employees, of course.

As everyone who has come forward fully expects to be hypnotized and the performer has been advertised as a master hypnotist, the prestige factor is all in his favor. Quite naturally, he is proficient or he never would have obtained booking.

Taking first the members of his company who are conditioned to instant hypnosis, he puts them into a trance. Having seen these people hypnotized so quickly, the genuine volunteers are thus prepared by indirect suggestion to yield easily. The induction method used by most stage hypnotists follows the laws of the science but usually is accomplished somewhat differently, though entirely through suggestion. The subjects are either frightened or confused into the trance state by a rapid-fire system—sometimes producing severe repercussions.

The troupe members having been hypnotized and left asleep in their chairs, a legitimate volunteer is invited to stand and the demonstrator proceeds with the falling test described in the next chapter, telling the subject he is going to fall backwards. A rapid delivery with emphatic tone and impressive manner is used, suggestions being accompanied by gestures and passes as stage dressing. When the volunteer topples over he is quickly placed on his feet again, and before he has had time to recover, eye closure, hand gripping or rotating, or similar tests are given, one following the other so rapidly that the subject has no chance to think. Finally he is again made to fall backwards and is eased into a chair, the operator leaning over him to give sleep suggestions somewhat as follows:

"You are going to sleep, deep sleep. You are sound asleep now, going deeper and deeper, asleep, sound asleep. Relax now and go deeper and deeper asleep. That's right. Now you are deep in sleep, fast asleep. Sleep! Sleep! You will sleep until I come back to you and will pay no attention to anything except my voice. I will come back to you in just a moment. Then you are to do just as I direct and carry out everything I tell you to do. Now sleep!"

Probably this process will be repeated with another subject or two, then the hypnotist passes from one to another of those remaining, who now need only a few words spoken to them after watching their companions go to sleep so easily. In ten or fifteen minutes the entire group will be asleep, more or less deeply. Should anyone prove a difficult subject, the hypnotist permits him to remain on the stage, for he probably will conform to the actions of the others even though not hypnotized, few wishing to make themselves conspicuous by not responding. With those not deeply affected, the operator is careful to call only for actions which will not embarrass, and thus he receives complete cooperation.

Then follows the usual performance: fantastic hallucinations are suggested, speeches are made by the subjects, a skit is enacted or a mass game played—all very amusing to the audience, which is sure to enjoy the buffoonery and marvel at the strange power of the hypnotist. Sometimes the stunts demanded of the subjects as a part of the show may be harmful, though it is the action and not the hypnosis itself which may be detrimental or injurious.

Variations of such a stage show have been broadcast over the radio. Few of these broadcasts have been made, owing to the danger of lawsuit should something happen to a listener over whom there would be no control if anything went wrong, as might possibly occur with someone suffering from a personality disturbance, his emotional situation perhaps affecting him adversely. (Again, the hypnosis itself could have no ill effect.)

# CHAPTER IV

# Suggestibility

AS VARIOUS ASPECTS of hypnotism are discussed herein, mention will be made of the more important laboratory experiments which have been reported. Of course these can be summarized only, and interested readers may find details in Hull's text on hypnotic research, *Hypnosis and Suggestibility,* and in various psychological and medical books and journals in which articles on investigations in hypnotism appear. The bibliography included at the end of the text lists all our references, though it is not a complete list of the available literature.

Suggestibility has been one of the most important studies in the laboratory, and the older literature is replete with records and statements to which one may refer. There is no doubt that every human being is more or less susceptible to suggestion, and most people could be hypnotized—perhaps all—if better methods were available.

The degree of suggestibility to hypnosis is measured by the depth of trance reached by the subject. Various trance stages are known and recognized, but where one leaves off and the other begins is hard to say, even for the expert. Since the earliest days of hypnotic history, writers have tried to differentiate between these stages, but no general acceptance as to classification or nomenclature has ever been made in psychological circles. Division of the trance into various stages is difficult because of the lack of definition between them and also because of the great variability in response of subjects. The hypnotist seldom can say positively whether a light or medium hypnosis was obtained, nor can the exact difference be told between the medium and the deep states, although a close approximation can be made by an experienced operator.

The older writers proposed a number of scales as to depth of hypnosis. Liebeault set up five stages, while Bernheim described nine. Forel,[26] Moll, Wetterstrand and others believed a three-stage classification sufficient for all practical purposes. There have been some attempts to devise a scale for rating susceptibility for laboratory purposes which included definitions of such trance stages, but none has been generally accepted by psychologists. Hull suggested a graduated scale based on a score of 2 points each for 50 selected symptoms, thus producing a 100-point scale. Undoubtedly this would have value for laboratory work, and something of this nature is definitely needed.

For general purposes, five divisions of the various stages of susceptibility are quite satisfactory, with three of these designating actual hypnosis.

1. Insusceptible.
2. Hypnoidal (some symptoms but no trance).
3. Light trance.
4. Medium trance.
5. Deep or somnambulistic trance.

On the basis of signs or "symptoms," Davis and Husband [27] worked out a point scoring system which is given here as a good general index and because it is often referred to in the literature. Other scales have been devised in studies at Wisconsin and Harvard Universities. Friedlander and Sarbin [28] at Ohio State University made a summation of several, reporting none as of much value in itself, but they regarded a grouping of them as worth while. For detailed discussion of these scales, the article itself should be consulted.

### DAVIS AND HUSBAND SUSCEPTIBILITY SCORING SYSTEM

| Depth | Score | Objective Symptoms |
|---|---|---|
| Insusceptible | 0 | |
| Hypnoidal | 2 | Relaxation |
| | 3 | Fluttering of lids |
| | 4 | Closing of eyes |
| | 5 | Complete physical relaxation |
| Light trance | 6 | Catalepsy of eyes |
| | 7 | Limb catalepsies |
| | 10 | Rigid catalepsy |
| | 11 | Anaesthesia (glove) * |
| Medium trance | 13 | Partial amnesia |
| | 15 | Posthypnotic anaesthesia |
| | 17 | Personality changes |
| | 18 | Simple posthypnotic suggestions |
| | 20 | Kinaesthetic delusions; complete amnesia † |
| Somnambulistic trance | 21 | Ability to open eyes without affecting trance |
| | 23 | Bizarre posthypnotic suggestions |
| | 25 | Complete somnambulism |
| | 26 | Positive visual hallucinations, posthypnotic |

* In our opinion true anaesthesia (analgesia) is unlikely in the light trance and should be attributed only to the medium stage.

† Complete amnesia is seldom possible in the medium stage and is generally regarded as a manifestation found only in the somnambulistic trance.

## DAVIS AND HUSBAND SUSCEPTIBILITY
### SCORING SYSTEM—Continued

| Depth | Score | Objective Symptoms |
|-------|-------|--------------------|
| | 27 | Positive auditory hallucinations, post-hypnotic |
| | 28 | Systematized posthypnotic amnesias |
| | 29 | Negative auditory hallucinations |
| | 30 | Negative visual hallucinations; hyperaesthesias |

This scheme of scoring phenomena fails to take into consideration many definite symptoms and sensations experienced by a hypnotized person. The inclusion of these would make a much better rating system and give a truer description of each stage of hypnosis. Following Hull's idea of a 100-point system listing 50 symptoms or signs, we offer a scoring chart separated into six divisions instead of five, the last being the addition of a deeper stage of hypnosis not often classified since it is so seldom invoked. It should be included, however, to make the score complete.

Based on 2 points for each symptom exhibited, a total score would indicate the depth of trance reached. From 2 to 12 points would be hypnoidal; 14 to 36 would show a light trance; 38 to 54 a medium stage; 56 or more a deep or somnambulistic trance.

## LeCRON-BORDEAUX SCORING SYSTEM FOR INDICATING DEPTH OF HYPNOSIS

| Depth | | Symptoms and Phenomena Exhibited |
|-------|---|----------------------------------|
| Insusceptible | 0 | Subject fails to react in any way |
| Hypnoidal | 1 | Physical relaxation |
| | 2 | Drowsiness apparent |
| | 3 | Fluttering of eyelids |

*LeCRON-BORDEAUX SCORING SYSTEM FOR INDICAT-ING DEPTH OF HYPNOSIS—Continued*

| *Depth* | | *Symptoms and Phenomena Exhibited* |
|---|---|---|
| | 4 | Closing of eyes |
| | 5 | Mental relaxation, partial lethargy of mind |
| | 6 | Heaviness of limbs |
| Light trance | 7 | Catalepsy of eyes |
| | 8 | Partial limb catalepsy |
| | 9 | Inhibition of small muscle groups |
| | 10 | Slower and deeper breathing, slower pulse |
| | 11 | Strong lassitude (disinclination to move, speak, think or act) |
| | 12 | Twitching of mouth or jaw during induction |
| | 13 | Rapport between subject and operator |
| | 14 | Simple posthypnotic suggestions heeded |
| | 15 | Involuntary start or eye twitch on awakening |
| | 16 | Personality changes |
| | 17 | Feeling of heaviness throughout entire body |
| | 18 | Partial feeling of detachment |
| Medium trance | 19 | Recognition of trance (difficult to describe but definitely felt) |
| | 20 | Complete muscular inhibitions (kinaesthetic delusions) |
| | 21 | Partial amnesia |
| | 22 | Glove anaesthesia |
| | 23 | Tactile illusions |
| | 24 | Gustatory illusions |
| | 25 | Olfactory illusions |
| | 26 | Hyperacuity to atmospheric conditions |
| | 27 | Complete catalepsy of limbs or body |

65

## LeCRON-BORDEAUX SCORING SYSTEM FOR INDICAT-
## ING DEPTH OF HYPNOSIS—Continued

| *Depth* | | *Symptoms and Phenomena Exhibited* |
|---|---|---|
| Deep or somnam-<br>bulistic trance | 28 | Ability to open eyes without affecting trance |
| | 29 | Fixed stare when eyes are open; pupillary dilation |
| | 30 | Somnambulism |
| | 31 | Complete amnesia |
| | 32 | Systematized posthypnotic amnesias |
| | 33 | Complete anaesthesia |
| | 34 | Posthypnotic anaesthesia |
| | 35 | Bizarre posthypnotic suggestions heeded |
| | 36 | Uncontrolled movements of eyeballs—eye coordination lost |
| | 37 | Sensation of lightness, floating, swinging, of being bloated or swollen, detached feeling |
| | 38 | Rigidity and lag in muscular movements and reactions |
| | 39 | Fading and increase in cycles of the sound of operator's voice (like radio station fading in and out) |
| | 40 | Control of organic body functions (heart beat, blood pressure, digestion, etc.) |
| | 41 | Recall of lost memories (hypermnesia) |
| | 42 | Age regression |
| | 43 | Positive visual hallucinations; posthypnotic |
| | 44 | Negative visual hallucinations; posthypnotic |
| | 45 | Positive auditory hallucinations; posthypnotic |
| | 46 | Negative auditory hallucinations; posthypnotic |
| | 47 | Stimulation of dreams (in trance or posthypnotic in natural sleep) |

## LeCRON-BORDEAUX SCORING SYSTEM FOR INDICATING DEPTH OF HYPNOSIS—Continued

| Depth | | Symptoms and Phenomena Exhibited |
|---|---|---|
| | 48 | Hyperaesthesias |
| | 49 | Color sensations experienced |
| Plenary trance | 50 | Stuporous condition in which all spontaneous activity is inhibited. Somnambulism can be developed by suggestion to that effect. |

While the general attributes of each state are here segregated, it must be remembered that individual reactions always vary greatly. Some symptoms of the deep state may be shown by a person in only a medium trance (perhaps even in the light stage), and possibly some of those listed as characteristic of the light or medium trances may not be evidenced by some individuals in the deep trance. Allocations thus must be considered as general only. Nevertheless, the total score indicates with fair accuracy the depth of trance reached.

Obviously there is a fault in such a grading that considers the plenary or stuporous trance as requiring a score of 100. Even in such a deep state some individuals might fail to evidence some symptoms or phenomena. This condition is so well marked and so much time is necessary to attain it even with excellent subjects that scoring it is a purely arbitrary matter. It has been described in detail by Erickson,[29] who remarks that even trained subjects must undergo further training to develop it. After securing subjects for his experiment who were capable of deep trances, he spent on an average of two hours of systematic suggestion to reach the stuporous condition which resembles closely a profound catatonic stupor.

Prior to undertaking the development of hypnosis, various susceptibility tests can be made. If successful, they suggest to the prospective subject that he will be easily hypnotized. They are indicators only, but when markedly positive, it can be assumed the testee will be a good subject.

On a piece of paper or cardboard, draw a heavy-lined 8-inch circle with four radii at right angles to each other, as shown:

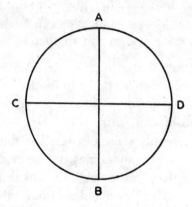

To a ring or some small light object, tie a thread about twelve inches long and seat the person to be tested at a table with the card in front of him. Have him hold the ring with arm extended so the ring dangles at the full length of the thread about four inches above the center of the circle as he looks at it. He is then to let his eye travel repeatedly up and down the full length of the line *A-B*. As he does so, he is told the ring will soon begin to swing in rhythm with the eye movement, though he is to pay no attention to the ring and is not to let his gaze wander to it. No matter how he tries to hold the thread motionless, the ring will swing in accompaniment to the eye movement if he is suggestible.

With approximately nine out of ten people, the ring will quickly commence to sway back and forth at gradually increasing speed. After it is moving briskly, he is asked to shift his gaze to line *C-D* (this may be omitted) or to let it travel completely around the circle as fast as possible in either a clockwise or counterclockwise direction. The ring will swing accordingly and shortly attain a speed matching the eye movement, swinging in a circle of about the same diameter as that of the circle drawn on the chart. This test is known as Chevreul's pendulum. It invariably proves extremely interesting and amusing to subject and spectators alike and exclamations of astonishment are heard as the ring picks up speed.

Another interesting test that may be made uses a color print of a room which can be cut from a magazine advertisement. The one chosen, let us say, shows a window with light blue drapes, and two chairs are visible. The prospective subject is handed the picture and allowed to inspect it briefly, say for one minute. Then it is taken away and he is asked the following questions, no information being given as to his accuracy until all the questions are answered.

"Are there two or three windows in the picture?" "What color is the window drapery, light yellow or light green?" "Are three or four chairs shown?"

Few people will answer the questions correctly. This is a test of observation as well as of suggestibility, but after answers have been given, many people, when told the drapes are blue, will say, "Of course, I remember now." The usual reply as to the number of windows will be two and as to the chairs, either three or four, more often three.

A further test is to draw two circles, about three inches apart, an inch or an inch and a half in diameter and identical. Write a figure 8 in one and in the other a slightly bigger 14, then ask which circle is the larger. Many will select the one with the higher number, thus indicating that they are influenced by suggestion.

Hypnotism is not involved in these tests but it is manifested slightly in the following, a very effective indicator of suggestibility. The subject is asked to stand erect with feet together, shoulders thrown back and face upturned so he looks at the ceiling at a point about two feet before him. The operator stands beside or directly behind him. If shorter in height than the subject, he should always stand to the rear. The following directions, or similar ones, are then given:

"I want you to think you are like a board standing on end. Let your knees be stiff, the whole body rigid and erect. Now close your eyes but hold the head level and keep the eyes still looking up. You cannot fall to the floor for I will catch you, but you are going to fall backwards. You will have a feeling of wanting to fall backwards. Do not resist it. You are teetering now, swaying, tipping over backwards. You are falling backwards! Backwards! Falling! Falling! Falling!"

The operator must be careful to catch the falling subject, and it is best to say "All right, all right" to arouse him when he has toppled over. The more susceptible fall with feet together and take no backward step, something almost impossible to do when wide awake.

When the operator is taller than his subject, it is more effective to have the subject's gaze fixed on the eyes of the hypnotist instead of looking up with eyes closed. Before beginning the talk, we make it a practice to rock the testee back and forth with our hands on his shoulders, disturbing his balance as the suggestion will later disturb it. The test may be varied by having the person fall forward instead of backwards.

Rarely an individual is encountered who will react in a negative way to both the falling and the pendulum test, falling forward when told to fall backwards or making the ring go in a direction opposite to the eye movement around the circle. Hull thinks this results from a complicating thought or emotion such as resistance to the suggestion. His tests were made with an apparatus which charted exact reactions in time, degree and direction. They showed that all persons tested were influenced to some extent by the suggestion, resistance being indicated by those who did not fall—a movement made and then halted.

When no tendency is shown to obey the suggestion and fall backwards, a very effective artifice may be used to bring results. Standing behind the subject, the operator places both hands on his shoulders, rocks him back and forth, then restores balance and presses down firmly on the shoulders, being careful not to exert any backward pull, which would be noticed at once. Further suggestions of falling are given and the hands suddenly lifted. In most cases, there will be a backward movement at once and the fall will continue until the person is caught. It is more impressive if he is allowed to go halfway to the floor before the movement is arrested.

When making the falling test, the operator must be alert for contingencies and must always prevent a fall to the floor. He must be prepared to catch the subject regardless of the direction of fall and must never neglect the possibility of the knees relaxing, for it is extremely difficult to support a wholly limp body. Also he must be ready for quick action because some subjects topple over at the first mention of falling, as we have found by experience.

Stage hypnotists and lecturers use this test to select good subjects from the audience, and the practitioner or laboratory worker can use it to prepare a subject for hypnosis. Most subjects will be impressed by the response aroused and thereafter accept more readily suggestive assurance of being an excellent subject. But the test is not always advisable with patients undergoing hypnotherapy, for it may intensify their fears or conflicts.

For demonstrations it is often possible to choose almost "sure-fire" subjects by questioning the spectators to find one who admits to sleep-walking. Usually sleep-walkers or sleep-talkers make excellent subjects, though sometimes subconscious resistances serve to prevent hypnosis. Though not an actual test, knowledge of this fact is extremely handy for the demonstrator.

Before attempting to hypnotize, it is usually best to make at least the pendulum and falling tests. Most people who know little about hypnotism are under the impression that they will not make good subjects, feeling that their own mind is too strong and that yielding to hypnosis would indicate a weakness. This idea must be counteracted by explanation, and then a positive test of suggestibility banishes the feeling. If the test fails, confirmation is felt and it may be difficult to obtain hypnosis.

As to suggestibility, a number of questions arise. What percentage of people can be hypnotized? To what extent? How quickly? The literature is full of references and statistics on these points, but it is impossible to reach exact figures because too many variables are involved. The physician who reports has dealt mostly with unhealthy people, who are therefore not average. The university psychologist, more likely to keep statistics and records, draws mostly from students in their teens or early twenties but above average in education. These are among the most readily hypnotizable subjects. The hypnotist's attitude, skill and prestige are highly important, and the selection of subjects is a vital factor. There being no generally accepted or standardized scale for rating depth of trance, it is impossible accurately to correlate and assay reports. Moreover, few reports indicate how many attempts have been necessary to produce hypnosis nor the number of trials which failed.

Perhaps the recorded failures could have been reversed by further trial.

Bramwell [30] writes at some length as to the findings of a number of the old-time hypnotists, most of whom were physicians. He gives his own results, which were somewhat surprising, for he claimed 100 per cent success in his early practicing at home in Boole, but after moving to London he found 22 per cent of his patients refractory. At Boole 48 per cent reached somnambulism; only 29 per cent in the London practice did so. Prestige probably is partly responsible, but he was more experienced when practicing in London. His results puzzled Bramwell himself. Perhaps country patients were more suggestible than the more sophisticated Londoners.

Liebeault, Schrenck-Notzing (Germany), Von Eden and Von Renterghen (Holland) were among the practitioners mentioned by Bramwell. He reported their experiences in a total of several thousand cases, summarized by Hull to show a mean percentage (including Bramwell's own figures) as follows:

| | |
|---|---|
| Refractory | 10.48% |
| Slight hypnosis | 32.68% |
| Deep hypnosis | 34.58% |
| Somnambulism | 22.26% |

Wetterstrand, who practiced in the latter part of the nineteenth century in Stockholm, obtained the best results statistically of the hypnotists of his era. He treated more than six thousand patients by hypnotic suggestion. His method was to hypnotize individually those who came to him, but only after they were allowed to see many others asleep in his offices. It was his custom to keep patients in hypnosis for hours at a time (sometimes for several days) and he would go from one to another, whispering suggestions into their ears. Patients undoubtedly found it most impressive when entering the doctor's offices to see sleepers scattered about on couches and in comfortable chairs in various rooms. This mass method was undoubtedly responsible, through suggestion, for the extraordinary percentage of subjects hypnotized. Out of 3148 cases, Wetterstrand reports only 97 failures, or 3 per cent, and he asserts that only one or two attempts were made with most of the failures.

Many years ago LeCron, shortly after graduation from college, was for a time an advertising salesman on a Denver newspaper. Among his customers was a professional hypnotist who employed Wetterstrand's mass method. The entire lower floor of an old brownstone residence was devoted to his offices, and patients were sleeping in every room. This operator resembled the storied Svengali in appearance, and his method certainly was effective. It was one of LeCron's first contacts with hypnotism and, noting his great interest, the "Doctor" often permitted him to observe the work. He referred to the scene as a "slumber party" and seemed thoroughly to enjoy his activities. Despite the Svengali appearance, he proved to be a kindly and pleasant individual on acquaintance, and a most adept hypnotist.

Hull's summary of Bramwell's report gives only three divisions of hypnosis aside from the refractory class. Conforming to the previous table of five classes and estimating from experience plus reports from the literature in general, the percentages of people susceptible may be tabulated approximately as follows:

| | |
|---|---|
| Uninfluenced | 5% |
| Hypnoidal | 10% |
| Light trance | 25% |
| Medium trance | 35% |
| Somnambulistic trance | 25% |

Analysis of the tables shows about one person out of four to be somnambulistic—able to reach an extremely deep state. Some 60 per cent, however, will reach a fairly deep hypnosis and a further one in four will enter a light trance. This means that about 85 per cent can be hypnotized although some estimate 90 per cent, and even more can be affected to a slight extent. While these estimates may err slightly, they are intentionally conservative. In all cases it is assumed that the operator is expert. If considerable time were devoted to the induction process, an adept operator probably could hypnotize almost any normal person and these figures would then be found to be much too low.

They must not be understood as indicating the results obtainable on first attempts at hypnosis. Bramwell mentions making sixty trials before hypnotizing one of his patients. Wetterstrand tried seventy times with a woman patient and finally succeeded. Vogt of Berlin, with typical Teutonic thoroughness, persevered through six hundred attempts with one subject, and seven hundred with another before reaching the goal. This would seem to be somewhat of a record.

As previously stated, the induction of hypnosis follows the laws of habit formation, the depth of trance usually increasing with subsequent attempts. The tables given represent the ultimate stage obtained. Braid, and most of those who followed, recognized that repetition of the trance makes induction easier and quicker and permits a deeper stage as facility is gained. Hull's experiments definitely prove this hypothesis, showing that the speed of induction is greater with repetition, slower early in practice than later. They also demonstrate that a period of disuse makes a slightly longer time necessary once more, followed by a recovery of ease of induction at a faster rate than in the first instance.

Ordinarily the greatest depth of trance which can be

reached will come in from eight to twelve sittings if the intervals between them are not too long. It is frequently impossible to secure proper relaxation and mental attitude in the first session, and usually a second or third is necessary before good results are possible. The subject should not be informed as to these points, however, before the first hypnosis is begun, for failure then would be suggested to him. Instead, complete confidence of success on the first attempt must be manifested. Only after failure is an explanation in order, and then suggestions of certain achievement at the next trial should be implanted.

It would be logical to assume that persons with a thorough knowledge of hypnotism and firmly convinced of the power of suggestion, understanding the phenomena and knowing the ease with which hypnosis can be brought on, would be easy to hypnotize. But here we have a paradox, for no one is so difficult to hypnotize as another hypnotist. With his knowledge, he is almost sure to be critical of another's technique. The same thing is seen in students who may be tractable before they acquire a knowledge of the subject, then become difficult and perhaps lose all susceptibility. If this attitude is overcome, the situation reverts to normal.

For almost eighty years the basis of inducing hypnosis has been the Nancy method of suggestion. It works effectively in many cases but only partially in others, and sometimes it fails completely. Having a fairly efficient means at hand, there has been little effort to find a better. While admitting failures, many old-timers stated that every normal person should be hypnotizable under proper conditions by a skilled operator. We fully agree with this opinion. The insane and feeble-minded are excepted, however. Suggestibility is undoubtedly an attribute of all mankind, though not to the same extent in all. If a better system of trance induction were to be discovered, it is our opinion that every normal individual could be hypnotized deeply in the course of not more than three attempts. We have indicated that massage, rhythmic breathing or the use of sound effects aid in producing hypnosis and sincerely hope laboratory psychologists will experiment to find a better, more effective method, perhaps something entirely different from those now practiced.

In popular opinion, women are generally regarded as more suggestible and more susceptible to hypnosis than are men. The literature is almost unanimous in rejecting this conception, and it seems as easy to hypnotize the male of the species as the female. Hull's tests corroborate this, though he found a slight difference in favor of women. As a matter of interest only, women are usually much more willing to be hypnotized, evidently not so timorous of the process and perhaps more curious than the so-called braver male.

All experts agree as to the great degree of susceptibility in children. Messerschmidt [31] made extensive research in this area and found the greatest degree at about eight years of age, from a study of those between the ages of five and sixteen. All investigation proves that children are almost 100 per cent hypnotizable, from the time they are able to understand and obey the necessary instructions up to fourteen years. Wetterstrand hypnotized a child of two and a half years, and bright children of three frequently can reach a trance state.

Adults grow less suggestible with advancing years, a graph of the tendency showing a gradual decline from fourteen on. It is far more difficult to obtain hypnosis with the elderly, though many oldsters can be hypnotized.

A statement frequently heard is, "I am sure I cannot be hypnotized because my mind is so strong and active." Almost everyone seems to have this idea, and the hypnotist must remove it in a prospective subject or he may have a failure. The suggestibility tests usually suffice. Also, most people tend to accept the word of one they regard as an expert, and will lose confidence in their invulnerability when told they are mistaken. The loudest skeptic may succumb readily, for he may be trying to reassure himself and is not really so sure of his invulnerability. He may even be skeptical in his conscious mind, yet the subconscious will retain a strong doubt and cause him to yield readily to hypnosis.

Among those hardest to hypnotize are the "bullheaded" ones who know it all and have no intention of following the directions of the hypnotist, even though they pretend to comply. Usually it is a waste of time to make any attempt with such people, but the adroit hypnotist with a good understanding of personality factors may be able to turn these traits and cause them to work for rather than against him.

One who is extremely anxious to be hypnotized, perhaps seeking relief from some painful or unpleasant condition, is also a most difficult subject. Just as the person troubled with insomnia becomes wider awake the more he tries to go to sleep, so it is with hypnosis. Passivity is needed; overactive cooperation has a negative effect. The hypnotherapist often encounters this situation.

Another refractory type is the person of keen, analytical mind. Even when he accepts the probability of being hypnotized and cooperates with the operator, during the process of hypnotization every suggestion will be weighed, each sensation studied, and thus he has difficulty in gaining the passivity which is so important. No matter how brilliant or intelligent, this kind of person has almost as much trouble either being passive or in centering attention on suggestions as does the flighty type of individual.

When it is important to hypnotize a difficult subject, as in a therapeutic case, a highly skilled hypnotist may direct his suggestions to utilize such personal characteristics and mental attitudes as bullheadedness, anxiety, too intense cooperation or an analytic type of mind. Naturally this requires great ingenuity, keen observation, and a good knowledge of personality and psychology. Erickson undoubtedly is a master of technique and explains that he orients himself entirely around what the subject himself does, making intense utilization of whatever he offers and of his personality pattern, feeling that what he (Erickson) does is extremely unimportant. Too often the hypnotist finds a good, workable formula which he likes and follows with all subjects. But success as a hypnotist lies primarily in knowledge, perspicacity and adaptability.

Popular belief in suggestibility as a mark of unintelligence or weak-mindedness is completely in error, and tests show that those of higher intelligence are more easily hypnotized. Suggestibility should not be confused with gullibility, although the credulous and gullible are, of course, highly suggestible. Gullibility implies the use of deceit, which is not involved in suggestibility. A giddy person with little control over his mind is usually unable to become mentally passive or to concentrate. His thoughts leap from one idea to another like a monkey in a tree jumping from bough to bough. An intelligent mind accepts logic and reason and, after a preliminary explanation, will understand the working of suggestion. By virtue of mental control he will become passive or will concentrate.

Friedlander and Sarbin found little relation between suggestibility and personality or traits of character. Davis and Husband report only small differences in the suggestibility of neurotic, introverted, extraverted, submissive or egoistic subjects. While theirs were controlled experiments, which ordinarily should carry more weight than mere opinions, additional study on these points is needed for clarification. The opinion of experts is based on extensive observation and in many instances does not check with the experiments mentioned, which were with a limited number of subjects, the suggestibility tests made having been arbitrary and artificial.

Among writers on hypnotism a general view is that introverts are more easily hypnotized than extraverts, McDougall [32] explaining the introvert as more liable to dissociation. Hysterical people are usually found to be excellent subjects, though there are exceptions, but there is a division of opinion as to those with other types of neuroses. This probably depends partially on the kind of neurosis and the objective symptoms displayed, as well as on other personality traits of the individual. The insomniac, for instance, may repel every idea of sleep. He is usually a most difficult subject with whom the word "sleep" must be carefully avoided. Anxiety frequently causes great resistance. The alcoholic generally is found a good subject unless suffering from a hangover at the time of attempted induction. Most neurotics are nervous and must be taught relaxation before good results are possible.

While the neurotic is extremely suggestible, that very factor may be one of the causes of his neurosis, though there is some disagreement as to this among authorities. Neurotics frequently are victims of negative or detrimental autosuggestion in connection with their neurotic difficulties. With these people, often there is great unconscious resistance, for the neurosis forms a defense mechanism which the subconscious mind wishes to retain. There may be extreme resistance not only to hypnosis but also to therapeutic suggestion and even to cure.

Position in life seems to have a direct bearing on suggestibility. Those who command or customarily give orders to subordinates are more difficult, while servants, workers, soldiers or sailors and those accustomed to obey as a rule make good subjects. Of course these are general statements only. The matter of prestige is important here. Owing to the prestige factor, most hypnotists usually find relatives, members of the family and close friends somewhat intractable. With any subject, familiarity lessens prestige and decreases suggestibility. The practitioner must always maintain prestige.

Little has been done in testing hypnotizability along racial lines. Among Europeans, we find the hard-headed Scandinavian as easily influenced as the more temperamental Latin. It is extremely doubtful if the more enlightened, allegedly "civilized" human being is any less susceptible than the aborigine. Latins and Hebrews have been regarded in psychiatric literature as somewhat more liable to neuroses, which may possibly indicate a greater susceptibility to suggestion.

Hypnotic drugs were mentioned earlier in the text and will be given further consideration in Part Two. Hull found that some drugs increase suggestibility in those who are normally suggestible. Alcohol certainly has this faculty when taken in small amounts, but one experience with a somnambulistic subject while very much intoxicated was entirely negative in our own experience. If the subject is still able to concentrate and give attention, alcoholic drinks remove inhibitions and release nervous tension, thus making it easier to "let go."

# CHAPTER V

# Principles of Suggestion

NO MATTER what objective use is to be made of hypnotism, whether in therapeutics, the laboratory, or merely for amusement, a thorough knowledge of the principles and practical application of suggestion is essential. Good results are improbable, if not impossible, when the operator does not know how to make suggestions properly. Although of great importance, entirely too little attention has been given this subject in the literature, perhaps because writers have withheld some of their more valuable information. If the response of the subject is to be as desired, the stimulus must be given with proper use of words and according to rule.

The exact meaning of the word "suggestion" should be understood. One dictionary definition is "the presentation of an idea or a belief or impulse to the mind." The psychological definition must go further. It must take into consideration both hetero and autosuggestion, direct and indirect, and waking and hypnotic suggestion. McDougall advanced a definition which we adopt with a slight change. "Suggestion is a process of communication resulting in the acceptance with conviction of an idea (or belief or impulse), and it may include an absence of logical grounds for its acceptance." This would answer our requirements on all points.

The reasoning power of the person to whom suggestion is to be given while in the waking state must always be considered, and it must be appreciated that anything illogical may not be accepted. When a person has been hypnotized, his mind is in a condition of increased suggestibility, as will be elaborated under the theories of hypnotism. Therefore the form of suggestion may be altered somewhat. Boris Sidis,[33] an expert in technique, recommended indirect suggestion as best in the waking state and the light trance state—a less positive phrasing of words with avoidance of definiteness and emphasis. In the deeper hypnotic states, direct suggestion is more effective and we may become positive and forceful. This does not necessarily mean the issuance of orders or commands. While commands may be more powerful, much depends on the character of the individual and the majority resent being ordered about or told what to do. Even in the trance this feeling is not lost. If the operator is peremptory and dictatorial, there may be obedience but there is always the possibility of refusal to accept a command, and better results in general will be obtained by not being abrupt or domineering. Positive, firm suggestion is different, and confidence of acceptance should be exhibited by the hypnotist. The word "must" should be avoided except with those who are by nature dependent in character.

A suggestion should be characterized by a firm belief or faith in the idea if it is to be accepted, and compliance is more likely when the suggestion is logical and a sound reason is given for its acceptance. This applies particularly to waking suggestion and is also true in hypnosis. An explanation tends to make it more acceptable and more powerful. We cannot spend time explaining every remark made, but if several suggestions are given, an explanation of the most important, the one which we particularly desire to have accepted, is more likely to bring its adoption.

A suggestion has the power of suppressing or inhibiting

the reverse idea in the mind. When there is acceptance an impulse to carry out the suggestion follows immediately, and that action temporarily bars any impulse to carry out an opposite action. The impulse to act suppresses the impulse not to act, and vice versa. Attention narrows the field of consciousness and increases suggestibility so that compliance with a suggestion is accomplished more easily. Belief in a proposed idea brings acceptance, and action to carry it out follows.

When suggesting, the wording must be carefully thought out in order to secure ready acceptance of the idea. If an obviously incorrect statement is made to a subject in the waking state as a suggestion, it will promptly be questioned and probably rejected. If made during the trance, it may be carried out but there is always the possibility of rejection.

For example, to eliminate a headache by hypnotic suggestion, it is futile to say, "Your headache has gone," for the patient has a headache and knows he has because discomfort is present. Even in hypnosis his immediate thought would be, "It certainly has not gone; I still feel it." A sensible person would then reject the suggestion and the headache would continue. Instead, if we say, "Your headache will gradually lessen and in a few moments will be entirely gone," the idea is implanted and the future tense allows time for it to become effective. If a logical reason is given why the headache will go away, the suggestion is almost certain to be accepted. Probable cause of the headache, such as fatigue, eyestrain or other reason, should be learned beforehand if possible. Whatever the cause, it can be woven into a statement that the subject's body is becoming relaxed, he is resting and there is no longer a reason for the headache to remain. Most subjects will report on awakening that the headache has disappeared.

It has been mentioned that an occasional person shows a negative reaction to suggestibility tests, usually some resistance.

With this type of individual the approach must be roundabout, for he will almost invariably resist a positive suggestion. Ingenuity is needed to formulate such suggestions.

The hypnotic practitioner soon learns that a trance state is not necessary in order to obtain good response to suggestion. It is very effective in the waking state with many who cannot be hypnotized or who reach only a hypnoidal condition. But as hypnosis is a state of increased suggestibility, suggestion is far quicker and stronger in action if the trance can be induced. The deeper the trance, the greater the degree of suggestibility. Those who cannot be hypnotized are less likely to accept suggestion, but when relaxed and attentive, good results frequently follow. Without the trance, advantage cannot be taken of the phenomenon of posthypnotic suggestion which permits a greatly increased range of effect. It will be discussed further in a separate chapter.

Baudouin,[34] a disciple of Coué,[35] pointed out several definite laws of suggestion which should be understood, his delineations clarifying principles long known but hitherto little understood.

*The Law of Concentrated Attention.* When spontaneous attention is concentrated on an idea, it tends to realize itself.

While conscious attention is desired in the waking state to secure full effect from suggestion, it is the attention of the subconscious mind which is sought during hypnosis and this part of the mind is more easily reached if there is no conscious attention. This important point is to be noted in connection with our remarks on attention.

*The Law of Reversed Effect.* Whenever anyone is in a state of mind in which he thinks, "I should like to do this but I cannot," he may wish as much as he pleases, but the more he tries, the less he is able.

The result of this law is seen in the person with insomnia

who tries to go to sleep. The harder he tries, the more wide awake he becomes. A similar situation arises in the induction of hypnosis. The more the subject tries to cooperate actively —the harder he tries to become hypnotized—the less chance there is of inducing the trance, since passive or directed cooperation is essential.

This law must be remembered when phrasing a suggestion—for instance, in the test where the subject is told to try to open his eyes but that he cannot because they are glued together. The harder he tries, the tighter they stick.

Coué said, "When the imagination and the will are at war, the imagination invariably wins. The force of the imagination is in direct ratio to the square of the will." This is so in principle, although it is not apparent how the mathematical relationship was figured.

Like Baudouin and Coué, Frederick Pierce [36] made an extensive study of suggestion and added another principle termed *The Law of Dominant Effect.* An idea always tends towards realization, according to Pierce. At any given time there is available in the brain only a certain amount of energy which is always attracted to the strongest emotional wish-feeling then present. Thus, when a person is experiencing the emotion of pleasure and danger intrudes, danger is stronger and subdues the pleasure instinct, which disappears—instantly if the danger is great. To achieve the greatest result from a suggestion, it must be attached to an emotion of the instinct group having such energy capacity as to surmount any other then likely to be active in the mind. The desire for success is an excellent motivation for use in connection with suggestion.

An emotion can best be aroused by employment of a visual image, a description or a story, emphasizing the content of the emotion rather than the feeling. This is noted, too, by Schilder and Kauders. As they point out, if acceleration of the heart beat is sought, suggestion is strengthened by having the subject visualize some terrifying concept. For overcoming insomnia, a visual image of being asleep combined with a suggestion to go to sleep helps to bring realization of that state.

The functioning of suggestion can be compared to the cutting of a sound track on a phonograph record. With the proper presentation of a suggestion, a deeper track is cut and acceptance becomes more certain. Actually the correct presentation of a suggestion causes a reorganization of thoughts and emotions which leads to a more ready acceptance of the idea. All human emotions, such as anger, fear, anxiety, disgust, love, hunger, serve to influence the mind. All are potent in result. Hence a greater effect can be obtained by combining suggestion with an emotion, deepening the impressed idea by stimulating an emotion which will tie in with it.

In the hypnotic treatment of alcoholism, for example, a feeling of disgust or aversion and nausea may be added as an accompaniment to the suggestion of loss of desire for alcohol. A good mental image to be applied in this case is to suggest that the subject will picture himself in a drunken state, reeling and staggering while onlookers show great disgust. This enlarges his view of himself and by making it inclusive he tends to become aware of what alcohol does to him. As another example, faith healers stimulate the emotions associated with religion in exactly the same manner in order to accomplish a cure.

Affirmations are far stronger than negations when making suggestions. For instance, to curb temper in a child it is practically useless to say during hypnosis, "You will not lose your temper." Instead, the youngster should be told again and again that he will be well, cheerful and happy, always in a good humor. He should be filled with the idea that he wants to and can be a good child.

Some old writers on hypnotism contended that only one idea at a time is accepted by a hypnotic subject. Our experience indicates that this is not entirely correct, though undoubtedly the fewer given, the easier it is to obtain acceptance. The main factor always is clarity. If there is not perfect understanding on the part of the subject, he cannot be expected to carry out suggestions. Simplicity is essential, for the subject's reasoning powers, though present, are limited in range to the idea suggested and literal in character.

There is sometimes a tendency for a hypnotized person to fall into a natural sleep, and a suggestion given a sleeping person may not reach either the conscious or the subconscious mind, although some authorities believe that the subconscious reacts to suggestion given during normal sleep. Since the point has not been positively determined and is doubtful, the subject should be brought back to the trance state and a check to ascertain which condition he is in can be made now and then by asking a question which requires an answer.

When suggestions have been given, the subject may be questioned to determine whether they have been understood and he may even be asked to repeat the suggestions. Curiously, when a promise is given during hypnosis to carry out a certain idea or action, it is usually fulfilled. For this reason, a request should often be made for such a promise. However, promises are not always carried out, particularly by alcoholics, drug addicts and certain neurotic types who may be deceitful in both the waking and hypnotic states. Even with them there is a strong tendency to keep a promise given in the trance.

The character of an individual cannot be expected to undergo material change in the hypnotic state. There is more of a tendency toward truthfulness in the untruthful and yet a liar is quite likely to falsify when hypnotized and even then he remains undependable. The normally truthful person who is essentially honest is likely to·be utterly truthful in hypnosis. The "rapport" factor, to be discussed later, undoubtedly tends to make a subject more truthful. Frequently secrets can be brought out if that is expedient, particularly by adroit questioning, and things may be confessed which never would be divulged in a waking condition. On the other hand, when a subject is queried in such a way, he is likely to awaken and may refuse to be hypnotized again even though there is amnesia for such questions. He may be unable to remember having been interrogated and yet continue recalcitrant. If willing to "tell all," as in the course of treatment for some condition such as a neurosis, things completely repressed and forgotten by the conscious mind can be brought to light. This is one advantage in favor of hypnotism for psychotherapy.

Under drug anaesthetics there is often a tendency to talk freely, and many people fear they may do so under hypnosis, but this is entirely a misconception. Frequently it is necessary to give assurance to a prospective subject on this point.

When a deep trance is reached and reasoning has been restricted, even the most bizarre suggestions may be accepted and carried out. Weird hallucinations can then be induced. These are real to the subject and no pretense is involved, as various investigations have demonstrated.

While there may seemingly be unquestioned obedience to the operator's will during the trance, nature has put a valuable safety factor or brake on the carrying out of harmful suggestions. A subject will never do anything directly in violation of his moral code. Ordinarily, a modest woman will flatly disobey a command to disrobe, probably awakening immediately, and no one will commit any act, criminal or otherwise, which he would not be willing to do when awake, if it ran contrary to his principles.

There has been great controversy on this subject and

countless experiments have been conducted to prove or disprove the contention. Perhaps an adroit hypnotist could in-
stigate any criminal act, including murder, but he would have
to proceed in an indirect manner rather than by using direct
suggestion, which would assuredly fail. But such a method can
also be successful with a person in the waking state.

An inconclusive but most interesting experiment to produce an act harmful to the subject was conducted by Rowland
at Tulsa University. He put a live rattlesnake in a box over
which was placed a cover of nonreflecting glass, almost invisible
to the eye. The snake was irritated and, rattling viciously,
coiled itself to strike. Several hypnotized subjects one at a time
were invited to reach in and pick up the serpent after an explanation that this was a real rattler. The suggestion was followed and they reached confidently for the snake, exhibiting
great bewilderment when their hands were stopped by the
nonvisible glass cover. The test would have been better if the
fangs of the serpent had been removed and it had been allowed
to strike with no glass to prevent it.

The same piece of glass was then placed in front of Dr.
Rowland's face and a subject handed a glass of sulfuric acid.
After being informed of the nature of the acid and its vitriolic
action, he was told to throw it in Rowland's face and promptly
carried out the suggestion, only the glass saving the doctor.

These experiments really demonstrate nothing. Possibly
the subjects were aware of the "invisible" glass, though all
denied seeing it. Undoubtedly there was complete confidence
in the operator, a certainty that nothing actually harmful
would be required of them, hence the willingness to comply.
His subjects were not stupid.

Apparently overlooked by Rowland, since he did not discuss it, was the complete absence of phobic reactions to the
snake on the part of his subjects while they were hypnotized,

yet the reptile caused them to become almost hysterical when they approached it while awake. In other words, the hypnotized subjects knew the situation was completely safe for them. Thus he seems to have been deceived into the belief that the experiment was decisive in proving that subjects would do something in hypnosis which they would not do in the waking state. Seemingly he confused "would not" and "could not."

Many experts have believed and tried to prove that a subject cannot be forced to commit any act against his code. Many are also positive that such acts could be successfully instigated hypnotically by use of subterfuge. Both views probably are correct, for it is possible to delude anyone into some such act even while in the waking state. Certainly hypnosis cannot cause and is a mere coincidental phenomenon in causing any antisocial behavior. Even if it were possible, there would be small likelihood of an unscrupulous hypnotist escaping the consequences. He could have no assurance of complete amnesia in the subject, although he might suggest forgetfulness of the suggestions, of the act, even of being hypnotized. If the subject were haled into court and subjected to the strain and emotion of a trial, these memories might be recalled in spite of the inhibitions suggested by the operator.

Several other experimental studies of possible harmful or antisocial use of hypnosis have been made, but with make-believe, pretended or "as if" situations hypnotically suggested which obviated the tests. Erickson, [37] however, conducted a long series of investigations using a total of fifty subjects trying to cause them to perform a number of different kinds of acts of unconventional, harmful, antisocial and criminal nature. All failed to respond. As Erickson reported, "Instead of blind, submissive, automatic, unthinking obedience and the acceptance of carefully given suggestions and commands, the subjects demonstrated a full capacity and ability for self-protection, ready and complete understanding with critical judgment, avoidance, evasion, or complete rejection of commands, resentment and objection to instrumentalization by the hypnotist, and for aggression and retaliation, direct and immediate, against the hypnotist for his objectionable suggestions and commands." In fact Erickson found more resistance to the carrying out of such suggested acts during hypnosis than in the waking state.

To the hypnotist prestige is a most important factor. Attorneys, physicians, professional men of all kinds learn by experience the importance of prestige in their practice. The psychologist, either clinical or medical, who practices hypnotherapy has even greater need of prestige. His personal appearance as well as his office, must be dignified. In addition, the hypnotist must exhibit complete confidence and a full knowledge of his subject. Suggestion depends too much on faith for these matters to be neglected, and mere faith in the physician has cured many an ailment.

Familiarity must be avoided, for it surely does not breed prestige even though it may not breed contempt. The hypnotist's attitude should be one of cooperative endeavor but with a teacher-pupil relationship maintained. Making a "house call" on a client should be avoided by the hypnotic practitioner because the prestige effect of his office is lost. For the same reason the consultant should not use his home as an office.

Prestige is used from the first attempt at induction of hypnosis. The subject is led to believe wholeheartedly in the ability of the operator to hypnotize him. It might be fatal to success if he were previously informed of the approximately one-in-five chance of deep trance induction on a first trial. That fact is never mentioned until a first attempt has failed. Then a full explanation of the reason for the failure can be coupled with assurances that the person will undoubtedly learn to be a good subject. Explanation will restore the prestige of the operator.

The consultant must never say, "Now I will try to hypnotize you," nor when engaged by a patient to overcome some physical or mental disturbance should he say, "I will try to cure you." Instead, the wise practitioner exudes confidence and gives the subject to understand that there is not the slightest doubt of success; that he will certainly be hypnotized and, if therapy is involved, that relief is certain. The same principle is important in laboratory experimentation. The neutral, would-be-scientific attitude of most laboratory hypnotists is proper for other sciences but in hypnotism will almost surely bring neutral results, defeating the entire purpose of many investigations.

To indicate the value of proper suggestion, let us analyze one of the experiments reported in Hull's book. It was performed to check further on the ability of a hypnotized person to resist muscular fatigue, such an investigation having previously been conducted by N. C. Nicholson [38] at Johns Hopkins Hospital. Nicholson found that fatigue could be largely inhibited by hypnotic suggestion. In Hull's test his operator, G. W. Williams, gave to each subject tested the following formula, the procedure being to have the subjects lift by one finger a weight of four and one half kilograms (about ten pounds) at a rate of eighty times per minute until fatigue prevented them from continuing:

"I want you to pull this weight and keep time with the metronome. I will start the metronome so that you can get the rhythm but do not wake up. You can now open your eyes but you are sound asleep. Now open your eyes and see your record. All right, eyes wide open, but sound asleep. There will be no fatigue in your arm and finger and you can make a good record. Ready—go."

Although there is some repetition as to the eyes opening without awakening, the most important suggestion of "no fatigue" is given once only as a mild direction. There was no emphasis or explanation as to why there would be no fatigue. The suggestion seems to have been given almost as an afterthought. Nothing is said as to monotony, and continued performance of the act certainly would be wearisome after a short time even if no fatigue were felt in the arm and finger. With an appreciation of the laws of suggestion, pride in achievement and strength should have been stimulated as an accompanying emotion, rather than a mere statement made that a good record could be made.

It would be truly astonishing if any positive result were obtained from such phrasing, which shows complete ignorance or disregard of all the principles of suggestion. This is typical of most of the Hull experiments. Yet in this particular one, the result was slightly positive, indicating the force of even a mild hypnotic suggestion.

Using proper phrases, Nicholson caused his subjects to continue the lifting exercise almost indefinitely even after they had previously carried on the same exercise in the waking state until their muscles were exhausted, and then had been put immediately into hypnosis and told they could continue without fatigue.

This is a perfect illustration of why one investigator has a positive result from experiments, yet another obtains the opposite. Without analysis we might conclude from Williams' test that "transcendency of voluntary motor capacity," as Hull calls it, could not be accomplished under hypnosis or would be slight. Nicholson definitely proves that it can. The difficulties of weighing hypnotic phenomena are thus apparent.

Ralph Winn,[39] in his book *Scientific Hypnotism,* has adopted a belief advanced by Schilder and Kauders as to the stage of hypnosis in which suggestion is most effective. They believe the light state best for most effective suggestion because the subject is more nearly in normal possession of his senses, as they put it. One of the reasons for Winn's preference for the light state when suggesting is that there is no subsequent amnesia. The subject remembers the suggestions and is more likely to carry them out when conscious of them.

We disagree entirely with this hypothesis, and most investigators support our opinion. Such conflicts are frequent and add zest to the study of the science! Logical argument and debate may clarify these disputes. There is not the slightest doubt of the efficacy of suggestion in the lighter stages of hypnosis or even in the waking state. Its force is great and the hypnotic practitioner quickly develops a healthy respect for suggestion, whether it is given in hypnosis or not.

But it is puzzling how such conclusions as to lesser effect in deeper trance could be reached. Experience demonstrates that suggestion given a subject in the deeper hypnotic states is far more powerful and effective. When there is complete, unconscious acceptance, the suggestion is almost certain to be acted upon. In most cases the less the conscious mind knows as to what has been suggested, the less interference there is and the easier it is for the subconscious to carry it out.

We believe the best results are obtained when amnesia after awakening is suggested, which requires a deeper trance. Hypnotic therapeutics involves posthypnotic suggestions, and they are certainly more likely to be accomplished when amnesia is invoked. Pitzer, [40] one of the best of the old-school medical hypnotists and highly skilled in the use of suggestion, always sought for amnesia after the trance, and we are in complete accord on this point. Then the subconscious can act to fulfill the suggestion without interference from conscious rationalizations and irrelevant considerations, for posthypnotic suggestion has a compulsive quality. Sometimes it is mild and sometimes very powerful. Pitzer advised an avoidance of all posthypnotic discussion with the subject, since it tends to weaken the amnesia and bring recall of the suggestion to mind.

To illustrate the proper application of the laws of suggestion, an analysis of the sleep formula given in the chapter on induction of hypnosis follows. We suggest that the reader turn back to it and review the phrasing (page 36).

In the first paragraph are directions to bring relaxation and mental passivity which will concentrate the attention automatically on the words being spoken. Even if instructed to pay no attention to the words, the subject hears and everything said will be registered in the mind. A passive mind will receive and accept suggestion better than a mind asked to concentrate on the words spoken, for the attention is then unconsciously fixed.

The symptoms which the subject will probably feel are next described, using the future tense and allowing time for the suggestion of these signs to take effect. Their subsequent appearance within the next few minutes confirms the suggestion and makes easier the acceptance of others. An assurance of comfort to allay nervousness or anxiety is quickly accepted because relaxation renders the subject physically comfortable. This is an indirect suggestion, for the feeling of comfort will automatically calm nervousness or self-consciousness, which is the end sought.

So far, no positive statements have been made nor any commands given. When we judge that the trance state is at hand, we become more positive and change the tense to the present, telling the subject he is sinking into sleep, going deeper with every breath. Emphasis and positive tones are now employed and he is told he will go to sleep, then that he is asleep and will go deeper asleep after a count of three has been made.

Up to this point the subject may have been hovering on the brink of the trance, and such a statement often acts as a push, causing him to "fall" into the hypnotic state. Commands may now be given, not brusquely nor too emphatically but as positive statements. The sleeper is not to awaken until told to; he is to do as directed (not ordered); and he will wake when instructed—wide awake with a refreshed feeling.

Great variations of wording can be used in the induction talk, but there must be conformation with the laws of suggestion in order to secure the best results. The skilled hypnotist studies the subject carefully before beginning the suggestions and sizes up his individual personality pattern as much as possible. Some people require more positive statements than others; some need more reassurance. The tone of voice is quite important. Few respond to loud tones, and a low, monotonous but emphatic voice is usually best. In some cases it is well to speak rapidly, thus preventing a subject's mind from wandering to other ideas or studying his feelings while listening. Many times the subject responds more easily to a slow, drawling delivery. Ordinarily he expects to be dominated and to be forced into the hypnotic state, although quite willing to comply. Toward this end delivery should be forceful, emphatic and certain, but not sternly commanding. However, and only in general, we prefer to keep the relationship between hypnotist and subject on more of a cooperative basis with a teacher-pupil relationship.

With many subjects, dominance is resented and then the induction talk must be more in the nature of a lullaby, slow and monotonous with a definite rhythm maintained. In the sample formula this would begin after the second paragraph, with the rhythm accompanying the subject's breathing on exhalation, which will be found extremely effective. A tone in the bass register is far preferable to a tenor. Certain words lend themselves to the rhythm and may be drawled throughout the exhalation of a breath—such words as "drow-w-w-w-sy," "heav-v-v-v-vy," "slee-e-e-e-py," "dee-e-e-e-p." When becoming more emphatic, a faster tempo should be used together with a louder voice, as when the count of three is started.

With suggestion given a subject in the trance state, speech should be definitely positive and direct suggestion should be used throughout, but with the word "must" avoided. During the trance, emphasis and clarity are important, and the most vital feature of hypnotic suggestion is repetition. Statements are reiterated over and over again, each single idea and group of ideas being constantly repeated. This cannot be emphasized too much, for repetition undoubtedly is the key to the use of hypnotic suggestion. Many hypnotists do not appreciate its importance. Usually there are a number of thoughts to be imparted to the subject as suggestions to gain our ends, and each one should be repeated when given, then the entire group repeated. The minor points should be mentioned first, the more important following and the one of greatest consequence reserved until the last, for the one last given will be most readily accepted.

# Hypnotic Phenomena

MOST PHENOMENA observed in hypnosis today were well known back in the days of animal magnetism. Modern investigation has merely analyzed and tested them. It has been the unusual elements and extraordinary capacities involved which have made the science so fascinating to practitioners and to laboratory psychologists alike. Their startling nature has made possible stage exhibitions for which audiences are willing to pay. With the great amount of interest exhibited by observers whenever shown a demonstration and with over one hundred years of experience with hypnotism in its more modern form, it is remarkable that there should be so much misunderstanding and ignorance of the subject.

The lecturer invariably finds his audience intensely curious and expectant, but almost entirely uninformed or misinformed as to hypnotism. A straightforward explanatory talk removes the mysticism and strips off the shroud of the occult, leaving interest increased by proper understanding. If the lecturer were to ask for volunteer subjects at the beginning of his talk, few would come forward. After an explanation, many listeners have lost their apprehension and fear and are willing, even eager, to experience hypnosis. This is particularly true of small audiences where the volunteer will not feel too conspicuous and self-conscious.

Although hypnotic phenomena may seem strange and unusual, examples duplicating every phase of hypnosis can be found in the waking state of everyday life. All may be seen or induced in completely normal persons. Often they are evidenced by those who have some mental abnormality which may run the scale from slight mental disturbance through neurosis and hysteria to actual psychosis or insanity. Every phenomenon can be manifested in entirely normal people by means of posthypnotic suggestions given during the trance, to be carried out in the waking state after the trance has ended, though sometimes such suggestion brings a new trance when acted upon. All phases can also be self-induced by individuals able to put themselves into a hypnotic state.

*Catalepsy* has already been discussed. Cataleptic rigidity of the entire body is a favorite feat of the stage hypnotist. The subject is asked to lie down while hypnotized, complete body rigidity is suggested and he soon becomes stiff and board-like. When fully rigid, he is lifted and placed across two chairs, remaining suspended between them. To make this more spectacular, several people may be invited to sit on his body, which is capable of supporting extraordinary weight. For this the chair must be placed under the shoulders and never under the head or neck. Sometimes the "professor" places a large stone on the victim's stomach and breaks it with a sledge hammer—a very dangerous procedure, as one stage hypnotist (Flint) of former days discovered, when his wife, acting as subject, was killed by a poorly aimed blow delivered by a volunteer from the audience. There is no condition in hypnosis which will change the composition of the body. Bones will break just as easily or the flesh bruise as badly in hypnosis as in the waking state.

Most of the conditions reported by the early writers as attributes of hypnosis have been confirmed in laboratory tests. One which is hard to analyze and is most puzzling is that known as *rapport*. It was long believed that a subject would respond only to the suggestions of the person who had hypnotized him and would pay no attention to anyone else unless so instructed by the hypnotizer. Such rapport could be transferred to a second person and the operator would then lose contact with the subject, or the rapport could be shared if a suggestion to that effect was given. The subject would respond to no one else and could not be awakened except by one with whom he was in rapport. This was a firm conviction of the magnetists and of many later hypnotists.

Braid and a few others in the early days questioned this feature and thought it entirely due to suggestion. They felt that most subjects must have heard of it and regarded it as true, or else they received some idea of it during hypnosis and consequently conformed in their actions. But when there was no knowledge, observant hypnotists noticed that this feature of rapport might be lacking and they decided it was a myth. They found that some responded to the suggestions of observers, answered their questions or woke at the command of a third party.

P. C. Young [41] and Hull in more recent times came to this same conclusion, but it would seem that experimental study of rapport which confirmed their belief was not close enough. Erickson investigated more thoroughly by testing a five-year-old girl who knew nothing of hypnosis and could have had no preconceived notions of rapport. To make the result more conclusive, a spontaneously induced posthypnotic trance was obtained with no suggestion as to rapport given. The little girl paid no attention to questions or to the actions of others than the hypnotist and seemed quite unconscious of them. Even her mother was unable to attract her attention in any way, but the child could walk around, talk to the hypnotist and see any particular object or person called directly to her attention by the hypnotist, though she made no response except to him.

It should be mentioned also that Erickson found a spontaneous catalepsy displayed by this same little girl, her limbs remaining motionless in any position in which they were placed.

Rapport is really a most remarkable phenomenon, and Erickson comments that one never knows what it actually may include. He feels that it is expressive of the subject's attitude towards his surroundings and very definitely a phenomenon of hypnosis.

There is another phase of rapport which seems to be unquestionable as to actuality. This is the desire on the part of the subject to please the hypnotist and to carry out his instructions even when they are obviously ridiculous or even unpleasant to the subject—a tendency to automatic obedience. Such a desire is quite abnormal even when submission to hypnosis is sought by the subject. It is seldom evidenced towards others than the hypnotist, and then genuine reluctance is shown. Towards the operator there may be an indication of sluggishness and passivity, a time lag in response, but none of reluctance, and lassitude or lethargy disappears if normal activeness is suggested. Desire and eagerness to please are quite definite, and complete cooperation is usually manifested. This phase of rapport is real and apparent.

Often there is a strange urge in the subject to act a part and to pretend. Simulation of hypnosis is an ever-present possibility for which the operator must watch. Even the most honest person may deceive in this way, apparently feeling it necessary. When questioned, the subject will often say, "Oh, I did not want to let you down. I really wasn't hypnotized at all," or he may remark, "I was just trying to cooperate." It is possible that he was unaffected but this desire to simulate is in itself a sign of hypnosis. It is connected with the phase of rapport just mentioned. Sometimes it serves as an adequate defense against the knowledge that one is in a trance. If post-hypnotic amnesia is not present, the subject may rationalize his behavior by an honest belief that he was simulating, this permitting him an understanding of his actions. Complete amnesia would make such rationalizing unnecessary and he could then accept the fact of having been hypnotized.

Not only may a pretense at being hypnotized be made but, in actual trance, trickery may be displayed in attempting to complete some suggestion—additional evidence of the desire to please the operator. Such behavior is more often observed in the light trance state, especially when it may not be deep enough to bring about actual performance without fraud. The operator may then be led to believe that the state is deeper than is really the case, hence the importance of tests which have been described. There may be deception during tests, but a skilled hypnotizer is likely to see through any fraud. When fraudulent, there is usually an exaggeration; the impostor will act too quickly in accepting suggestions and not show the natural deliberateness he should evidence. If there is any indication of feigning, physical signs should be closely observed, particularly those of catalepsy.

Some tests make good checks against deceit, as they cannot be simulated. If the subject is told he is to smell a delightful perfume and an uncorked bottle of strong ammonia is then held beneath his nose, he will sniff it appreciatively while hypnotized, for the sense of smell has been hallucinated. If he is pretending to be hypnotized, he will be unable to refrain from drawing his head away. A better proof is to induce anaesthesia in the hands or arms and then tell the subject he is to be given a strong electrical shock which will not be felt because of his anaesthesia, but much too powerful to take if he were awake.

If there is no real hypnosis the sleeper will suddenly awaken, for few subjects care to continue a fraudulent performance to such an extreme.

*Anaesthesia* has been frequently mentioned heretofore. Technically the word means loss of sensory perception, but it is commonly used to denote loss of the feeling of pain. While the proper term for absence of sensibility to pain is *analgesia*, we will continue to use the word "anaesthesia" in its more ordinary sense.

Anaesthesia is one of the most interesting phases of hypnosis, and it has definite practical value. It can be readily induced in a good subject during the trance. Any part of the body may be anaesthetized; an arm or a limb or even a limited area may be marked off so that no sensation of pain can be perceived under stimulus, while sensation is normal outside the designated area. When induced over a limited space it is technically designated a glove or stocking anaesthesia.

Induction is accomplished by repetitive suggestion with phrasing such as, "I am going to anaesthetize your right arm. When I have counted up to three, you will be unable to feel any pain in that arm if it is pinched or pricked with a needle or even cut with a knife. You will be unable to feel any sensation of pain at all. *One*—your right arm is losing the ability to feel pain. *Two*—you will not be able to feel pain of any kind in the right arm. *Three*—the arm is now completely anaesthetized."

For best results, and so that the subject can reorganize his processes of mental behavior, there should be distinct pauses between the counts and a lapse of time before anaesthesia is tested. In such a demonstration it seems easier to cut off the pain nerves if the tactile sense is employed. The arm is stroked gently while suggestions are given, accompanying the count by running the hand down the arm of the subject. It should not be assumed that this has anything to do with mesmeric passes, for it is merely the addition of touch to the suggestion.

With the phrasing given, the subject would still have a sensation of touch, but not of pain. If a test is made by electric shock, phraseology should include a statement that no shock will be felt. If told there will be no feeling at all in the arm, even the sense of touch would be inhibited and nothing at all would be perceived so far as that limb was concerned.

Ordinarily a pinch will effectively show whether anaesthesia has been evoked, at least to the subject. Breaking the skin in any way leaves a possibility of infection. Not to be condoned is the stage practice of running long needles through the cheeks or arms of the subject. Electric shock is excellent as a test, and spectacular to onlookers allowed to feel the strength of the shock. A surprising voltage may be taken, one which would be unbearable in the waking state. Estabrooks reported using a variac device with which voltage can be regulated, the contacts placed in the palm and on the back of the hand over blotting paper soaked in a saturated salt solution, making an excellent contact. He found fifteen volts painful and twenty unbearable in the normal state, but up to one hundred and twenty taken without flinching when hypnotic anaesthesia was induced. Certainly this is proof of the reality of the anaesthesia. The many surgical operations performed with it offer even better proof of the genuineness of the phenomena.

One precaution should be observed when testing anaesthesia. Intensely interested and curious at the absence of pain, a subject may injure himself when invited to try the anaesthesia with a needle or other sharp instrument. Subjects who cut themselves deeply instead of pricking lightly with a knife handed them for the purpose have been reported. LeCron had this experience when a young lady subject was given a sterilized needle and promptly plunged it deep into her arm, much to his surprise. With some, this tendency may indicate complete confidence while in others it may show a trace of masochism. We do not make it a practice to allow the subject to do more than pinch himself, and even then we caution against too hard a pinch.

In the laboratory, investigations of anaesthesia have been made by Bechterev and confirmed by Hull. Subjects displayed no signs of suffering when pain stimuli were given nor in such semi-involuntary processes as change of respiration. Some positive indications were obtained with galvanic skin reaction and with the pulse rate by Hull. Bechterev [42] reported the pulse unaffected and no contraction of the pupil of the eye noted, these being usual accompaniments of pain.

The technical question has been asked, "Is the pain really not felt or is there amnesia? Does the subject feel it, later forgetting the pain?" Laboratory findings demonstrate that no pain is felt. Under drug anaesthesia, it is generally believed the pain is felt but immediately forgotten. That is why operating tables are equipped with straps to prevent movements of the patients who often groan during operations. Esdaile found that hypnotized patients did not move or indicate pain in any way even when a limb was amputated.

Under drug anaesthesia there is a postoperative shock which has been reported by some of the old writers as absent in hypnotic anaesthesia. Esdaile noted the rate of healing in his surgical patients as being greatly accelerated when hypnotic anaesthesia was used.

A subject in whom anaesthesia can be produced in the trance may be conditioned by means of posthypnotic suggestion so that it can be applied in the waking state, either by the operator or by the subject himself. This conditioning has a practical and desirable aspect, particularly when dental work is to be performed, in case of accident, or in childbirth. The wife of one of the writers is able to do this regularly when in the dental chair. One of our subjects has been taught this feat and employs it at will. He was employed in an aircraft factory where a heavy forging one day slipped from his hands and fell, tearing the flesh and causing a painful injury to his foot. The company physician found no broken bones so our subject anaesthetized the part and found instant relief from the pain, returning to work after the wound was dressed.

The ability to apply anaesthesia in this way usually requires several repeated suggestions. The subject must be conditioned to it, although this is sometimes possible on the first attempt. At first there may be only partial anaesthesia, which becomes more complete with practice. Furthermore, it must be practiced from time to time or the ability may be lost. Some report no sensation when anaesthesia is induced, while others report a tingling or numbness much like the effect of novocain, perhaps by reason of association of ideas.

A precaution should be mentioned. After anaesthesia has been invoked, it must always be removed and that part of the body returned to a normal condition of sensitivity. The operator must never forget this, nor should the subject, if it is self-induced. Pain is a natural danger signal and while this is an excellent method of gaining comfort by removal of pain, the cause of the pain should not be neglected. In the cited case, had there been a broken bone it would certainly have caused serious injury to the foot to have walked on it. Before removing the pain it was incumbent on the victim to be sure no break in any of the bones had occurred.

There is a logical theory as to how anaesthesia of this nature is established, though actual proof is impossible with our present knowledge of neurology. The nerves of the human body carry faint electrical currents or impulses to and from the brain. The nerves are made up of innumerable minute fleshly "wires" called neurons which connect with each other at points called synapses. These are infinitesimal brushes much like those of electric generators. Electrical impulses traveling along the nerves can be cut off when the synapses are opened, and the neurons seem to have the ability to break the contacts. The theory advanced by Travis et al. is that during sleep or when unconscious from other causes such as a blow on the head, there is a shorting out of some nerve impulses. Under anaesthesia produced by suggestion, probably there is a similar short-circuiting and the impulses never reach the brain. Hence no pain is felt, no mental image seen, no sound heard and no taste or smell discerned if anaesthesia for any of these senses is suggested. It is exactly as though we had thrown open a switch to shut off the current. This theory is entirely feasible and adequately explains what happens, although we cannot prove the accuracy of the explanation.

Anaesthesia is applicable to all the senses as well as to tactility. Functional blindness may be induced in one or both eyes and its actuality can be proved. Of course nothing is wrong with the eye; the sight is simply inhibited and visual images do not reach the brain. Erickson [43, 44] induced color-blindness hypnotically in tests and also induced hallucinations of color vision so that his subjects saw white sheets of paper as red, blue, green or yellow when it was suggested, describing interleaved white sheets as of the complementary color appropriate to the hallucinated color of the preceding sheet.

Erickson also made experiments as to the sense of hearing and proved that it is possible to induce complete functional deafness with the subject hearing nothing, not even the voice of the operator or his own voice. One way of testing the induced deafness was by establishing a conditioned reflex where response was to an auditory stimulus and would thus be automatic and involuntary. When hypnotic deafness was then induced, no response to the conditioned reflex was made by the subject, which would seem to be conclusive proof of the deafness being actual. An interesting side light to this experiment was the finding in one subject of a spontaneous deafness for all sounds except the experimenter's voice. Thus no conditioned reflex could be established, for the subject did not hear the stimulus sound.

Auditory anaesthesia has also been tested by firing a gun unexpectedly behind the hypnotized person in whom deafness had been induced. Even when instrument tests were made, no sudden start was noted nor any reaction seen. Subjects may be conditioned to induce such deafness or other sense anaesthesia in themselves in the waking state, just as described for anaesthesia to pain.

The practical value of hypnotic anaesthesia is unfortunately limited, for it can be produced by today's methods only in about one person out of three or four and even then it may not be complete. Its use in surgery or dentistry is thus restricted. However, drugs are not effective with a number of people and some are allergic to them. They cannot be used in certain physical conditions such as a weak heart. Obstetricians find drugs of only partial value in almost 50 per cent of childbirth cases, as many mothers will testify.

Another drawback to the use of hypnotic anaesthesia is the time element. Several sessions with most subjects are needed before it can be brought on and relative completeness developed, and this would serve to make it an expensive matter as well. And of course few hypnotic anaesthetists are available. Should the medical profession adopt hypnosis as a therapeutic agent, most of these hindrances will be eliminated.

Two Australian physicians have recently reported [44a] an interesting application of hypnotic anaesthesia. Held captive by the Japanese in a Singapore prison camp, they were called upon to perform many operations on their fellow captives. As no medical supplies were available and anaesthetic drugs were thus lacking, they resorted to hypnosis for anaesthesia. A number of operations were performed, including major ones, without pain to the patients and the results of 29 such cases are described by them. Although only a very light hypnosis was obtained in some instances, even in these suggestion induced the desired anaesthesia. Among the advantages they found in their work were the elimination of nervousness; full cooperation on the part of the patient; eradication of postoperative complications such as nausea; reduction or removal of postoperative pain; and less bleeding and more rapid healing of wounds.

The opposite of anaesthesia is *hyperaesthesia*. Instead of inhibiting the various senses, we render them superacute—or do we? Here again we run into controversy. It would seem quite possible to demonstrate such "superman" qualities if they can be produced, but laboratory experiments of this nature are a difficult matter. There is always the possibility that hyperaesthesia credited to hypnotic subjects may result from the underestimation of normal waking powers and the absolute refusal of the individual in the normal waking state to extend himself to the full limit of his capacities. Superior concentration under hypnosis may also be concerned. Perhaps hyperaesthesia is impossible to establish in most of us, yet a small percentage might show a positive response and tend to prove the point.

Tests by Rhine [45] at Duke University on extrasensory perception seemed to indicate that most people lack it, although a small number appeared to evidence varying degrees of extrasensory perception. Rhine's work has been vigorously attacked by psychologists, particularly as to the statistical accuracy of the findings, and has not been accepted as factual.

It is never easy to find somnambulistic subjects willing to serve as guinea-pigs. Otherwise investigation would be facilitated. Hyperacuity of vision under hypnotic stimulation could easily be tested with eye charts; hearing by means of vibrators.

Hyperacuity is sometimes found among people in the normal waking state, though rarely, which would indicate that it might possibly be established by hypnotic suggestion. We know of one such person shown by college laboratory tests to have definite superacuity of hearing, in that he can detect sounds above the normal human register. The playing of a violin or the singing of a canary will produce a violent headache in this individual if he listens to it for a few moments. Undergoing tests, a vibrator was started with control in another room beyond his range of vision. When the instrument was set in higher registers than can normally be heard, he responded to the stimulus each time. These upper range vibrations he describes as felt rather than heard. Tests in hypnosis could include not only suggestion for hyperacuity of tones in the upper register, but for sharpness of hearing—the distance at which sounds can be heard.

Hypnotists of the old days often demonstrated an interesting matter which we have also performed successfully. A number of new playing cards with presumably identical backs are placed face down on a table. The hypnotized person is shown the cards on the table but each is described as a photograph, a landscape, a portrait or anything which comes to mind. One of the imaginary photos is designated as a picture of the subject's home, for example, and he is asked to recognize and select that card from among the others. The cards are then shuffled with the subject not permitted to see the faces, though the operator and witnesses are shown the face of the indicated one for identification. Again placed face down before the subject, he selects the correct one. Frequently there is failure with this test, but some subjects have an uncanny ability to pick the right card.

Hyperacuity of vision under hypnosis would be a likely explanation, but there are other possible ones. Cards are not identical and have infinitesimal differences in the markings. Gamblers make a practice of learning such markings and some can readily distinguish them. So could anyone else, either in hypnosis or wide awake, but few are aware of such differences or could distinguish them without a few moments of study. After making this experiment, Erickson took the sensible but often overlooked step of questioning hypnotized subjects as to how they identified the card. They reported the hallucination of the suggested photograph as seen but were able to connect a part of it, such as the smoke from the chimney of a suggested house, with a single line on the actual card which would then be looked for in recognizing that card. A photograph of a portrait would have an earring associated with another line or mark.

Many instances of various sense hyperaesthesias are cited in hypnotic literature, and the phenomenon was generally accepted in earlier days, though controlled investigations never were made and such reports cannot be regarded as proved. Moll and others experimented with increased sensitivity to touch, pressing the points of a drawing compass against the skin. Moll found that by use of hypnotic suggestion he could cause an increase of skin sensitivity in a subject who could then distinguish the points as two instead of one at a less distance apart.

One kind of increased sensitivity has been noted by us. At an evening with friends, a young lady was hypnotized and placed in a deep trance. She was reclining on a couch and at once began to show signs of distress, tossing her head from side to side with a pained expression on her face. When questioned, she complained of being unable to breathe comfortably—the air hurt her throat and lungs. As she was very uncomfortable and suggestion did not make her feel better, she was awakened. Later in the evening another girl who had arrived after the first episode, and knew nothing of it, asked to be hypnotized and showed the same signs, asking to be awakened. She complained of a feeling of suffocation. All present then noticed that the air was foul and filled with tobacco smoke.

Comfort and enjoyment had been suggested during the induction process in these two instances. Superacuity toward the foul air, if that is the explanation, must have been spontaneous and would seem then to be an attribute of the trance, not the result of heightened sensitivity due to suggestion. It may be said that passivity or concentrated attention was responsible, the foul air being unnoticed until the subject relaxed and reclined for the induction process. Yet the exhibited distress appeared out of all proportion and vanished on awakening. Mention has been made previously of the importance of room temperature and that a draft of air, particularly if cold, hindered hypnotic induction. This is also perhaps a matter of hypersensitivity and indicates that it may be present in the earlier stages of the trance.

There have been many reports showing increased ability to reckon elapsed time under hypnosis. Many seem to possess a mental alarm clock which is apparently aware of the hour or appreciates the passing of time with extraordinary accuracy. This is usually exhibited as an ability to awaken from normal sleep at a given time, one of the authors being able to do this regularly. The facility is not rare and probably is a conditioned reflex developed by the individual over a period of time.

Delboeuf in 1886 experimented with the time sense in hypnosis, and Bramwell, after reading of this, tried it in 1895 with a female subject. As a posthypnotic suggestion, she was told to mark a cross on a sheet of paper together with the time of day, and this was to be done some definite number of minutes after the suggestion was made, amounting in some instances to several days or weeks later. Out of fifty-five attempts, most were recorded exactly at the proper moment, and there never was more than a five-minute error on any one test.

Bramwell cites other such investigations but, having no controls and not having checked the results of similar tests on the same subjects in the waking state, he proved nothing save an abnormally accurate sense of time perception on the part of these particular subjects. He does claim that the woman subject was unable to show such time appreciation in the waking state, but he made no record of having tested it.

Hull reports Stalnaker's and Richardson's study along this line, clinical observation indicating no such increase in power to estimate passage of time. However, only nine subjects were examined, so the matter may be regarded as unproved either positively or negatively.

Everything experienced in the process of living is perceived first by the consciousness and then recorded in the brain. The recording is spoken of as a memory and the strength of the impression determines whether or not it is retained. Almost all experiences are in all probability promptly discarded as unimportant and do not remain in the memory, only the stronger ones being recallable. We are constantly undergoing new or repeated experiences, and it would be impractical to retain more than a tiny fraction of them. In "experiences" we include every move a human being makes and every thought that occurs. All of these are mentally recorded, but only the more striking are subject to recall at will or through stimulus such as an association of ideas. Often these memorable experiences are connected with an emotion which may be pleasant or unpleasant.

Human memory consists primarily of four factors: assimilation, retention, recollection and recognition. Unless an experience is assimilated, it will not be retained. Evidently there is a sort of mental filing system for the process of retention, because a memory leaves the consciousness and seemingly is forgotten until the need to recall makes it desirable for that memory to be brought forth again into consciousness. All strong memories and experiences are assimilated and probably retained, but most of them are never recalled for lack of need. Under hypnosis, memories completely forgotten in the waking state and not subject to conscious recall can be brought out of the subconscious filing cabinet. Pending recall, what becomes of these memories?

Psychologists have various terms for the subconscious mind such as "unconscious," "subjective," "superconscious," "subliminal" and others. Regardless of terms, there is an area of the mind which differs from that which we use consciously. Someone has compared the mind to an iceberg floating in the sea with the conscious mind or awareness above the water line, the greater bulk being below and ordinarily unreachable. We term this submerged portion the subconscious. It controls the various functions of the body outside of consciousness, all the semivoluntary and involuntary actions of the organs, glands and muscles. The autonomic nervous system is the vehicle through which it acts. Memory is a part of the subconscious, Rivers [46] having termed it the "storehouse of memory." Hypnotism provides a means of reaching the subconscious, as we shall learn when considering theory.

One of the most remarkable of hypnotic phenomena is the ability to bring back lost memories, those completely missing from consciousness and no longer subject to voluntary recall in the waking state. This special hypnotic ability is termed *hypermnesia*—the opposite of amnesia. There are several normal types of memory loss, including ordinary forgetting and the amnesias, with some of the latter abnormal. Among the latter are repressed memories which cannot usually be recalled. These memories are of experiences or emotions which cause a mental conflict within, perhaps with an accompanying feeling of guilt. As such memories are undesirable, they may be pushed from the consciousness deliberately.

Memories of very early childhood ordinarily are lost through the passing of time, or perhaps because the tiny child cannot assimilate and hence cannot retain or recall. Freud theorized that a mental block develops, preventing the recollection of all childhood memories occurring before the age of five or six except the very strongest emotional experiences. This block is presumed to inhibit the recall of childhood memories prior to that age. At any rate, most people have only sketchy memories of their early childhood, and there is always the possibility that some supposedly recalled memories were obtained at second hand from stories told by parents or relatives. This acquired knowledge is not an actual memory.

Hull has summarized some examples of hypnotic recall of childhood memories as cited by commentators. Of these, Bramwell instances the recollection under hypnosis of events which happened to a subject at the age of two; in one case a first birthday party was remembered. Wingfield [47] states that he caused a lady of thirty-two to remember herself in swaddling clothes. Moll says if a person is told he has never been born, the consciousness becomes a complete blank. LeCron obtained a description of a birthday at the age of two from a woman subject of twenty-eight. She named the children present and the kinds of refreshments served, the mother of the subject confirming much of the story.

It must be remembered that these are merely statements which were not verified by controlled experiment. Extremely early memories supposedly recalled by a subject may be conscious or unconscious fabrications.

The claims mentioned here are modest if we can believe some of the writers on "psychic"matters. According to them hypnotized persons have been carried back into past lives and previous incarnations and have relived them in memory! Needless to say, this has never been done in the laboratory.

When considering the hypnotic recall of memories, two possible aspects are present. There may be a lowering of the threshold for remote memories or the removal of an inhibition or mental block. Hull's experiments along these lines gave inconclusive results, though there is no doubt of the ability in hypnosis to recall lost memories. Not only can childhood memories be brought back to conscious recognition, but we have had instances where mislaid papers were found after resort to hypnosis for remembrance of their disposal. However, even under hypnosis, a subject will seldom recall events happening before the age of two.

In the case of amnesias following physical or emotional shock, the normal memory often can be restored by hypnosis. This type of amnesia will be considered further under dissociation, where the theories of hypnosis are discussed.

Another kind of amnesia frequently develops following a hypnotic trance. It is the forgetfulness of the trance happenings and seems to be similar to the amnesia for dreams which follows normal sleep at times. Dreams in normal sleep often are so vivid as to seem like actual experiences, yet on awakening only a few are remembered and most are completely forgotten. There are many people who claim they never dream. This can be regarded as the result of an amnesia, one so complete that the person never remembers anything about the dreams. Sometimes we awaken immediately after a dream and dwell on it momentarily, but on rising in the morning find we cannot recall it or else recollect only parts of it.

Amnesia after hypnosis may be complete or partial. Even when complete, it may disappear entirely or in part should there be any discussion of the occurrences in the trance or if a strong effort is made to recall them. Generally this amnesia is spontaneous, coming without suggestive prompting and as a definite phenomenon of the deep trance. A few may reach the deep state and have no subsequent amnesia. It will almost always be evidenced after deep hypnosis if forgetfulness is suggested, while on the other hand there will be no amnesia if suggestion to remember on awakening is given. Thus the operator may cause or inhibit amnesia at his discretion. The subject can be told he will not have any remembrance even of being hypnotized and subsequently will indignantly deny that he was. As mentioned in Chapter V, amnesia appears to strengthen posthypnotic suggestion.

Boris Sidis and other observers considered amnesia the main identifying sign of the somnambulistic trance, believing only a light state reached unless amnesia could be established. Such a conclusion is essentially correct, although our experience indicates that amnesia is not an invariable accompaniment of somnambulism.

Occasionally there is complete amnesia after only a medium trance, but much oftener it is only partial or is not experienced at all. With the exception of anaesthesia, amnesia undoubtedly offers the most convincing proof to the subject that he has been hypnotized. When he is unable to remember, there is little doubt in his mind of having been hypnotized.

Even with complete amnesia, upon rehypnotization every event of previous trances can readily be recalled and this fact has induced some to accept the dissociation theory of hypnosis.

Somewhat along the same line as memory recall is *age regression,* a really strange phenomenon. A mature adult in hypnosis can be told that he has become a child once more—perhaps it is stated that he is six years old. Thereupon he will give every indication of being that age, acting the part perfectly and speaking like a little boy. Asked to remember events of that period, he will describe in detail experiences which are completely forgotten in the normal conscious state. Given a toy, he will sit on the floor and play, then cry if it is snatched away. With systematic regression to different ages, intelligence tests for the different ages have been given the hypnotized subject, and the mental age and intelligence quotient have been found to correspond very closely.

When a person is taken step by step back through several age periods successively and is required to write his name at each age, the handwriting gradually changes until it becomes childish. At five or six the words may be printed if this was learned before writing was mastered. Comparisons of handwriting during regression with that actually written at known ages will show identical features, it is claimed. In one such experiment a different name was written at the age of six, and investigation disclosed that the man had been adopted and the new parents had changed his name.

Just how far back in a person's life regression may be extended is difficult to say, and no doubt it varies with the personality pattern of the individual. It probably is similar in scope to the recall of lost memories. Wolberg[48] states: "In several cases I have succeeded in regressing subjects to an infantile level, so that they lost the capacity of expressive speech and for ambulation, producing at the same time typical sucking and grasping movements."

In the second part of this volume will be found a description of the therapeutic use of age regression together with methods of procedure and a discussion of types of regression. It is a phenomenon of considerable value in hypnoanalysis.

Stage hypnotists make frequent use of hallucinations, illusions and delusions in their entertainments. A delusion is a persistent error of perception due to a false belief, commonly about things which are themselves real, while an illusion is a perception which fails to give the true character of an object perceived, a false impression. An illusion is closely related to a hallucination, but the latter differs in that it has no external source or object and is an imaginary perception, while the illusion is of an objective reality. All may occur in connection with any of the five senses, and may be either positive or negative. Stage technique always involves the suggestion of bizarre hallucinations, and the audience rocks with laughter when some dignified gentleman plays the clown while under hypnotic inducement.

It is easy to think of hallucinations which will be amusing to onlookers but inoffensive to the subject, and such suggestions are more likely to be carried out. Normally no one enjoys being made to appear foolish, and the operator must remember that the subject is not a lump of clay but a conscious human being who undoubtedly will resent being forced to perform a repugnant or disagreeable act. He deserves the same treatment he would receive if awake. When the operator plans to invoke hallucinations, it is best to ask prior permission and never to experiment without the subject's approval. Mild hallucinations are quite possible with only a moderate degree of hypnosis; when the more fantastic ones are seen, we can be sure a deep state has been reached.

For example, taste hallucinations may be given, and an imaginary meal will be eaten with great relish. Incidentally, the subject's stomach will enter into the fun, performing the normal movements of digestion and secreting the juices necessary for proper digestion of such foods as are suggested. Laboratory tests have confirmed this. If the subject is told that a glass of water is lemonade he will comment on its pleasant taste, or if informed that it is whisky he will show signs of inebriation.

An interesting example of negative visual hallucination is the suggestion that a spectator has left the room. The subject is to open his eyes, notice the absence of this person, and comment on it. This will be carried out, with blank gaze at the "absentee" who may be sitting directly in front of him. If addressed by the invisible one, no attention will be paid, and if asked to sit in the chair occupied by him, the subject will express astonishment and be much puzzled at finding himself on an invisible lap.

In another of Erickson's [49] experiments adroitly arranged tests proved the reality of the hallucinations when this kind of suggestion is given. Both auditory and visual unawareness was induced.

One of the few dangers in hypnotism is neglect on the part of the operator to remove any hallucination, delusion or illusion before dismissing the subject, and there must be no "amnesia" on this point by the hypnotist. This is especially important when a number of people have been hypnotized and hallucinated, for the hypnotist may forget just what has been suggested to each. Estabrooks cites the case of a stage hypnotist making such a mistake, the awakened subject believing a black dog was following him as had been suggested on the stage. The victim was thought ready for the asylum until a physician learned the cause of the unwanted canine presence. It was necessary to call in another hypnotist to remove the hallucination.

The hypnotist who is thoughtful of his subjects should be careful in inducing hallucinations. Amusing ones will cause no resentment in some people; other subjects may become indignant and take out their ire on the hypnotist. Good judgment on his part should be displayed.

*Dream induction.* Although dreams are a commonplace to all of us, their psychological aspect is not thoroughly known and we can only theorize about them. By means of suggestion, dreams can be made to occur in the hypnotic state or later during normal sleep. Not only the content of the dream will appear as directed but the exact time of dreaming may be set. In fact, setting a certain time for the dream to appear seems to make the manifestation more sure.

Stimulation of dreams might seem to have no practical value, but in psychotherapy, dreams and their interpretation are important. By their hypnotic instigation much can be learned. Klein [50] has made a study of dreams caused to occur in the hypnotic state rather than in normal sleep, stimulated in a variety of ways. This subject will be considered further in the second part of the text.

There are other phenomena hitherto unmentioned which can be more appropriately dealt with later, among them dissociation, skin blistering, healing of tissue and certain physical conditions which can be produced or influenced by hypnotic suggestion.

When describing their sensations under hypnosis, subjects have often mentioned experiencing a feeling which, to our knowledge, has not been noted in the literature yet which seems to arise spontaneously without the stimulus of suggestion. The matter has been voluntarily reported so frequently that it is puzzling to find it previously unmentioned. It would seem to be an attribute of deep hypnosis only.

The subject describes the occurrence as the sensing of a rise and fall in depth of the trance following a wave pattern; a feeling of slipping down deep into the trough of the wave, then slowly rising up the slope of the next wave to a crest and again slipping down to a depth. Concomitantly, the voice of the operator is heard to fade and increase in tonal volume, just like the volume of a distant radio station. The operator's voice may blank out completely at the bottom of the trough, then gradually swell to a normal tone again.

This is similar to one of the phenomena of fluctuation of attention which is often noted in nonhypnotic situations. It is frequently seen when one's attention is concentrated, but the feeling in hypnosis seems to be more definite or stronger and more regular, a matter of mental passivity rather than concentrated attention. It may or may not be a real hypnotic phenomenon. Laboratory investigation might be worth while.

Turning to things which *cannot* be done with hypnotism, it is sufficient to say that miracles cannot be performed; all hypnotic accomplishments are strictly in accordance with natural laws. No one in hypnosis can suddenly speak in a foreign language which is not already known, nor can suggestion convert a subject into a musician if he is not one. George du Maurier's novel *Trilby,* written years ago, was responsible for disseminating much misinformation about hypnotism. Trilby, the heroine, under the influence of the hypnotist Svengali was able to sing in hypnosis with the beautiful tones of a Jenny Lind but croaked dismally when she was her normal self. This is impossible except in fiction, just as was Svengali's complete power over her.

A current comic strip features as hero a hypnotist whose powers are depicted as unlimited. Foes are paralyzed at a glance, hallucinations produced by a "hypnotic gesture" and all manner of wonders performed. Our experience has failed to give us knowledge of any hypnotic gesture. The "artist" evidently has not bothered to learn even the rudiments of hypnotism, and consequently the "hypnotic" adventures illustrated are ridiculous in the extreme. No wonder the public has a complete misconception of the science!

# CHAPTER VII

# Posthypnotic Suggestion, Auto-hypnosis and Autosuggestion

MOST IMPORTANT of all hypnotic phenomena is posthypnotic suggestion, whereby we are able to transfer all the conditions of the trance to the waking state. Taking advantage of this faculty, one may implant suggestions in the mind during hypnosis to take effect later at any specified time. By stipulating a definite time for the action, it will be performed almost at the exact moment designated.

We may say to a subject, "The back of your right hand will begin to itch five minutes after I awaken you, and the itching will quickly become intolerable. You can relieve it only by scratching, and until you have scratched it you will be most uncomfortable. The back of your right hand will itch until you scratch it. It will begin to itch five minutes after I awaken you."

The subject will be quite at ease for five minutes after awakening, then will begin to move his right hand, inspecting it and rubbing the skin while showing signs of discomfort. Quickly the itching will become unbearable. Within a moment or two he will scratch vigorously with obvious satisfaction.

Should the subject be told of the suggestion and invited to resist, or if there is no amnesia subsequent to the trance and he is therefore aware of the suggestion, the force is scarcely lessened. Should he decide to fight the feeling, he is due for a struggle. He may succeed in controlling his actions, but generally the impulse will be too strong; in this case the hand will keep right on itching until he yields and scratches it. He may think the impulse has been overcome but it tends to return and with a compulsion to scratch he probably will yield eventually and scratch. Even with another idea or counter-suggestion present in his mind acting to prevent acceptance of the suggestion, a vague feeling of discomfort may persist for some time, and no such suggestion should be permitted to remain in a subject's mind following the sitting. There must be compliance or rehypnotization to remove it.

Instructions to carry out an idea upon waking may be set for a future time weeks away, not just a matter of moments or hours. Liebeault told one patient during hypnosis to return at the same hour exactly one year later, specifying certain things which he would then do. Everything was carried out on that date almost exactly as had been directed. When such a long period of time is involved, there is a likelihood of failure unless the suggestion has been repeated several times, yet Estabrooks notes a most astonishing instance from his personal experience. A friend to whom he had several times given a particular posthypnotic suggestion in the nature of a "stunt" to be performed whenever a certain signal was given, was encountered by Estabrooks after a lapse of twenty years. When the signal was given again, there was instant response to the stimulus.

An opportunity for such a test would seldom arise and a response after so long a period would hardly be expected, as the retention of the idea in memory over that interval is remarkable and reveals the compelling force involved.

Patten (one of Hull's associates) made tests on the duration of posthypnotic suggestion. His results bore out the clinical experiences reported by many writers of the past. From his investigation Patten concluded that several repetitions of the suggestion tend to lead to its indefinite persistence, a conditioned reflex having been established. This seems to refute one of the greatest criticisms of hypnotherapy—that the strength of suggestion wears off rapidly and effects are only transient. Instead, they are found to be practically permanent when there has been sufficient repetition, again indicating the extreme importance of repetition in giving suggestion.

Instruction to complete some action after awakening is far more likely to be fulfilled when coupled with a definite signal, or if a specific time is set. We may say, "Three weeks from today on March 8 at ten o'clock in the morning, you will phone me at my office," and in all probability the phone will ring at that hour. When the suggested action is to be consummated soon after arousal, it may be tied to a signal such as, "Your mouth will be dry and you will feel thirsty when you wake up. When I tap the table three times, you will ask for a glass of water. You will be so thirsty that you will ask for a glass of water." In this instance, more force is given the idea by stimulating thirst and a desire to satisfy it; also by providing a reason for the carrying out of the action. Of course the phrasing in these examples would require more repetition to be most effective.

This type of posthypnotic suggestion can be utilized to speed up later trance induction by telling the subject to enter immediately a deep sleep at a given signal such as has been mentioned previously—moving the hand in front of his eyes, for instance. Depth of hypnosis in later trances may also be increased by use of posthypnotic suggestion.

Without repetition and any signal or definite statement as to time, posthypnotic suggestion has a tendency to lose its force. A pictorial graph would show a downward curve sharp at first in point of time, then gradually straightening. The more repetition used, the greater the radius of the curve and the flatter its arc. When a conditioned reflex has been established, the curve tends to become a straight line descending slowly as the reflex is lost or extinguished.

Some observers claim to have noted a tendency for the strength of suggestion to become reduced with too frequent repetition and too many sittings. This is an argumentative point which does not check with Patten's findings. However, we have noticed it in a few subjects, and the answer may be a difference in the response of individuals and in their behavior patterns. Certainly response differs greatly in the carrying out of posthypnotic suggestions. Some will complete each suggestion, while others resist or for some other reason fail to comply, and there may be compliance in one sitting and failure at some other, although the trance seems as deep.

An obvious way to continue the full effect of posthypnotic suggestion without the necessity of renewal by the hypnotist is employment of autosuggestion in autohypnosis. Any suggestion can thus be kept active for an indefinite period.

Posthypnotic suggestion seems to incite a time-limited, situation-limited form of compulsive behavior even when the idea is recognized and comprehended as suggestion. Then there is no need felt to rationalize the carrying out of the action, but the case is different when there is amnesia for the suggestion. No matter how silly or ridiculous the action involved may be, it must be carried out, and the subject feels that he must provide himself with a reason for doing it to make the action logical and to explain his behavior, since he is aware of the action.

This rationalization is often most ingenious and amusing to the onlooker who appreciates that compulsion is at work. Always the person must justify himself. When questioned as to the reason for odd behavior he may reply, "Oh, I just wanted to do it. It seemed like a good idea."

At a sitting with several people present, LeCron suggested to a young lady that she would remove her left shoe when awakened and place it on a coffee table in front of her. Then she would take some flowers from a vase on the table and arrange them artistically in her shoe. This might well have been resisted as embarrassing to her, but all was accomplished as directed and the lady sat back to admire the floral masterpiece.

"Why have you put those flowers in your shoe?" she was asked.

"The flowers? Well, a nice floral arrangement just occurred to me and I wanted to see how it would look."

"But why use your shoe?"

"Oh, I have a vase at home shaped something like a shoe, and I wanted to try the arrangement with that vase in mind."

Probably the vase mentioned had only the slightest resemblance to a shoe, but rationalization was called for, and one quite satisfactory to her was devised on the spur of the moment.

Following the performance of a posthypnotic suggestion, there is sometimes immediate amnesia for the act as soon as it has been completed, particularly if it has been an absurd one. If questioned, the subject may indignantly deny ever having done such a thing although the action was performed only a moment or two before. The amnesia is probably real and serves as a defense to avoid the difficulty of explaining the absurdity, though it may sometimes be a pretense for the same purpose.

The question has arisen as to the exact condition of the subject when he is carrying out a posthypnotic suggestion. Is he in a normal state, or has a new hypnosis been produced at the time specified for execution of the suggestion? There had been comment and expressions of opinion on this matter by writers, but it remained for Dr. Erickson and his wife to undertake a systematic investigation of the posthypnotic state and behavior. Until then there had been much study of post-hypnotic acts and effects, but the state in which they were carried out had been almost completely ignored. As a result of their findings, the Ericksons say: "The hypnotized subject, instructed to execute some act post-hypnotically, invariably develops spontaneously a hypnotic trance. This trance is of brief duration, occurs in direct relation to the performance of the posthypnotic act, and apparently constitutes an essential part of the process of response to and execution of the post-hypnotic command. . . . Furthermore, the development of a trance state as a part of the posthypnotic performance re-quires for its appearance neither suggestion nor instruction . . . [it] develops at the moment of initiation of the post-hypnotic act, and persists usually for only a moment or two; hence it is easily overlooked." If there is no amnesia for the original trance and the posthypnotic suggestion made at that time or if the amnesia is weakened and the suggestion is re-membered before the posthypnotic act is to be carried out, this spontaneous trance may not develop even though the suggested act is carried out, which may be done voluntarily or through a feeling of compulsion.

To quote further from the Ericksons' report: "Demon-stration and testing of the spontaneous posthypnotic trance are usually best accomplished at the moment of the initiation of the posthypnotic performance by interference either with the subject or with the suggested act. Properly given, such interference ordinarily leads to an immediate arrest in the subject's behavior, and a prolongation of the spontaneous posthypnotic trance, permitting a direct evocation of hypnotic phenomena typical of the ordinary induced hypnotic trance."

Practically, this spontaneous trance if developed will serve as a criterion of the validity of the previous trance. For experimental and therapeutic purposes it offers possibilities, because it automatically removes some of the difficulties present in the usual method of trance induction—for instance the overcoming of subconscious resistances in psychotherapy.

## AUTOHYPNOSIS

Certain people seem to have the ability to hypnotize themselves readily. Among them are the spiritualistic mediums who place themselves in a trance at will; this refers to the few who believe themselves to be real mediums, not the large number of "phonies." Some individuals learn the process by accident or develop it during periods of daydreaming, although it is difficult for most of us. It may be learned through practice, but it develops readily by means of posthypnotic suggestion. Probably only a light trance will be achieved on first attempts, but in the course of more the state will become as deep as in hypnosis previously induced by another—i. e., in heterohypnosis.

When teaching self-hypnosis by this means, a definite procedure for the subject to follow should be outlined and he must be impressed with the idea that he can induce hypnosis in himself without difficulty. Here is an example of one method of procedure and accompanying suggestion.

"You may induce in yourself at any time you wish as deep a stage of hypnosis as the one you have now reached, or even deeper. To do this, take any comfortable position, seated or lying down, and relax as you have been taught. Take a deep breath to aid in relaxing. When thoroughly relaxed and comfortable, close your eyes and say to yourself, 'Now I am going into the hypnotic state,' either thinking the phrase or repeating it aloud. Then begin to breathe slowly and deeply. You do not need to count, but by the time you have taken ten deep breaths you will be in a deep hypnotic condition. Should you have any difficulty in making the mind passive and quiet, fix your open eyes on some spot on the ceiling or keep them closed and look at an imaginary spot or indefinitely at an imagined gray field of general vision.

"While in hypnosis you will be alert and able to give yourself any suggestions you wish. You will be able to induce any hypnotic phenomena in yourself.

"When you wish to awaken, say to yourself, 'I am now going to wake up.' You will then count to three and be wide awake. If for any reason you should need to awaken to answer the phone or in the event of an emergency such as a fire, you will awaken automatically and at once. In this self-induced hypnosis you will always be able to listen to me and to follow any instructions I give you."

The last sentence will maintain rapport which might otherwise be lost, permitting the operator to arouse the subject if necessary. Sometimes there is considerable mental sluggishness in the first trial at self-hypnosis, making it difficult for the sleeper to awaken himself. The student ought to practice two or three times with the operator present before putting himself in hypnosis while alone. He will then be sufficiently experienced to proceed by himself.

As hypnotic phenomena are usually fascinating to one who has just learned to hypnotize himself, no doubt he will want to experiment, and a few precautions should be observed. To give oneself hallucinations is not desirable, particularly repeated ones, though a well-balanced individual probably would suffer no harm and might try them for the experience. There is a possibility of such hallucinations becoming persistent and difficult to oust from the mind. Estabrooks mentions a personal experience of this nature.

Some authorities believe that there is a possible danger of dissociation or splitting of personality arising from self-hypnosis. But such a danger is most unlikely, since hypnotism itself has been found to be one of the best means for correcting and welding dissociations. So far as we know there has never been a report of a dissociation due to self-hypnosis. Dissociation will be discussed further under theory.

Autohypnosis is quite harmless and can be of benefit to the ordinary person who is reasonably prudent. The only potential risk is with flighty, hysterical or neurotic people who might get into trouble through misuse. Therefore discretion should be observed in teaching it. Many neurotics are highly intelligent, and for them it may be valuable in aiding the overcoming of their neurotic difficulties.

The formula given here for teaching self-hypnosis is really a combination of auto- and heterohypnotic technique. The response is not merely autohypnosis but comes as posthypnotic response to posthypnotic suggestion. With repetition of such self-induced hypnosis, the response becomes more and more actual self-induction rather than a response to the original heterosuggestion.

## Autosuggestion

Autohypnosis and autosuggestion are phenomena whose value has been recognized from the earliest days of hypnotic history. The self-given variety of suggestion may be applied in the waking state or in autohypnosis. While well known, it was not fully appreciated until the second decade of the nineteenth century, when Émile Coué brought it into world prominence. Coué was a pharmacist in Nancy, France, and came into contact with the work of Liebeault and Bernheim when Nancy was the capital of the hypnotic world, mecca of all hypnotic practitioners and students. He studied the science and was deeply impressed with the power of suggestion, particularly noting its strong effect even when no trance condition was present. This being true and with the consideration that some cannot be hypnotized, Coué decided that hypnosis was unnecessary and a waste of time. Anyone could benefit himself by autosuggestion, he reasoned, and began teaching autosuggestive methods. Results were so excellent that he opened a clinic and soon was swamped with patients. The New Nancy School, as Coué called his system, rapidly became a fad in France and spread all over Europe. Thousands made pilgrimages to Nancy to learn how to cure themselves of their ailments. Soon Coué was world-famous.

It is always thus when a new faith cure is developed. All are based entirely on suggestion and autosuggestion, usually with a mystical or religious tinge added. The world is filled with neurotics whose pains and troubles are functional, and others with ailments not yet curable by medicine. Failing to find relief through orthodox curative methods, they desert the physician for the practitioners of other persuasions—the osteopath, the chiropractor, naturopath, herbalist, and the entire gamut of more or less sincere healers. They turn in despair to the quack, the charlatan, the fake psychologist, the sincere but unscientific Christian Science practitioner, or other religious faith healers. And many are cured—by suggestion, no matter under what name it is disguised.

The Coué fad is recent enough to be well remembered today, as is the catch phrase taught his pupils for use in giving themselves suggestion—"Day by day, in every way, I'm getting better and better." Ribald Americans changed the phrase to

"Hells bells, I'm well!" Coué's expression was broad and adaptable as a stimulus to cover any ailment or condition. The French suggestionist made repetition the very heart of the ritual he taught and insisted that you could never say the formula too often.

Coué wrote a book on the method, and his disciple Baudouin followed with a better one, both including treatises on the laws of suggestion. Their work, with that of Sidis, Pierce, Pitzer and Parkyn, represents about the sum total of worthwhile literature on suggestion. Since their day almost no attention has been given the scientific basis of suggestion, by either university or medical psychologists with few exceptions—Erickson emphasizes the extreme importance of suggestion and its careful wording. So far as we are aware, suggestion is not mentioned except vaguely in any college or university psychology class, at least in the United States.

With the fad at its height, Coué was prevailed upon to visit America and he toured this country giving lectures. However, overenthusiastic promoters led the vast crowds who turned out to expect a continual series of miracles of healing, although Coué promised nothing of the sort and was entirely sincere. His ideas were essentially sound, with no religious motive or quackery involved. But the American tour was a fiasco, so Coué returned to France disappointed and discouraged. As a result, his following dwindled almost as rapidly as it had accumulated.

While his teachings were taken up to some extent in the United States and some charlatans set themselves up as exponents of the system, no craze developed here and autosuggestion was not accepted as a general panacea as it had been in Europe.

Coué advanced nothing new, but he did clarify the laws of suggestion and call attention to its worth, particularly that of the self-given variety. While disclaiming hypnotism as unnecessary, he tried to obtain a sleep state when dealing with patients and some entered the deeper trance. Thus his actual method was inconsistent with his writings and lectures.

Autosuggestion may be combined advantageously with autohypnosis, and a systematic use of the two may be beneficial at times in hypnotic psychotherapy. Theoretically it should be of value in enabling some patients to continue their own treatment without necessity of returning too often to the practitioner, maintaining the suggestions given. There is a further value in the therapy through the active participation which it forces upon the patient.

The actual worth of autosuggestion is not clearly known because it has had almost no scientific investigation. There are many conflicting factors involved. One's frame of mind must be positive in giving suggestions, but to receive and act on these one must be completely negative. It is impossible to be both at the same time, and thus autosuggestion might seem to be valueless. On the other hand, Coué certainly had great success. The authors are in mild disagreement over this point, Bordeaux believing autosuggestion worthless in nearly all cases, while LeCron is convinced it has merit at times, although of far less potency than heterosuggestion. Faith undoubtedly is the vital element. Whenever a person believes implicitly that autosuggestion will help him, Bordeaux agrees that it is practically certain to be effective.

Whether or not autosuggestion is effective, the average person wishing to use it cannot acquire sufficient knowledge to treat himself properly and safely without expert advice, unless he devotes some time to study. Too often it is employed by a sick person who knows he should receive treatment but attempts to treat himself without even knowing the nature of his ills. In such cases autosuggestion is a blind, hopeless and stupid procedure. Intelligent direction is a requisite.

Here the situation is similar to the use of medicine. Certain home remedies and medicines may be used safely, but a physician is needed when there is something really wrong with an individual's health. Except for simple, obvious matters, the psychiatrist or psychologist (only after diagnosis) should always be consulted before attempting to cure one's self at home by using autosuggestion or autohypnosis. Autosuggestion wrongly applied can create serious problems, as will be elaborated in the chapters on therapeutics. As with poisons in the home medicine cabinet, autosuggestion is a prescription to be labeled with the skull and crossbones of danger. It is hazardous unless the precept "Apply only as directed" is followed.

As is true in hetero-induced hypnosis, suggestion is more effective with self-hypnosis than without a trance. The laws of suggestion apply to the self-given kind just as they do to heterosuggestion, and these principles should be taught in connection with lessons in autohypnosis. Hypnotic suggestion works best without the presence of conscious attention. Autosuggestion requires the control of attention. Since it is impossible to surrender attention and at the same time to fix it on the desired result, this tends to diminish the value of autosuggestion.

To apply autosuggestion with or without hypnosis, it has been found best first to think out the suggestion and then to frame it with actual words—spoken ones. This adds to the imagination the reinforcement of speech and the auditory effect of the spoken words. Many writers have noted this fact, and Fink [51] reported the use of spoken words as increasing the effect of the relaxation exercises advocated and described by him.

In some cases autosuggestion and autohypnosis offer a

means of self-improvement both physically and mentally; a means of strengthening the personality and the powers of the user. Thus will power sometimes can be increased and self-confidence intensified. Primarily autosuggestion is a means of repressing, suppressing, and to some extent of augmenting mental attitudes.

# CHAPTER VIII

# Theories of Hypnosis

HYPNOTIC PRACTITIONERS, psychiatrists and psychologists have long sought to formulate a workable theory which would explain hypnosis satisfactorily. Having an understanding of the phenomena, knowledge is needed as to their causative factors, how they work and why they appear. There should be sensible answers to the questions "What is hypnotism?" "What is hypnosis?" but our present knowledge of mind and body and human behavior is insufficient to provide an explanation.

The chief difficulty in seeking a logical theory is the lack of general acceptance of any accurate definition of either hypnotism or hypnosis. Hypnotism as used by the authors refers to the entire science, and hypnosis indicates the trance state. However, there is no scientific way to measure the trance definitely nor to ascertain exactly when it begins or even what it actually is. The light trance is considered as hypnosis, yet the subject is only slightly affected. Ordinarily he can awaken at will, and there still remains the question of whether or not he was actually "hypnotized."

In considering the general field of hypnotism, undoubtedly suggestion is very effective in the waking and hypnoidal conditions, and if suggestion is the basis of hypnotism—which definitely is true—should we consider hypnotism as including all suggestion or only that dispensed during a trance? The general conception of hypnotism has been to consider hypnosis as the most integral part of the science, and suggestion unaccompanied by trance has not been treated as hypnotism. However, Bernheim held that hypnotism was suggestion and that there was no marked difference between normal acts carried out under suggestion and acts brought about hypnotically. Furthermore, all the phenomena of the trance can be evidenced in at least a minor form in the waking state as well.

If we accept this idea, an excellent definition of hypnotism would be "the control of thought and action through suggestion." This is quite broad but it covers the field. It would include every form of suggestion, spoken or written or however presented, and we could then class as hypnotism the various mild forms of suggestion continually met with in everyday life. Such a classification to us seems justified. It would include the mother lulling a child to sleep by singing softly while cradling it in her arms. Incessantly our daily lives are influenced by suggestion from government and other propaganda agencies, from the press and radio, dealt out to us by writers, orators, politicians and preachers. All work through suggestion, and the listener or reader is swayed, sometimes deeply, by them. According to our definition, this is hypnotism in mild form. Nowadays we even speak of an audience listening as though hypnotized. A soap-box orator frequently turns the crowd into an angry mob, some in actual trance. As Estabrooks has indicated, Hitler seemed to exert hypnotic influence over the entire German nation by oratory and his understanding of mass psychology.

The only real danger from hypnotism, in our opinion, is uncurbed propaganda regardless of its source. And what is salesmanship but the hypnotic influence of suggestive words and illustrations? Only the mystical and magical connotations still remaining in the word "hypnotism" retard acceptance of this interpretation.

Somewhat stronger in degree but definitely hypnotic is the religious fervor seen at camp meetings and revivals, where hallucinations and actual trance are frequently induced in susceptible participants. Such revivals usually include faith healing—cure of the ailing while crutches and braces are thrown away. Dowie, of the past generation, and the late Aimee Semple McPherson, of the present, seemed able to exert hypnotic influence through mass psychology and shrewd showmanship. Suggestion is the basis of all faith healing. God may work the cure, but suggestion is the means and the mechanism. The priesthood always has used suggestion. Even the most orthodox physician employs it constantly in daily practice, though he may never have heard of its laws. Frequently he resorts to "bread-pill" medication, staging a little act for the patient and assuring him, "This will fix you up." The little deception is usually successful and well worth while. Isn't this hypnotism even though trance is not involved?

Many psychologists believe with us that suggestion invoked by propagandists, orators and preachers is as much hypnotism as is suggestion given a subject in a trance. Estabrooks says, "It is he [the orator] who leads humanity by the nose into bloody wars. We must learn to discount him, to refuse to be stampeded by his appeals to hatred and prejudice."

In discussing hypnotic theory, R. W. White [52] insists that an acceptable explanation of three facts is essential in formulating a scientific hypothesis:

1. That a hypnotized person transcends the normal limits of volitional control.

2. That he behaves without the experience of will or intention or self-consciousness and without subsequent memory.

3. That these changes occur because the hypnotist says they will.

According to White, when these three factors are answered satisfactorily, we shall have a workable theory even if it cannot be considered certain. Discussion of all theories yet advanced reveals that none meets these requirements. White's own theory, tentatively accepted by Dorcus [53] also, in our opinion fails to meet the requirements.

Before considering the White-Dorcus hypothesis, let us look at some earlier ones. Bernheim, Liebeault, Forel, Bechterev, Pavlov and other distinguished scientists believed that hypnosis was a modified form of sleep. Probably this was because the appearance of the hypnotized person resembles that of the sleeping person in most respects, but as this is due to eye closure and to sleep suggestions given during induction and such appearance can be entirely removed by further suggestion, the theory is untenable.

While consciousness is entirely suspended in natural sleep (or partially when dreaming), it is definitely present in hypnosis—a great difference. Additional evidence of differences in the two states has been demonstrated by laboratory experiments. Wible and Jenness [54, 55] studied respiration and heart action in hypnosis and found them the same as in the waking state. They are quite different in sleep. Bass [56] made a most important contribution to the understanding of hypnosis and to the technique of laboratory tests in hypnosis when he found the patellar reflex (knee-jerk when tapped) to be the same in hypnosis and the waking state. In sleep there is almost no response to this stimulus.

It is possible that somnambulism or sleep-walking may be a state akin to hypnosis, though there has been little study along this line. However, when this condition occurs during slumber, it certainly is not natural sleep and is, in fact, quite abnormal.

Charcot's theory that hypnosis is an artificially induced hysteria has been mentioned. Mainly because Pierre Janet accepted it, a few years later psychologists subscribed to it, William Brown [57] of Oxford being one. They believed that anyone who was hypnotizable was a hysteric and that no normal person could be hypnotized. Also, they claimed that in hypnosis (as in hysteria) there was a narrowing or restriction of the field of consciousness. This is a phenomenon of hypnosis but certainly is not an explanation. Its occurrence in hysteria is not a proof that the conditions are the same, for other elements are found in both states and also in the waking state.

It seems incredible that a man of Brown's experience in hypnotism would not have hypnotized many perfectly normal people, and the same applies to Janet. But Brown's work to a great extent was with "shell shock" patients of the first World War and later with civilian neurotics, and it is perhaps understandable that he should have reached his odd conclusion. Psychological tests in the laboratory refute the theory, since perfectly normal people make good hypnotic subjects. Furthermore, some hysterics and neurotics cannot be hypnotized.

Other theories which have had support from well-known scientists can be dismissed as disproved or illogical with present knowledge. One is the parental theory of Ferenczi.[58] He declared that a hypnotized person has accepted the hypnotist as occupying the place of one of his or her parents—the favored parent. McDougall refuted this by saying that if it were true, a woman could then be expected to hypnotize only those who favored their mother and a man only those partial to their father. Certainly a good subject is hypnotizable by either a male or female practitioner.

Another inconsistent view is that hypnosis results only from brain fatigue caused by monotonous stimulation. Since trance in many instances can be induced almost instantaneously, as either hetero- or autohypnosis, with the subject fresh both mentally and physically, this is quite unsound.

Quite popular for a time was a supposition that the subject must carry out the will of the hypnotist in spite of himself. Thus he was thought to be an automaton. Such a belief fails to consider the lighter states of hypnosis, where there is no evidence of automatism. Even in the deep state, as every practicing hypnotist discovers to his chagrin, a subject often fails to carry out suggestions and may even awaken when he considers a suggestion improper. While volition may be partially inhibited, the subject is anything but an automaton!

Many authorities have held to the theory of dissociation, mentioned several times heretofore. The idea probably was first advanced by Max Dessoir, though it was more thoroughly formulated by Pierre Janet [59] and was embraced by prominent psychologists such as Coriat, Prince, Sidis, McDougall and others. It is accepted and approved by many today.

The normal act of recalling memories is a result of the association of ideas. If there is a failure of the power to recall events which normally should be remembered, this is termed "dissociation"—an interruption or repression of the memory. Amnesia is therefore an essential element in the theory.

We have postulated the mind as made up of two parts, the consciousness, which can be considered as awareness, and the subconsciousness. The subconscious part of the mind seems able to perform many of the acts of the conscious, such as thinking, computing, etc., as well as serving to control the autonomic nervous system. These matters can be demonstrated through automatic writing or speaking or drawing (they are basically the same).

In automatic writing an individual can consciously converse intelligently on a topic, and at the same time his hand holding a pencil will write automatically and coherently on some entirely unrelated subject, the person having no conscious knowledge of what the hand writes. This is not a rare ability for many are able to do it in the waking state. During hypnosis it can often be invoked in others.

From this fact it has been reasoned that the mind is dual or even multiple. Janet thought a dissociated memory or group of memories might develop into a kind of second personality. This is best exemplified by those strange cases of dual personality which sometimes come to light, where the individual is at different times under the control of entirely distinct conscious entities. Stevenson's Dr. Jekyll and Mr. Hyde is the classic fictional example of this condition, and there have been a number of cases in real life, though they did not portray the good versus bad characters of Stevenson's fantasy. One of the most famous of these was Miss Beauchamp, studied by Morton Prince.[60] His report describes four different personalities all becoming conscious and in control at one time or another.

More familiar are the amnesia cases which show such a dual personality, with the second entity developing as a result of trauma—either an emotional or mental shock or a physical injury such as a blow on the head. The new personality may persist for a short time or for years, the second consciousness in control and the normal self completely forgotten with all memories of life before the trauma gone and not subject to recall.

It has been claimed that hypnosis produces a similar

splitting of personality, the subconscious part of the mind becoming the dominant one. Sidis contended that the two parts of the nervous system were dissociated, with the primary inhibited and the autonomic open to suggestion. He believed that dissociation begins with light hypnosis, that it is completed when a deep trance is reached, and that the boundary marker for the depth of trance is amnesia for events therein. A similar and simpler comparison would be to visualize the mind as a see-saw with the conscious part normally at the elevated end. During hypnosis this end would descend and the subconscious mind at the other end of the plank would rise to become the dominant one.

This seems reasonable, because we definitely can reach and influence the subconscious to a much greater extent during hypnosis. However, in hypnosis the two sections of the mind cannot be regarded as having changed in any way since consciousness is retained, though the power to reason and think is restricted unless there is a stimulus for it to act. Suggestion can dissolve the curb, and questioning serves as a stimulus. When questioned, the subject is able to think, to compute, and to reason, and events normally not possible of recall can then be brought out. Except for memory recall and perhaps reasoning, either part of the mind can perform these functions.

The dissociation theory is mainly based on the amnesia subsequent to the trance, and the functions mentioned above are considered by proponents of the theory to be performed by the subconscious mind. Since amnesia may be removed entirely by suggestion and often is not present after even the deepest trance unless there is suggestion of amnesia, and since automatic writing can be carried on equally well in the waking state, it would seem to be the original consciousness which in hypnosis thinks, reasons and computes. This would seem to weaken the dissociation hypothesis. Hull rejected it, but his experiments were too inconclusive to be assigned validity. He regarded the hypnotic recall of lost memories as a type of dissociation, but having no connection with the idea of dissociation into two independent consciousnesses.

The whole subject of dissociation is difficult of explanation and as a theory has many logical and satisfactory points. While it does not seem to us completely acceptable, it is difficult to refute. A clear definition of dissociation is almost impossible, since conceptions of the term are seldom identical. Amnesia is one thing, dissociation is another, the first often influencing the second.

It is important for the reader to appreciate the psychological situation in hypnosis. Ordinarily we have a wide field of conscious awareness which is indefinitely and vaguely bounded. Within this field of awareness is a general focus of attention which is fairly well defined, though it may be irregularly shaped. In hypnosis the field of attention closely approaches in size and shape the field of conscious awareness. The limitation of the field of awareness is drawn into the limitation of the field of attention.

It has been advanced as a theory that the hypnotic trance is nothing but a conditioned reflex, an idea taken to some extent from Bechterev and Pavlov,[61] who thought suggestion the simplest form of conditioned reflex, though Pavlov accepted the theory that normal and hypnotic sleep were essentially like conditions.

According to this surmise, the sleep formula acts as a stimulus corresponding to Pavlov's bell which caused a flow of saliva in the mouths of dogs on which he experimented. The bell was rung at the same time a dog was given food, and after several such feedings, accompanied by a ringing of the bell, saliva would flow when the bell was rung whether or not any food was offered.

Hypnosis does follow the laws of habit formation in induction, as was shown by Hull (Kreuger's experiments). Training makes hypnosis appear more quickly and makes the trance deeper. But to regard hypnosis as a conditioned reflex fails to take into consideration the fact that some respond to sleep suggestions almost instantly and become hypnotized when induction is first attempted, and without previous experience. With them there has been no conditioning and no conditioned reflex has been established. This situation would be comparable in Pavlov's dog experiment to the animal salivating the first time he ever heard the bell ring, without the presence of meat. Therefore this theory is unacceptable.

In considering hypnotic theory, both Dorcus and White arrived at the same conclusion. Differing from other conjectures, it has some points in its favor. White summed it up as follows:

"As a first step it is proposed that hypnotic behavior be regarded as meaningful, goal-directed striving, its most general goal being to behave like a hypnotized person as this is continually defined by the operator and understood by the subject. . . . The subject, it is held, is ruled by a wish to behave like a hypnotized person, his regnant motive is submission to the operator's demands, he understands at all times what the operator intends, and his behavior is a striving to put these intentions into execution."

The explanation is ingenious and also ingenuous, indicating skepticism as to the authenticity of many hypnotic phenomena. Dorcus says it does not necessarily follow that one hypnotized is simulating response to a suggestion, but that he may instead be carrying out the act suggested to the best of his ability. He qualifies his acceptance of the theory by admitting, "If modifications of processes not under voluntary control occur, then some revision of the notions set forth above will have to be made. Our knowledge of voluntary control of so-called involuntary processes is so limited for the waking state that no clear-cut statements can be made."

Estabrooks' tests of anaesthesia by electric shock are a direct refutation of the Dorcus-White theory, since he found that subjects in hypnosis could withstand without discomfort currents almost ten times as strong as those that could be tolerated in the waking state. No matter how much one might try to behave like a hypnotized person, hypnotic anaesthesia is certainly an involuntary matter in such a test.

Amnesia also would seem to refute the theory. According to this belief, hypnotic hallucinations could scarcely be regarded as actual, yet investigation has proved that they are. Dorcus cites the case of one of his own subjects who was instructed to walk through an hallucinatory open doorway in a solid wall. Obediently walking into the wall, he struck his face against it so hard as to cause a nosebleed.

This theory also fails to consider the behavior of a person who has no conceptions as to hypnosis, such as the little girl in the experiments in posthypnotic behavior made by the Ericksons. How can such a child be instructed by the hypnotist as to the mental process involved in recovering a forgotten memory? With no knowledge of how a hypnotized person should act, no child is able to behave as it believes a hypnotized person should, yet many three-year-old children are hypnotizable.

Hull concluded that our present knowledge of human behavior is too little developed to formulate a complete and ultimate theory of hypnosis. Erickson has the same opinion, and we agree. Since most of the effects obtainable in hypnosis can be realized in the waking state, Hull believes that the chief characteristic of hypnosis is the heightened suggestibility. This merely shows that it is easier to evoke the phenomena during hypnosis. Although heightened suggestibility apparently has been regarded as a theory by Estabrooks, it should undoubtedly be considered only as an attribute of hypnosis.

To understand the physiological functioning of hypnosis and suggestion, a comprehension of the nervous system is necessary. This is composed essentially of two parts: the primary system centering in the brain cortex and the secondary (or autonomic) system consisting of a network of nerves running from two trunk lines extending along the spinal column. These two lines are referred to as the sympathetic and parasympathetic divisions, one inhibiting and the other exciting all the functions controlled by the system. One acts as the brake and the other as the throttle of our fleshly motor vehicle. The focal point of the autonomic system is the thalamus, or midbrain as it is sometimes called, located near the center of the cerebral mass.

Most bodily functions and activities are performed automatically by the various organs and glands, no volition being required. They are controlled and correlated by the subconscious, acting through the thalamus on the autonomic nervous system. Some actions such as breathing are subject to more or less voluntary control. Apparently the two nervous systems are closely related and linked together. Breathing is mostly automatic, and we do not make any conscious effort to breathe, yet we can voluntarily slow down or speed up the respiratory rate.

Under the control of the autonomic system are the eyes, the heart and blood vessels, lungs, stomach, liver, kidneys, bladder, genitals, intestines, sphincter muscles of the anus and bladder, and perhaps the glands. Our knowledge of the glands is still extremely limited, although their normal functions are becoming better known with additional research in endocrinology. All muscular movements and secretions and most of the intricate operations of the body are under autonomic control, including body temperature, production of blood corpuscles and antibodies, the action in growth and healing of the billions of cells composing the body.

The activity of the organs and glands can be influenced directly either by emotion or by suggestion, particularly hypnotic suggestion. The feeling of embarrassment or shame, for instance, is a simple emotional influence usually displayed in a blush. Extreme fear affects the adrenals and perhaps all the organs and glands, but there are insufficient data to make definite statements.

Suggestion exerts the same effect as emotions and is much stronger when emotion is stimulated by the suggestion, being then supercharged. As suggestibility is so greatly increased in hypnosis, control of the organs and probably of the glands hypnotically is readily understandable—we can excite or inhibit as we wish, at least theoretically. Control of the activities of the organs has been proved, but almost nothing has been done experimentally in testing glandular control.

According to Pierce, who stresses the relationship of emotions and suggestions, the correct use of the latter depends to a large extent on understanding how the various emotions are translated into physiological reactions and appreciating how to inhibit certain elements of the mind so that there is no diminution of energy due to attention or concentration. It is difficult to increase emotion voluntarily, and some emotions are lessened when attention is drawn to them.

Emotions stimulate the production of nervous energy in

the body, particularly in the nerves activating the muscles used to express that emotion. If there is repression of an emotion with no action taken to release the nervous tension thus created, another outlet must be found, and failing this, other emotions may become intensified. A repressed emotion is always replaced or displaced by another, often its opposite; love by hate, horror by humor. There can be no vacuum, and nature demands that balance be maintained.

Even without a definite theory of hypnosis, it is thus possible to understand the control by suggestion of the mind and of the body, and to appreciate why regulation is strongest under hypnosis. The subconscious mind undoubtedly controls the autonomic nervous system either by inhibition or by excitation, and hypnotic influence of the subject is due to the ability to reach the subconscious more directly in the hypnotic state. Exactly how this happens is beyond our present knowledge.

# CHAPTER IX

# Hypnotism and the Psychic Sciences

OWING TO its admittedly unusual characteristics, hypnotism has always been deemed mysterious and mystical by the popular mind. That idea has been fostered by stage performers and the charlatans who prey on and mislead the paying public. Even in the days of the animal magnetists, interest in the science was based chiefly on profits to be derived from the supposedly occult and esoteric phases rather than the therapeutic or practical aspects. Every conceivable experiment was conducted along psychic lines, and the most extravagant claims were advanced as to its possibilities in connection with telepathy, clairvoyance and the various psychic "arts," primarily because it was a quick way to make easy money from a gullible public. Through hypnotic means the mind could be wafted from the body and directed to go anywhere on earth and report what it saw and heard; by age regression the events of former lives could be recalled; in hypnosis a subject without the slightest knowledge of medicine or anatomy could unfailingly diagnose any ailment and prescribe the proper treatment for cure!

Always the occult has appealed even to the brightest minds, and curiosity is always keen about the supernatural. Great scientists and Joe Doakes have had the same interest in psychic phenomena. Hence it is not strange that hypnotism should have been linked with the supernatural.

Science has long studied and investigated psychic matters, and protracted arguments have been waged as to the validity of all psychic phenomena. Science is skeptical and rightly demands proof, and most scientists refuse to believe. Some men of integrity and high renown have become convinced after delving into psychic research. Still others remain cautious of acceptance but open-mindedly admit that some things are inexplicable by known natural laws. Whole libraries exist on psychic research and strange events have been reported, but if we knew more there probably would be a natural explanation for these things.

Spiritualism has been the field for much investigation. Here we can consider it only as it relates to hypnotism, and there is little relevance.

The spiritualistic medium is usually classed as either a physical or a mental medium. The former deals with manifestations and physical occurrences supposedly resulting from spirit activities. Here we find the greatest evidence of fraud, and materialistic spiritualist phenomena should be considered as almost entirely faked for the benefit of those willing to pay highly in an earnest and pathetic hope of communicating with their dead. Since these mediums set up conditions that debar a scientific investigation to prove or disprove their contentions, physical manifestations may be regarded essentially as fraudulent.

The situation is somewhat different with the mental mediums. Here there is also fraud and trickery, sometimes blatant but often cunning and difficult to expose. Yet many skeptical investigators who deride spiritualism admit that some mental mediums are earnest and sincere, their séances genuine even if nothing supernatural is implicated. Mrs.

Piper, Mrs. Chenoweth, Mrs. Leonard and David Hume, great mediums of the past, were usually so regarded by scientific investigators who studied them.

Mental mediums operate in a so-called trance, probably faked for the most part. The honest few can be considered scientifically to be self-hypnotized in a state apparently identical with the hypnotic trance. When in a trance, whether feigned or real, the medium seems to come under the control of another personality, purportedly the spirit of a departed soul, and a genuine medium undoubtedly believes the "control" to be a spiritual entity. About 80 per cent of all mediums are women, and Sadler [62] believes that "the phenomena in question [in women] are due to the posterior pituitary body and other factors of an endocrine or chemical nature which directly serve in subjecting the nervous system of the female to periodic upheavals and disturbances of both psychologic and physiologic nature. I have never yet observed these phenomena to survive the menopause."

Sadler made an intensive study of spiritualism and mediums from both the psychologic and the physiologic angles as a physician, a different approach from that of most scientists, who instead investigate the phenomena directly. Whether or not his observations are correct, we shall leave to medical men.

In the trance the medium often enters a cataleptic state marked by extreme rigidity. The control then takes over, the voice may change completely, perhaps becoming like that of one of the opposite sex or of a child, and the supposed spirit answers the questions of the sitter, telling of things "on the other plane" and giving messages from those who have "passed over."

These messages are generally vague or subject to any interpretation desired, and the attitude or reactions of the sitter may give the medium clues which are quickly followed up. Very rarely are these messages difficult to explain, though some remarkable ones are noted throughout the literature.

The accepted scientific explanation of mediumistic controls is dissociation—the same dissociation dealt with in the last chapter. Instead of deriving from the spirit world, the new consciousness in the medium is another facet of the personality which comes to the surface. In other words, all the information imparted to the sitter is thought to come from the subconsciousness of the medium, although he may be sincere in his belief of spirit control.

In the instances of dual or multiple personality encountered in life, the individual seldom has had control as to which entity would possess him at any time. Either may come and go with long or short periods of possession. But a medium can apparently invoke the second side of the personality at will and banish it by ending the trance.

Recently LeCron had an opportunity to study informally the relationship of the hypnotic and mediumistic trances in two different instances. One was with a client who is well known in spiritualistic circles, a nonprofessional and entirely sincere. Under certain conditions this man is able to enter the mediumistic trance and to be "controlled." A first attempt at hypnosis with him failed because of certain emotional factors, and these also prevented him from going into a self-induced trance. In order to save time, because the client was making trips from another city for treatment, narcosis with pentothal was resorted to. While in narcosis it was strongly suggested that hypnosis could thereafter be easily induced. The suggestion was effective, and several subsequent hypnotic sessions were held with a deep hypnosis attained by the subject.

Having now had experience with all three states, narcosis,

mediumistic trance and hypnosis, the subject while hypnotized was asked to explain their differences. He remarked that he would compare it to an onion. Under pentothal he felt that a couple of outer layers had been peeled off, but under hypnosis it seemed as though additional layers had been removed and a greater depth attained. He found it harder to think clearly in narcosis and under hypnosis felt he was able to draw more directly on the subconscious. The mediumistic trance and hypnosis are identical, he declared positively.

Recently LeCron also was able to discuss this relationship with the late Stewart Edward White, famous writer whose latest works were devoted to spiritualism. Sincere and completely convinced as to the validity of spiritualism after a quarter century of intensive study of the subject, White volunteered to try to obtain information on hypnosis from his control, whom he termed "the Gaelic." In a subsequent séance this entity from the "Unobstructed Universe," which White believed controlled him during a trance, undertook an explanation which was a new interpretation and one of great interest. It was stated by him that hypnosis and the mediumistic trance are definitely identical but that they should not be considered autohypnosis. The medium having made himself relaxed and receptive, the Invisibles (as White termed them) from their plane induce the hypnotic state! And they often find it as difficult as does a corporeal hypnotist, according to the Gaelic control.

As was true after the first World War, spiritualism will undoubtedly go through a period of great popularity following World War II. Reports from England already tell of a great surge of interest in that country, and the same can be expected in the United States.

Akin to the mediumistic trance, though no trance is implicated in most cases, is automatic writing carried out either directly with the hand or indirectly through a Ouija board or planchette. The means of communication may be automatic speech instead, or automatic drawing. Sadler cites some of the more prominent automatic writers—the mother of George Bernard Shaw, the dramatist Sardou, and Flammarion the scientist. Coleridge is said to have written "Kubla Khan" automatically, a product of his subconscious mind.

Many spiritualists have indulged in automatic writing. Like those of the trance medium, their messages are assigned to spirit origin, the information thereby disclosed assertedly being unknown to the conscious mind of the writer. Often it can be shown to be a matter of the recall of lost memories. Also the subconscious at times can be unbelievably adroit and sensitive to small cues, subliminal stimuli, minor changes in facial expression, in breathing, etc. Even vocal intonations may betray things to the subconscious of another. No intentional fraud or deceit may be involved, merely subconscious promptings. No scientific proof of spirit origin has ever been produced, and the psychological explanation of dissociation, minimal cues and recall of lost memories is entirely consistent and adequate.

In scrying, or crystal gazing, an actual crystal is not necessary for the production of the visions. A glass of water, a glass bowl or a mirror will serve instead, although a crystal may facilitate the vision to some extent. The crystal gazer relates that the crystal clouds up and becomes smoky or misty after attention has been fixed on the ball for a few moments. The mist effect then clears and visions appear as though projected on a motion-picture screen, usually with movement and sometimes in color. When crystal gazing is attempted under hypnosis, the subject may hallucinate the crystal instead of gazing into an actual one and will see the suggested visions.

While the mediumistic trance is a form of hypnosis, in

the case of automatic writing, crystal gazing and the like, no trance ordinarily ensues. By means of hypnotic suggestion the ability to attain the necessary dissociation may be greatly increased, and many who cannot perform these feats in the waking state find themselves able to do so in hypnosis. By posthypnotic suggestion the ability may then be developed in the waking state.

These factors may all be put to practical use in psychotherapy, as will be elaborated in that section of the text. They can be employed as tools to bring out repressed and forgotten memories or conflicts. Mühl [63] has written of employing automatic writing and describes the development of the ability. Although she believes the process is perhaps dangerous because it may cause too much dissociation, Dr. Mühl tells of patients reading a book aloud while carrying on automatic writing with both hands at once, each writing of a different matter—a triangle of mental activity. Erickson, however, feels there is no danger in automatic writing itself, only that a person suffering from a mental disorder or disturbance may find automatic writing a delightful way of slipping into schizophrenic fantasies.

Quite different from spiritualistic matters is telepathy or thought transference, commonly called mind reading. It may be defined as the communication of ideas or impressions by other than the normal means through the five senses. The most common instances of telepathy are those in which two people (who may be relatives or married or intimate friends, most likely) think simultaneously of the same thing. This is by no means a rare occurrence. Skeptics maintain that it comes about through chance or coincidence, or because the two people are influenced by environment and perhaps heredity to think along the same lines. Undoubtedly such cases do arise from these factors, but believers in telepathy claim that too many have such identical ideas or thoughts at the same time to consider them as coincidental, the mathematical odds against the coincidence being enormous.

A few scientists have believed telepathy possible and supernormal only because its operation is inexplicable. A favorite theory, advanced by Sir William Crookes, has been that some kind of "brain wave" may be involved, with one mind intercepting the thoughts of another just as radio waves are received and transmitted. Somewhat similar to Crookes' theory is the theosophical idea of telepathy as the projection of thought forms from one mind to another through an etheric vibration or force.

Of course there has been much fraud in demonstrations of telepathy, and stage performances can be regarded as deception, cleverly executed. Most scientists are unconvinced of the actuality of telepathy, though more open-minded than towards spiritualism. J. B. Rhine has done much laboratory experiment at Duke University on extrasensory perception, but results as published in books and in the *Journal of Parapsychology* are the subject of great controversy.

Rhine believes that he has demonstrated possession of extrasensory perceptive powers in certain individuals. The Rhine tests were largely concerned with the naming of special cards by one person as they were drawn by another in a different room. More recently Rhine made tests as to mental influence on the results of dice throwing. Positive results are claimed for both, but opponents (notably John Scarne) decry them as mathematically in error and most psychologists have refused to accept the findings.

Telepathic tests under hypnosis have been conducted by nearly every dabbler in hypnotism, mostly with no controls and unscientifically. Results reported are often astounding—and completely worthless as proof that hypnosis increases a telepathic faculty. Rhine had little success with hypnotized subjects in his tests, but his reports indicate a lack of proper technique in suggesting. If he is ever able to prove his contentions, it is possible that extrasensory perception may be developed and increased by hypnotic suggestion, but all is purely speculative today so far as telepathy is concerned.

The ability to see distant scenes through mental eyes is known as clairvoyance. It is often demonstrated by hypnotists with apparently successful results. The hypnotized subject is directed to project his mind to some location and to report what he sees (clairvoyance) and/or what he hears (clairaudience). Usually a far-off locale is chosen, as distance seems to add to the interest.

The situation is exactly the same as in crystal gazing without a crystal, the subject experiencing only a visual hallucination. Almost invariably he will expatiate at length on what he believes he sees and hears, but usually it is impossible to ascertain whether the events actually occurred as described. It should be easy to prove such a matter scientifically, but no acceptable evidence of such abilities has ever been offered, to our knowledge.

Actually, hypnotism has little relationship to the psychic arts even though the mediumistic and hypnotic trances seem to be identical. Automatic writing, crystal gazing and the like are all performed equally well in the waking state, the ability merely being increased by hypnotic suggestion. Discussion of psychic matters is made here only because hypnotism has so often been connected with them in the mind of the public, one of the many popular misconceptions as to the science.

## PART TWO

HYPNOTHERAPY

AT PRESENT there are several million persons in the United States suffering from neurotic difficulties. Most of these sufferers are financially unable to afford expensive treatment. For them hypnotism offers the hope of relatively quick relief, a fact unknown to most laymen and seldom appreciated by physicians, even many of those engaged in psychotherapy. Millions of dollars are being spent in a search for relief from the diseases which afflict mankind, but scant attention is paid to the neuroses, among the most common illnesses. Many forms are serious and neuroses present one of the greatest problems in medicine. With our present knowledge it is not easy to overcome personality disorders, although brief treatment may suffice if the short-cuts afforded by hypnotism are utilized. To show the way to such brief psychotherapy, the following pages describe the practical applications of hypnotism.

Employment of hypnotic phenomena in psychotherapy involves a study of general and abnormal psychology, psychiatry, psychoanalysis, psychosomatic medicine and mental hygiene. Each is a field in itself with a literature of its own. While only brief mention can be made of even important matters, a condensed survey of pertinent sections of these fields will aid the average reader in understanding the usefulness of hypnotism. Mention of some technical terms is unavoidable in, for instance, the glossology of psychoanalysis. As space does not permit many definitions, readers unfamiliar with the terminology should consult a text such as Conklin's [1] *Principles of Abnormal Psychology* for further information.

Those professionally trained in medicine and psychotherapy are reminded that the authors are not physicians. However, we have followed standard texts throughout. Since there is so much room for argument as to many things in abnormal psychology and psychotherapy, we have tried to refrain from dogmatism.

Conditions in medicine pointed out here have repeatedly been called to our attention by physicians with whom we work. Most practicing physicians are aware of the deficiencies mentioned, and the thoughtful will understand that all criticisms are meant to be constructive.

# CHAPTER X

# Abnormal Psychology—
# Functional Diseases

UNUSUAL MENTAL ACTIVITY and behavior are a part of the study of abnormal psychology, but demarcation between the normal and the abnormal has never been satisfactorily drawn, owing to lack of knowledge of the so-called normal individual, his personality and his behavior. Abnormal means a deviation from the usual, and personality adjustments outside the medial range are considered abnormal. This being true, everyone is more or less abnormal in one way or another. Most of us have some neurotic tendencies, making it extremely difficult to establish a norm or to draft a definite average mental pattern.

For example, the emotion of fear is a normal feeling until it becomes too intense or is present in a situation where the average individual is not afraid, whereupon that fear is definitely abnormal. The average person has a normal fear of falling when near the brink of a high cliff and is cautious in approaching the edge. Let this fear become intense, perhaps accompanied by an impulse to jump off, and the emotion becomes abnormal.

Behavior abnormality may be so slight as to cause little or no distress or it may reach such an extreme as to constitute a psychosis (insanity), termed a major abnormality. Psychoses are not in our province because there is little opportunity for employing hypnotism in their treatment, since the insane seldom can be hypnotized. In fact no form of psychotherapy has been found very efficacious in treating psychoses, although cures are made and there is progress towards understanding them. The application of hypnotherapy, if attempted, would be the same as with the neuroses.

It is with the lesser functional disturbances that hypnotism is concerned. These have not been well defined, nor has their classification and nomenclature been stabilized, but there is a tendency to group all under the general term "psychoneuroses" or, more briefly, "neuroses," which will be the word employed here.

The milder functional disturbances differ from psychoses but no definite dividing line exists between the two nor is there such a demarcation between the neuroses and the normal. In many respects the symptomatology is not the same, but the essential difference between them is in reality relationships and the capacity to function.

Whether a neurotic tendency is hereditary or a result of environment has been much discussed but remains undetermined. Janet [2] regarded heredity as a definite element in hysteria; Sidis [3] was positive that it is not implicated in any neurosis. A neurotic person may have had a long line of neurotic ancestors, yet each may have become neurotic because of environment and association with a neurotic parent, and certainly environment is a potent factor. An adopted child is likely to become neurotic when either foster parent is neurotic.

The neurotic personality is well defined, Karen Horney [4] having written at length on the neurotic characteristics. Neurotics usually are egocentric and extremely self-conscious, burdened with strong feelings of inferiority, dependency, insecurity, frustration and discontent, sometimes accompanied by despondency and melancholia. Army draft statistics show neurotics to be slightly lower than average in mental age, but many are decidedly brilliant and gifted with superior intelligence. When the intelligence is high, it frequently is easier to overcome the condition, though sometimes high intelligence serves further to elaborate the neurosis.

Many psychologists and psychotherapists believe the motivation of all human activity is based on Freud's "pleasure principle"—the search for pleasure and the avoidance of pain. Hoping to escape from painful reality, the psychotic may avoid his problems by occupying himself with introspection, daydreaming and fantasies. He actively resists treatment by refusing all cooperation. This attitude makes it extremely difficult to hypnotize most of those suffering from a psychosis.

On the other hand, a neurotic seldom loses touch with reality. Though maladjusted, he usually realizes that something is wrong and he seeks relief. In fact, he may fear he is going insane. Because fear is painful, the neurotic seldom takes pleasure in his symptoms, though there are exceptions. He adjusts himself to existing in spite of his discomfort and subconsciously fears any change which may upset his defenses. Because his symptoms are defensive attitudes, he may subconsciously resist attempts at cure while consciously wishing to be well.

The hysterical personality differs from both the psychotic and the neurotic. Although physically mature, he remains emotionally arrested and inadequate but does not retreat entirely from reality. Barred by maladjustment from properly facing life, his symptoms become an excuse permitting partial escape. They tend to create the attention and sympathy which he craves and offer an alibi to avoid work—he is too ill. Such symptoms are a shield and he therefore takes pleasure in them. They may be anything such as the simulation of the symptoms of some disease, or they may be convulsive attacks, blindness, deafness, mutism, paralysis, contractures, bodily pains, etc. While the deception may be deliberate, more often it is unconscious.

There are wide differences in hysterical behavior, but many sufferers from the condition loudly inveigh against their illness, proclaiming to family and friends how miserable they are and asserting that they would do anything to be well again. But the hysterical individual subconsciously prefers to remain ill because he finds it advantageous. Therefore he resists cure. Unlike the psychotic, he usually is highly suggestible and easily hypnotized, though sometimes resistant. No matter what psychotherapy is employed, the hysteric finds pleasure in his condition, so that cure becomes difficult. Apparently relieved, he tends to relapse. When one symptom is eliminated, another crops out. If his symptoms are removed by hypnotic suggestion, which is often readily accomplished, the next day they are reanimated or new ones have taken their place. Although the condition is sometimes cured, the hysteric is the despair of all practitioners.

In studying the etiology (causation) of neuroses, differences between the various types are found to be due primarily to the causative factors. Many theories as to causation have been advanced, all similar in some ways, each quite logical in general, making it difficult to draw definite conclusions as to which is correct. Much depends on one's viewpoint. All the theories are probably correct in part, arriving at the same conclusions along divergent paths of thought. Knowledge of mental abnormality and of the subconscious mind is still too limited to permit proof of many of the ideas advanced and they remain conjectural only. Psychoanalytic theory is highly complicated and only a brief sketch of its contentions can be set forth here.

The Freudian school of thought is basic, though many psycho-analysts have divergent ideas.

In order to understand mental reactions it is necessary to consider the motives behind them. Those instinctive drives and impulses conflicting with our codes of morals and the taboos of society produce tension. Tension seeks an outlet for discharge which will then give relaxation, but discharge may be prevented by opposing tendencies which then dam up the energy. Inhibitions and repressions are the preventive factors, control resting in the "id," "ego" and "superego." When control breaks down or is insufficient, neurotic symptoms appear which the individual finds are strange and incomprehensible, apparently without reason. The symptoms are a result of the energy seeking an outlet, the prevention of normal discharge causing diversion to other channels, or "conversion." Thus neuroses are primarily the result of conflicts between instinctual drives and inhibiting forces.

Throughout his existence every individual faces the problem of solving conflicts which arise from environment and life's activities. Instincts, desires and impulses urge him along some path across which the dictates of society, morality and training may have erected a wall. For example, the problem of sexual desire creates such a situation. The individual feels instinctive need of gratification, but the social code of civilization forbids and a conflict ensues. Warfare offers another illustration. Even the bravest man is fearful in battle and at times that fear becomes extreme. Yet duty beckons him into the fray. If he yields to fear and runs away, he is liable to scorn and punishment. If he remains at his post, he may be killed or badly injured. Thus a mental conflict arises as emotion opposes reason.

Facing any mental conflict, the well-adjusted person confronts the problem, weighs and studies it, then decides on a course of action and pursues it even though it be unpleasant, thus resolving the conflict and suffering no harm to his personality. Alternatively, the person who is not properly adjusted may evade the issue and repress the idea in an effort to escape; or he may yield to desires and wishes, involving a lowering of moral values and creating a feeling of guilt which must then be repressed as repugnant and disagreeable. The latter courses open the door to a neurosis, particularly if they are repeatedly followed.

Conflict, repression and frustration of course begin in earliest infancy. According to Freudian tenets, they are complicated by instinctual, "archaic" urges which develop into complexes common to all infants and children. Most important of these are the "Oedipus" and "castration" complexes reputedly found in every child. It is the failure to resolve these complexes, together with other causes such as guilt over masturbation and eroticism, which lies behind every neurosis—according to Freudian theory. Many less orthodox analysts believe that infantile sexual matters are not overly important and should not be stressed, preferring instead to emphasize the precipitating causes. Finding many other emotions concerned as well as sexual urges, many are skeptical of the Freudian ideas of infant eroticism which orthodox analysts view as always deeply involved in neuroses.

Maladjustment to the realities of life arising from childhood development and environment is one of the main underlying factors in all neuroses. Irregularity in discipline of the child is one reason for maladjustment. Too great indulgence and too much restriction in training are equally harmful. When a parent has an erratic and indecisive temperament, the child does not know what reaction to expect from that parent. As a result, the child feels insecure and uncertain. What he regards as correct behavior is punished one day, the next it may be disregarded or perhaps even praised, leaving him continually apprehensive and in doubt.

One of the greatest needs of a child is for love and affection, which neurotic parents may not be able to supply because of their own difficulties. If training involves too much frustration of the child's wishes or if jealousy is felt towards a parent or brothers or sisters, hostility is aroused. Feelings of guilt, of helplessness and dependency, together with unjust punishments and fear all serve to provoke hostility. The child then through fear or guilt feels that the hostility must be repressed, and from repressed hostility anxiety may develop. Horney has described this process and believes that anxiety is the basis of every neurosis, though it may be concealed so the neurotic individual does not realize its presence. Horney stresses the importance of culture and customs as well as genetic influences in the development of neuroses. Freudians also regard anxiety as basic in neuroses but think that it generates from repressed energy, arising when the discharge of the energy is inhibited.

When a conflict or a wish repugnant to the ego is repressed, Freud termed the resulting neurosis a conversion hysteria if the repression is complete, the emotional symptoms being converted into the physical sphere. When the repression changes to fear, it becomes a phobia. Should the repression be displaced or transformed into another idea, it becomes an obsession or compulsion.

A conflict may arise from an emotional shock or trauma (or a series of them), an extremely unpleasant or frightening experience which arouses great emotion or terror in the individual. The insecure ego tries to protect itself by repressing the memory of the experience which threatens it. An example of these traumata is the experience of the soldier in battle who finds himself in great danger from shells and bursting bombs and his fear grows until he becomes terror-stricken. Unable to hold up any longer, he becomes a battle casualty suffering from war neurosis. Traumatic experiences in civilian life have similar results, especially those occurring in childhood. Then the event may be one terrifying to a youngster but not greatly disturbing to an adult.

Consider the case of Roy T——, a young man twenty-seven years old who had stuttered ever since he could remember. Though unable to recall consciously an event which had been completely repressed in memory, the clue to his trauma was supplied by his parents. Then, during hypnosis he was regressed to the age of three and described the event in detail. The house next door to his home had caught fire and Roy's mother carried him out to watch as fire engines arrived with shrieking sirens. In the window of the burning building appeared a dog, the pet of the neighborhood children. Unable to escape, the animal perished in the flames while they watched. Roy became hysterical, almost in convulsions, and had stuttered ever since. One obvious moral to the story is that parents should not permit children to witness extremely emotional scenes if it can be prevented, for children may not be able to handle their reactions adequately. Incidentally, Roy ceased stuttering after a few hypnoanalytic sessions.

When a situation, traumatic or environmental, becomes such that the individual cannot cope with it, there is a breakdown and a neurosis develops. Usually both contributing and precipitating causes are involved. Thus latent neurotic tendencies or trends become active when the power to adjust or adapt is insufficient. Probably everyone has some point at which he can no longer bear up, but most people do not encounter circumstances which cause such a breakdown.

Grinker and Spiegel believe that the neurosis is a psychosomatic problem  the psychological or emotional causation being as described in psychoanalytic theory but operating dynamically in a physiological way. Essentially this is a neurological explanation.

To sketch it briefly, the cortex or seat of consciousness and the thalamus, thought to be concerned with the subconscious, are in close harmony and relationship. Between them they coordinate all bodily activity and behavior, each stimulating the other in various ways and each reacting to the other. Under stress this relationship between the cortex and the thalamus, between the primary and autonomic nervous systems, may become disturbed and break down, many factors being involved. Consequently the autonomic nervous system performs erratically and various mental and somatic neurotic symptoms develop, together with anxiety and fear. This neurological disturbance upsets the proper functioning of the autonomic nervous system, operating through the hypothalamus —the central regulator which effects a coordination of responses. It is misfunctioning of the hypothalamus which causes the symptoms.

Some psychologists familiar with hypnotism and suggestion in some cases view the causes of neuroses partly from a slightly different angle than has been presented heretofore. In this conception suggestion is one of the factors involved, although the basic causes are those that have been described. All the emotions implicated in a neurosis, particularly any emotional shock or shocks which may precipitate it, act upon the mind. There is suggestion that fear should be felt whenever the object or situation associated with the shock is encountered again. Repetition establishes a neurotic symptom which is perhaps symbolic of the trauma or of the terrifying object, or perhaps it is projected as a phobia, an obsession, or a compulsion. Estabrooks calls attention to the working of conflicts and repressions as almost identical to that of posthypnotic suggestion in actuating the mind, symptoms then arising like suggested actions. Adopting Pavlov's theory, Fink believes that repetition of the association to such objects or situations establishes a conditioned reflex, the symptoms then appearing when the object or situation is met again.

Suggestion is sometimes an evident factor in a neurosis. One of our clients, a twenty-year-old girl, developed a whole series of phobias partly as a result of extreme suggestibility. In a number of different situations she would experience extreme anxiety—whenever a streetcar approached as she waited for it; when riding on a bus; whenever she passed a cemetery; if she found herself in any large open space such as a vacant lot; and there were others. A schoolteacher, she had anxiety attacks in the classroom; and a particularly unpleasant symptom was a feeling that she was about to faint whenever she walked alone along the street.

In the course of hypnoanalysis some mild emotional experience was found behind each one and when it was laid bare and she had reacted to it again, with insight each fear would vanish. It was much like peeling an onion to uncover the fears, most of them centering around her main conflict—hostility towards her father with consequent feelings of guilt. Each phobia seemed to have evolved as the result of a suggestion. She had seen another teacher faint on the sidewalk, and witnessing it gave her the suggestion of fainting when she walked alone. On a picnic in an open space in the mountains a bear had appeared and frightened the picnic party. Each such episode suggested that she should feel anxiety again in a similar situation. Eventually, education and insight released the hostility towards her father, and the difficulty was overcome with resolution of her conflict.

All the conceptions of the causative factors in neuroses which have been described are observed to fit together, and there is actually no conflict between them. Each interpretation provides a clearer view of the problem as a whole. They are mainly a matter of viewpoint.

## CLASSIFICATION OF THE NEUROSES

There is little agreement as to the classification of the types and varieties of neuroses encountered and no standard terms have been adopted, but those given below frequently are used. For convenience this listing follows in general that of Dorcus and Shaffer. All types are closely related and often overlap. The symptoms and tendencies are legion but only the more common are mentioned.

*Neurasthenia* is sometimes called the fatigue neurosis, for its outstanding symptom is fatigue, both mental and physical. Other symptoms are depression, irritability, insomnia, headache, indigestion, extreme nervousness and often inability to fix the attention on anything. General hypochondria may also be shown.

Overwork formerly was believed to be one of the main causes, but that idea has been discarded because rest brings no improvement. More certain origins are worry, profound emotional strain, and it may be that the disease is an escape reaction since the neurasthenic person is often very self-centered and may show little desire to recover.

*Anxiety states.* This condition is marked by morbid apprehension and intense fear—perhaps of death or of becoming insane. The sufferer is often unable to concentrate, exhibits much irritability and may be elated or depressed at times. Almost any physical symptom may also be present.

Freud believed that the condition arises from sexual conflicts generated in the present rather than in early childhood, as in the case of compulsion-obsessive neuroses. More probably the anxiety arises from conflict over other needs and desires as well, and particularly from financial or domestic worry.

The term *psychasthenia* is sometimes used to designate several closely related types of neuroses—the phobias, obsessions, compulsions and tics.

*Phobias* are morbid fears of abnormal intensity perhaps amounting at times to paralyzing terror. Classification is according to their stimuli, the list of different phobias being too long to enumerate here. Most common are claustrophobia (fear of closed places), acrophobia (fear of high places), achlophobia (fear of crowds), and frequently met with is zoophobia (fear of animals), particularly of snakes.

*Obsessions* are ideas persistently recurring which the individual is unable to ignore although the idea may be irrational and so recognized. The variety seen is innumerable. Usually the idea is unpleasant, though it may be merely annoying. Severe obsessions are invariably unpleasant and are accompanied by anxiety and nervousness.

*Compulsions.* If the obsessional idea is an irresistible impulse to carry out an act, it is a compulsion. These uncontrollable actions are sometimes termed manias, such as kleptomania (the impulse to steal), pyromania (the impulse to set fire to things) and dipsomania (compulsive drinking of alcoholic liquors). Other common compulsions are the need to wash the hands, as unclean or contaminated, and the counting or touching of objects; the variety is infinite.

Most people are able to remember having had as children mild forms of compulsion which they have outgrown. A frequent childhood compulsion is the urge to step on certain cracks in concrete sidewalks or to touch certain fence or telephone posts. Numerous compulsions show a background of superstition. There is a feeling of obligation to perform the act or else something unpleasant or evil will befall the person or someone close to him. He must take the compulsive action "or else."

*Psychasthenic tics* may be related to the compulsions but there seems not to be any purpose behind the action, which is a form of motor disturbance involving a small group of muscles, such as an involuntary twitching of the eye, of facial muscles, of the arms or hands, or almost any portion of the body. There is a consciousness of the movement but it is uncontrollable and distinctly uncomfortable. When the psychological genesis is not recognized, there may be resort to an operation severing the nerves which control the affected part; then, as a rule, the tic promptly reappears in some other location, the former one being paralyzed.

In all psychasthenic conditions there is a recognition of the absurdity involved but control is impossible and there is an accompanying feeling of incompetency and inferiority.

Dorcus and Shaffer briefly summarize the etiology of psychasthenic conditions as follows: "The specific causes appear to be stresses of prolonged emotional insecurity resulting from external threats or induced by attitude and example of dominant figures in the individual's environment. These emotional tensions become associated with certain objects or situations as the result of conditioning experiences, and this association gives rise to phobias, obsessions and compulsions. A group of defense reactions is then developed, including primarily the fundamental biological reactions of defense and avoidance and, in addition, partial adaptive defense reactions, the form and content of which are determined by conditioning experiences."

*Hysteria* has often been classed separately but is now generally regarded as a type of neurosis rather than a distinct disease. The term covers a wide range of conditions, from hysterical crying or laughing to complex disturbances. What is commonly termed "hysterics" is only one of a great variety of forms encountered and need not be regarded as abnormal when it follows a deep emotional shock.

Practically any kind of symptom, mental or physical, may be displayed. It may be sensory, such as functional blindness, deafness or any anaesthesia, hyperaesthesia or paraesthesia. Motor symptoms may be paralyses, contractures, tics or tremors. Mental symptoms may include amnesias, fugues, somnambulisms, etc. There may be a simulation of organic illness such as heart disease, tumor, tuberculosis; in fact, according to Janet the hysteric may simulate the symptoms of almost any disease.

Hysteria has been recognized since the earliest days of medical history and until recently was believed to be a condition peculiar to women (the term comes from the Greek word for womb) though it is now known that men also suffer from it, the incidence being greater in women.

Janet devoted much study to hysteria and outlined the hysterical personality as marked by imperfect integration which is further weakened by an emotional shock. He noted a restricted field of consciousness, which signifies that suggestibility is greatly increased. According to his belief, the emotional shock produces a dissociation of memory for the events of the trauma, amnesia then developing together with varied hysterical symptoms.

Babinski [5] agreed with Janet in believing that every hysteric is characterized by one most important trait—suggestibility. He thought that the development of hysterical symptoms was a result of this suggestibility. Probably it was this factor which led Charcot, Brown and others to consider hypnosis and hysteria relatively the same condition.

The theory of hysteria evolved by Freud was that its basis lay in a sexual trauma of early childhood which was repressed and then revived later in life by another emotional shock. There is a conflict between a distasteful wish and the ego, which is repressed, but only partially, with conversion into the hysterical symptoms.

*War neuroses.* All of these can be classified according to the types of neuroses previously defined, the term describing the cause rather than designating the kind. They have offered an excellent opportunity for investigation of the whole neurosis problem because the precipitating factor can be learned and its nature recognized more effectively.

Experimental induction of a neurosis might enable us to track the beast to its lair and study all its aspects at close range to reach a better understanding. Much investigation has been conducted with animals and neuroses have been developed in dogs, cats, pigs and rats by means of conflicts, frustrations and monotonous auditory stimuli. But human behavior is so different from that of animals that little can be learned from the results.

With human beings, a Russian psychologist, A. R. Luria [6] of the State Institute of Experimental Psychology in Moscow, was able to induce experimental neuroses by the use of hypnosis. His method was to suggest a complex to the hypnotized subject, something contrary to his moral code which would create a conflict and subsequent repression. The repression was brought about artificially by suggesting amnesia.

The causes were known exactly in these experimental situations, so that all reactions could be studied carefully with knowledge of what could be expected. One result was to prove the value of word association tests. The experimental neurosis, like the war neuroses, has served to prove other instincts and emotions as well as sexual ones concerned in neurotic etiology.

More recently, leading proponents of hypnoanalysis have followed Luria's lead and have induced conflicts during the treatment of neuroses. By means of these induced conflicts, strong emotional experiences are produced which may later be studied by both patient and therapist to provide insight into the patient's actual difficulty. Wolberg gives an excellent discussion of induced conflicts, saying, ". . . induction of an experimental conflict can play a decisive role by demonstrating to the patient how unconscious impulses and emotions are responsible for his symptoms."

As early as 1935 Erickson used this technique.[7] He has described [8] in detail its therapeutic use. A fictitious story was suggested to the subject as being an actual past forgotten social error committed by him. Each word of the story was carefully thought out in advance with all the intonations, inflections, emphases and pauses which were to be used, and an analysis is made at length of the whole story by word and phrase. Erickson regards such a carefully thought out suggestion as much superior to haphazard ones to induce extensive changes in the behavior of hypnotized subjects.

In this case no study of causes or analysis of the patient's neurosis was made, the induced conflict being suggested without the subject's knowledge while he was presumably acting as a subject in a hypnotic experiment. The artificial conflict was simply used to give him insight, the patient being well acquainted with psychotherapy himself. As a result of the conflict, he exhibited neurotic behavior as had been expected, found his emotions the same for the actual neurosis and the induced complex, and his real difficulty was overcome.

# CHAPTER XI

# Psychotherapeutic Methods

MODERN MEDICINE has been primarily interested in organic disease, and many physicians still adhere to the doctrine of Hippocrates, believing there is no sickness without organic cause. To them, mental abnormality results only from a diseased or an injured brain. The psychological aspects of disease have only recently been recognized. The transformation of psychiatry into psychological medicine has come almost wholly within the past fifty years, with its greatest development only in the last quarter century. Emil Kraepelin [9] (1856-1926), first modern student of the abnormal, led the way in showing the relationship between mind and body in disease, the effect of one upon the other, and demonstrating them as two parts making up a whole instead of considering them as two different entities to be treated separately.

Medical research until recently was concentrated mainly on physiology, and most psychologists have investigated normal behavior rather than abnormal. Hence our knowledge of mental illness is limited. Even today there is no commonly accepted, consistently effective system of psychotherapy available for the general public.

Medical history discloses that suggestion and herbal remedies have been the main weapons in the fight against disease. Since prehistoric times medicine men and witch doctors have treated organic illness with herbs, using suggestion as mental therapy, and often combining the two. The esoteric knowledge of the ancient priesthoods always comprehended suggestion as therapeutically potent.

Faith healing has long been a common psychotherapeutic method. From time to time over thousands of years, great religious healers have appeared to perform seeming miracles of healing by suggestion and religious faith. Many were deified —Zoroaster, Christ, Mohammed and others in many lands and ages. Today these methods are still employed by evangelists, Christian Science practitioners, healers of many cults.

As a matter of indirect suggestion, every physician has resorted to placebos with success. Sometimes a bad-tasting and entirely powerless "tonic" may be prescribed. Hysterical pains without organic basis have been cured by a simulated operation. Intentionally painful electric shock may be resorted to in the same way.

Ever since Benjamin Franklin flew his kite, medical men have had recourse to electrical treatment, hoping that a current through a diseased part of the body would work a cure in some way. The suggestion of cure often brought beneficial results, confirming the hopes of the physician, who then was convinced that electricity was wholly responsible. The same therapy is much in vogue today, as shown by the elaborate and awe-inspiring machines with highly technical names employed by chiropractors to diagnose or to cure anything and everything—neurocalometers, gravitonic rays, bio-electronic mechanisms, electrometabiographs. Such H. G. Wellsian contrivances surely must be potent for whatever ails you!

Treatment for insanity and other mental disturbances not very long ago included whirling the patient violently until consciousness was lost, thus "restoring the brain particles to proper arrangement." Bleeding, purging, and dehydration were all regarded as effective at one time. Less than a hundred years ago a shock treatment became popular—the victim was plunged into a tub of ice water! All were sometimes beneficial, and underneath them we find hidden that persistent "old debbil," suggestion.

Today there is a different kind of shock treatment in vogue among psychiatrists. Insulin, metrazol and electricity are the agents used to produce convulsions in the patient, a terrific physical shock. Theoretically a biological, chemical or other effect is exerted on the brain, bringing a cure or alleviation of the treated condition.

How it actually operates and why it succeeds is not clearly understood, but shock treatment has been found relatively effective. Apparently it is valuable for the treatment of psychoses, especially manic-depressive and other melancholic conditions. Shock treatment has now been used for a long enough time to permit evaluation of the method, and it is becoming more and more popular with psychiatrists. When psychotherapy fails, it may be resorted to for those neuroses where deep depression is manifested, but it has been found of little value in the treatment of most neuroses.

Auxiliary employment of the drug curare has reduced the chances of physical damage from the convulsions. Most recently a method of giving electric shock termed "electronarcosis" has been developed at the California Institute of Technology. With a current of much less intensity, the shock is applied for seven or eight minutes, producing a sleep-like state. Danger is thus eliminated and it is claimed that the therapeutic effects are greatly increased. The present trend is to give electric shock preference over insulin and metrazol.

The effects of the usual shock treatment are terrific. Symptoms are literally jarred out. The normal mental processes are effected to a degree, and the patient is often dazed. Memory is badly disturbed for some time, particularly if a series of three or more shocks are given. Having lost some or all of his symptoms, the patient may decide that he is cured. Shock treatment for neuroses frequently seems to remove symptoms but with subsequent relapse, perhaps because a busy psychiatrist considers shock sufficient and fails to follow it up with reeducation and readjustment, which are essential parts of psychotherapy.

Reassurance and encouragement constitute a direct method of suggestion which ought to be employed in every type of therapy, both functional and organic. Many physicians appreciate its importance and value, while others untutored in psychology are too often impatient with the neurotic and dismiss him with the statement, "There is nothing wrong with you but imagination. Just forget about your trouble." Yet neurotic pains and symptoms are not imaginary. They are actually felt although their basis may be entirely functional. Reassurance may not cure, but it is a valuable aid in paving the way to a cure. Every patient needs to be convinced that, with his cooperation, proper therapy will bring the desired results.

Simplest of all psychotherapeutic methods was that of persuasion, formulated in the latter part of the nineteenth century by Paul DuBois of Switzerland. DuBois [10] observed the cures of Bernheim and others using direct hypnotic suggestion but deemed the method unscientific. He considered hypnotism and suggestion unethical, tinged with charlatanism and something only for the gullible. While DuBois realized that mental disturbances might be caused by disease, he believed that if nothing was organically wrong a sufferer could give up his symptoms voluntarily and be well again. Therefore, he undertook persuasion by reassurance and rationalization.

In his book DuBois disclaimed emphatically the use of suggestion, contending that it weakened the subject's will, especially if hypnotism was employed. But when he described his system, it was suggestion and nothing else! As he used it, persuasion became synonymous with suggestion.

Until Freud made psychoanalysis popular early in the present century, probably the best available method of psychotherapy was hypnotism. Direct suggestion under hypnosis was employed by the old-time medical hypnotists such as Braid, Liebeault, Bernheim, Wetterstrand and their associates and successors who practiced before the development of psychoanalytic theory made available a better knowledge of the neuroses. Their system differed from modern hypnotherapy. The patient was hypnotized and given repetitious suggestions that his symptoms would disappear and that he would be cured. The writings of these old-school hypnotic practitioners certify to the efficacy of this system. In their survey of hypnotherapy, Brenman and Gill note the success and the permanency of many of their cures.

More orthodox medical men deprecated such an unscientific method, claiming that it only removed symptoms and effected no cure. Today, similar criticism is made by many psychotherapists and others unfamiliar with modern hypnotic methods. Undoubtedly some cures were only temporary, yet this is true also of every system of psychotherapy, for relapses are frequent regardless of the system employed. With little understanding of mental abnormalities and personality disorders, it is remarkable how many patients were permanently relieved. The method must be regarded as moderately effective, although modern hypnotherapy offers far greater possibilities.

Basically, direct hypnotic suggestion of cure is much like faith healing. The patient is benefited principally because he accepts the suggestion of cure. Unlike faith healing, suggestion is applied scientifically according to its laws and is aimed directly at the difficulty, its force increased because of the increased suggestibility of the patient under hypnosis.

In speaking of the cure of neurotic conditions, it is necessary to explain the use here of the word "cure." It is doubtful if anyone suffering from neurotic difficulties can ever be so completely "cured" as to be entirely free of all neurotic tendencies and traits. In a medical sense cure would imply that a particular disease has ceased to exist in the treated patient. In speaking here of the cure of a neurosis, we mean that the patient has recovered to an extent sufficient to permit him to exist comfortably without suffering and to occupy himself normally.

Modern systems of psychotherapy seek to apply a rational and scientific approach to the problem of cure and to remove the causes of the condition. According to Dorcus and Shaffer, to understand the functional mental illness, "It is necessary to find the answers to the following questions: (a) Why did the patient have a mental illness at this time? (b) Why did the mental illness take the particular form exhibited, and (c) What accounts for the symptoms manifested?" If these questions can be answered, they believe it should be possible to overcome and remedy the condition, although reeducation and readjustment are essential to complete the cure. Certainly these important questions require an answer, but we believe that other considerations are involved.

In order to find the answers, it is imperative to obtain a thorough case history in the nature of a detailed biography of the individual, no matter what system of psychotherapy is to be undertaken. This is an essential part of any effective treatment. Not only the disturbance itself but the environment and the entire personality pattern of the person must be studied.

To save time in sittings and to facilitate study of the case history, some psychotherapists find it expedient to have the patient write an itemized autobiography. He is urged to incorporate everything pertinent and to write at great length. A few paragraphs are insufficient. The longer and more detailed the report, the more time will be saved and the more advantageous it will be to the psychotherapist, who can study the material at leisure, going back over it from time to time in the light of subsequent disclosures which are made in sittings with the patient.

The patient must understand that no information is to be held back; he must be completely frank and open as to everything, even of the most intimate nature. An outline of salient points which should be incorporated in this report follows:

1. Family relationships; description of father, mother, sisters and brothers; attitude and feeling toward each.

2. Education, occupations, particularly the present business.

3. Residences and why moves were made.

4. A statement as to all illnesses, operations and accidents.

5. Religious beliefs.

6. Detailed description of any strong emotional episodes in the past.

7. Sexual history from childhood, including past and present affairs and marriages, if any.

8. Description of present difficulty; when the condition developed, all symptoms, previous medical or other treatment of the trouble.

9. Age, weight, height; date of last physical examination.

Often there is embarrassment over the seventh topic and frank detail is omitted. The material wanted should therefore be defined to the patient. Sometimes it is best to touch lightly on this at the start, and when he has become more accustomed to unburdening himself in subsequent sittings, then the sexual topic can be enlarged upon.

This written case history serves as a basis from which the practitioner may make a beginning, and he may refer to it during later sessions, adding notes to make it more complete. Repressed material divulged later will illuminate the original narrative.

*Psychoanalysis.* In the past there has been some tendency to consider psychoanalysis as strictly a matter of the theories advanced by Freud. Only the orthodox Freudian analyst was a psychoanalyst. With the passing of time and clarification of theory and therapy through experience, some of Freud's ideas have been modified and new ones have been advanced. Therefore it would seem that the definition of the term should be broadened and made more flexible. Horney has called psychoanalysis the theories as to the role of unconscious processes and the ways in which they find expression, and a form of therapeutic treatment that brings these processes to awareness. The Chicago Institute for Psychoanalysis uses the term for "any therapy based on psychodynamic principles which attempts to bring the patient into a more satisfactory adjustment to his environment and to assist the harmonious development of his capacities," according to Alexander and French.[11] By them the Freudian school is termed classical, standard, or orthodox, but other methods of analysis are still designated as psychoanalysis.

According to psychoanalytic theory, in the normal waking state the neurotic person cannot recall memories of traumatic experiences or emotional conflicts because they have been repressed. Sometimes the experience is remembered and only the emotional effect has been repressed. One of the aims of psychotherapy is to uncover these experiences; to bring them back into the patient's consciousness and permit discharge of their emotional effect. This has been called *abreaction,* and the process is known as mental *catharsis.*

This idea was originated by Josef Breuer of Vienna, Freud [12] collaborating with him in its development. Originally they thought abreaction would cause the neurotic symptoms to vanish, but they discovered that more treatment was needed although the symptoms sometimes would disappear with catharsis. After the discovery of the buried memories, the patient must be given insight in order to understand his neurotic drives, be educated as to how they operate, and his personality and reactions must be changed so that he becomes mentally mature and can face reality. Originally Freud and Breuer used hypnosis to bring out the memory of these repressions, but Freud was dissatisfied with results and soon gave it up for other methods. In standard psychoanalysis, the two main ways of learning the nature of hidden conflicts and traumas and discharging their emotional energy are free association and dream analysis.

*Free association.* In using this method, the patient is asked to assume a comfortable position, usually to recline on a couch, the analyst sitting at the head of the couch or in some location where he is not seen by the patient. The subject is told to relax completely, perhaps with eyes closed, and to give free expression to anything which comes into his consciousness, no matter what it is or how irrelevant it may seem. Everything is to be divulged. According to the Freudian school of thought, the analyst seldom interrupts and remains passive, noting carefully what is disclosed. However, many analysts have found it better to give some stimulation so as to direct the patient's thoughts into channels regarded as significant, and to become more active in the analysis.

A mass of material is disgorged over a long period of sittings. In the earlier ones the patient finds it unpleasant to "tell all" but later becomes accustomed to it. There is much unconscious resistance to the uncovering of repressed material, which may cause mental blocks and much delay.

Free association has value and is necessary in ordinary psychoanalysis, but the waste of time is enormous, much of what is told being inapplicable and worthless. This is one of the main reasons for the interminable time needed in orthodox psychoanalysis, amounting literally to hundreds of hours—for which the patient of course pays. The Catholic Church has realized for hundreds of years the therapeutic value of confession, and the "talking it out" process of free association operates similarly.

Association which is stimulated arbitrarily instead of being free is preferred by some analysts. One of Freud's earliest disciples, Carl Jung, prepared a list of one hundred carefully selected words likely to have a relationship to the complexes, conflicts and repressions which might be most expected to result from the usual activities of life. Jung's list was in German and has been modified and improved for English use, that of Eder now being generally employed.

The words are read to the patient one at a time, and he responds with another word which he associates with the stimulus word. A record is kept of the replies and of the time required for response, noted in split seconds by means of a stop watch. The patient's answer and physical reaction to the stimulus word should give a clue to the hidden repression when a number of indicant factors are considered. Luria's tests of word association in experimentally induced neuroses proved the value and accuracy of this method.

*Dream analysis.* According to Freud,[13] desires and wishes unacceptable to the ego and inhibited in the waking state appear under symbolic disguise during sleep as dreams. In sleep, inhibitions are relaxed but still in force so the content of the dream appears in symbolic form to make the wishes more acceptable to the superego. The *manifest content* of the dream is that which is remembered by the dreamer; the *latent content* is the unconscious underlying wish symbolically distorted. Dreams are defined by Freud as the concealed expressions of repressed wishes.

Klein, however, found that dreams could be stimulated by noises, discomfort, insufficient bed-covering, odors, tactile sensations and many other stimuli. If one side of the sleeper's bed was depressed slightly, a dream of the familiar falling type ensued. Analysis of 171 test dreams showed less than 10 per cent of sexual nature, although several of the stimuli were intended to have sexual significance.

Other causes of dreams are physical conditions such as thirst, indigestion and bladder distention, and moods and experiences of the day are frequently carried over into the dreams of the night. They may arise as the aftereffect of various emotions.

Undoubtedly many dreams are a product of unfulfilled wishes and there is much symbolism involved. For analysis, it is necessary to interpret the dream symbolism to learn the nature of the repressions. More will be said of this subject in the next chapter.

There are more direct methods of delving into the subconscious, but they are seldom employed in the more orthodox methods of psychoanalysis. Direct questioning is a method so obvious that it is often overlooked—the forest cannot be seen because of the trees. Though the patient may not be able consciously to recall the needed material, the stimulus of direct and persistent questioning may yield helpful clues and sometimes cause the repressed knowledge to appear.

Another approach is the use of automatic writing or crystal and mirror gazing, discussed previously in relation to hypnotism. With the dissociation here at hand, they can very profitably be utilized at times. The writing or visions may well be motivated by a complex seeking release.

In the course of standard psychoanalysis, a patient projects upon the therapist the affection and dependence or perhaps the hostility felt towards a parent, sometimes with a sexual attachment. This may take a positive form or, if the attitude is hostile, the transference is negative.

By means of transference, a conflict between the patient and the analyst is substituted for the real neurotic conflict, being denoted a transference neurosis. The analyst must resolve this situation and give the patient insight and education by means of interpretations, so that he understands the emotional attitudes involved.

During the phase of analysis known as conclusion the transference relationship is handled, with the affection for the therapist being directed outwardly into normal channels. This must be done with great tact and skill or failure of the analysis may result.

Some modifications and improvements on standard Freudian technique have been advanced. In the early days of psychoanalysis schisms developed between Freud and some of his closest associates, who evolved other ideas and methods, although they retained the basic Freudian conceptions. Jung,[14] Adler,[15] Rank,[16] and Stekel [17] each worked out a different school of thought, Stekel in particular emphasizing short analysis, using a direct approach and making a close investigation of the character traits of the individual.

One of the shortest and most effective systems of psychotherapy is that formulated by Adolf Meyer, called by him *psychobiology* and known also as *distributive analysis*. It is so well suited to supplemental employment of hypnosis that a summary of the method is given here, quoted almost in toto from Dorcus and Shaffer.[18]

"The goal of this therapy . . . is a synthesis of the various factors and strivings which will offer the patient security.

"Although the pathologic reactions which bring a patient to the doctor may be given special significance, the material for the synthesis is obtained by analysis of all of the factors and situations which are of importance in the study of human personality. The analysis is distributed along the lines of psychobiological integration, and the treatment is guided by the need to achieve a wholesome integration of the total personality as well as of various functions. In contradistinction to psychoanalysis, a constant effort to gain synthesis is maintained. Consequently, at the close of each consultation, an attempt is made to formulate constructively the material obtained by the analysis. The treatment is elastic enough to be applied to psychotic as well as psychoneurotic and minor personality disorders. The patient's complaints are seriously investigated and, though never minimized, are reduced to their actual value by careful formulation.

"This form of therapy is not carried out along preconceived lines of leading situations, but emphasizes plasticity in procedure. No rigid, systematic outline is followed, the therapeutic attacks being directed according to the opportunities that present themselves in the course of treatment. All situations are investigated regardless of whether they deal with present, past or possible future of the patient. The therapy also recognizes the possible destructiveness of mere analysis without the physician's taking a guiding hand. . . .

"Suggestion, hypnosis, catharsis, reeducation and desensitization may all be utilized in this therapy. In fact the therapy not only recognizes the need for frank reeducation procedures with some patients, but offers in the procedure itself some reeducative values. The procedure stresses the wisdom of putting the patient under responsibility to produce something new in each consultation. This is designed not only to give the patient a better understanding of himself, but to serve as a reeducation of faulty habits of thinking and of tendencies to evasion and procrastination.

"The illness is treated as a whole and the doctor decides whether he should attempt to eliminate symptoms at a particular time or to neglect them and utilize their disagreeable influence as incentives for the patient to get well. The therapy emphasizes the need of securing early in the course of treatment a careful account of the development of the illness, the life setting and a preliminary understanding of the personality. Emphasis is also placed on the need for each therapist to have a good knowledge of his own personality so that he may better understand his patients and be able to avoid the many pitfalls that will present themselves, particularly the tendency to become emotionally involved in the patient or his problems.

"Distributive analysis is usually carried out in a direct approach, the patient and doctor discussing problems in the form of ordinary conversation. In view of the fact that there is usually a greater tolerance for the past than for the present, the objective attitude is more easily established by beginning with analysis of past occurrences.

"The direct method may be supplemented by indirect procedures in which dream material, symptomatic acts, association tests and Rorschach's ink blot tests may be utilized. Interpretations are fundamental to the treatment, but are avoided until the patient has proceeded far enough in the understanding of the problem to be able to accept them as possibilities which he has to consider. Although the treatment is one in which the doctor plays an active role, the method is exceptionally elastic, and its type is determined by the patient's problems and personality. The analysis and synthesis are terminated when it seems wisest, a brief analysis sometimes being sufficient to achieve personality synthesis.

"In such instances much attention may then need to be paid to outside adjustment. When it appears evident that a more or less permanent relationship between patient and doctor is to be necessary, an attempt is made to put this relationship on the basis of cooperation and collaboration rather than on dependence upon the doctor. The above statement indicates one of the fundamental differences between this therapy and the Freudian analytic treatment. The help-seeking attitude of the patient is recognized and treated, but is not encouraged, and an attempt is made from the beginning to prevent the attitude of dependence upon the doctor. An actual fostering and utilization of the transference in the sense of the psychoanalytic transference neurosis is considered undesirable and particularly so in the sexual realm.

"While the contributions of the psychoanalytic school are recognized, the detection of unconscious attitudes and mechanisms is secondary to an interest in the actual situation and symptoms. The analysis is not arranged for a search of repression, regression and resistance, but these factors are recognized and dealt with when they appear."

Depending upon the particular case, this type of analysis is usually brief but the patient emerges with a feeling of security based on self-dependence developed from his reeducation. Distributive analysis seems to be a sensible and logical system of analytical therapy. The present trend in psychotherapy is towards brevity and simplification of treatment in most neurotic cases, such as that afforded by this system.

# CHAPTER XII

# Functional Hypnotherapy

THE EMPLOYMENT of hypnotism in the treatment of disease is properly termed *hypnotherapy* regardless of whether the ailment is organic or functional in origin and regardless of the method employed. *Hypnoanalysis* is a system of treating the mental aspects of disease combining any form of psychoanalysis with hypnotism. Brevity is implied because hypnosis provides a short-cut to hidden complexes and repressed material.

Direct persuasive suggestion under hypnosis was the type of hypnotherapy used by the old medical practitioners of hypnotism, as has been mentioned. Criticism of the therapeutic use of hypnotism has been almost entirely directed at this method, hypnotism and suggestion being considered as identical. But criticism should be aimed at suggestion, since that is the method and hypnotism is only a scalpel in the hands of the therapist. It is a tool, not a method. It would be comparable to term dream interpretation a method.

The factor which has been most criticized is that direct suggestion is supposedly aimed at removing the symptom or symptoms by suggesting their disappearance. Critics claim that removal of the symptoms is a temporary expedient, since the cause of the trouble is not removed, and therefore hypnotism is not satisfactory. It is true that a patient may relapse and his symptoms return or others may develop, yet patients relapse in exactly the same way with any method of psychotherapy employed, even when the causes are clearly evident and education and insight have supposedly readjusted the patient. This is explained as resistance to cure, but apparently resistance is not applicable to the suggestive method.

Illogically, it is said that a relapse comes because the post-hypnotic suggestions lose strength, thereby permitting return of the symptoms. But Hull demonstrated that repetitious post-hypnotic suggestions can be maintained almost indefinitely. This, plus the fact that there are relapses with any method of psychotherapy, proves that resistance was not overcome and cure was not complete in these cases. It does not prove that suggestion had lost its power. Perhaps, too, education and readjustment were insufficient or environmental situations were not corrected, or the neurotic desire to remain ill outweighed the desire to be well.

Criticism erroneously assumes that the removal of symptoms is the basic principle in suggestive therapy. Suggestive therapy uses every effort to remove the symptoms because there is no cure if they continue and none is possible until they are eradicated. Adequate suggestion will include reeducation, and it should be directed at the causes.

One of the chief defects in the old-time hypnotherapy was the failure to reeducate the patient to adjust to reality and life. Since there was no knowledge of the genesis of neurotic conditions until Freud pointed them out, little could be done to help the patient in this respect. Failure to resolve past and present conflicts and those he might have to face subsequent to cure made relapse or new difficulty a real possibility.

In general, as will be seen, hypnoanalysis offers a superior method of psychotherapy to that of direct hypnotic suggestion. However, there are situations where the older method can advantageously be employed in hypnoanalysis, and it can sometimes be used alone with the addition of reeducation. It is therefore important to understand the method and to know its proper application.

In our opinion, a fundamental principle is the development of a strong faith in the patient that he will be cured. Before attempting to remove symptoms, a belief must be created that cure is inevitable. Until the patient believes he will be cured, he probably will remain ill. Firm faith in cure is essential for success with the direct suggestion method. The competent therapist never says to a patient, "I'll try to cure you"; instead he declares positively, "Certainly I can cure you; you will soon be well." This is direct suggestion. Regardless of the difficulty of cure or the possibility of failure, the practitioner should have no reluctance in making such positive statements. He might as well refuse the case if he does not make every effort to suggest cure. No deception is intended by such emphatic statements, for they are a means to an end. When hypnosis is induced, hypnotic suggestion should reinforce this idea of certain cure.

However, some neurotic patients would be made apprehensive by such confidence, it must be remembered, and at the beginning of treatment they may have a need for uncertainty and time to assimilate the idea of therapy and to dispel unconscious resistances to cure. The discerning hypnotherapist will manifest whatever degree of confidence is necessary to reassure a particular patient, perhaps postponing presentation of the idea of certain cure.

To some extent the direct suggestion method resembles faith healing, but with faith directed at cure instead of dependence on divinity. The patient must be convinced by suggestion that he will be made well, and relief should then follow. Of course there must be reeducation and adjustment to make the relief permanent.

In our opinion a firm belief in cure is essential for good results with any psychotherapy, and too often this basic principle is ignored, though some psychotherapists have recognized its importance. Mayo [19] has said, "The patient is not fully cured until he is himself certain of his restoration to health"; and Sadler [20] comments, "It is the reiteration and repeated inculcation of this truth [that he is going to get well] into and upon the patient's mind until it becomes a settled conviction in his soul that constitutes the very basis of cure."

What seems to be proof of this is to be found in the faith cures, Christian Science being one example, the "miracle" cures at Lourdes an even better one. The paralytic (probably suffering from hysteria) throws away his crutches and walks; the blind see; the neurotic throws off the demon of compulsion. Such cures often seem instantaneous, though the patient goes through a process of self-preparation with everything delayed until the psychological moment, but with the way prepared. Describing such cures, Alexis Carrel [21] mentions the "sudden sensation of being cured. In a few seconds, a few minutes, at the most a few hours, wounds are cicatrized, pathological symptoms disappear, appetite returns. . . . The miracle is chiefly characterized by an extreme acceleration of the processes of organic repair."

While there are often relapses after such cures, many seem to be complete and permanent. There is no removal of causes for they remain unknown, nor is there education or any readjustment other than emotional as a result of faith. Sometimes only repression or alteration of symptoms has occurred.

Functional diseases respond more readily to faith cures or direct hypnotic suggestion because nothing is physically wrong with the body, while organic cases are physiological. But it seems certain from reports that some organic disease may also be remedied if the patient accepts the belief that he will be healed.

In the practice of hypnotherapy by direct suggestion with a patient who has accepted the idea that he will be cured, the next step is to suggest disappearance of the symptoms. Complying with the laws of suggestion, repetition is employed and emotion is supplementally stimulated. A desire for health is provoked and pride or any other emotion applicable to the situation is aroused to reinforce the suggestion. Consideration is given to the patient's general physical condition, and he is told there will be general improvement in his health. Though no attempt is usually made to remove it at once, the symptom is attacked directly by statements that it will gradually diminish or be alleviated. Time for the suggestions to take effect is thus allowed and the idea is also implanted that there will never be a return of the ailment or symptoms, once cure has been made. In the course of treatment it may later be decided to set a specific date when all symptoms will have disappeared, but this procedure is warranted only if there has been a satisfactory response and the symptoms have diminished; otherwise failure might result which would retard or prevent cure.

A case history illustrative of both the method and a situation proper for its use is that of Jerry F——, sent to LeCron by a urologist. His physical condition was reported as excellent and neurotic traits were not apparent. In general, he was well adjusted and intelligent, but he was in a humiliating situation.

Fourteen months prior to his first visit, he had married. Owing to several factors, the few days before the ceremony were a period of great emotional disturbance. Two days before the wedding, his mother died of a heart attack and was buried the morning of the nuptials. Although it would have been advisable to postpone it, circumstances prevented and the ceremony was performed, the couple leaving immediately by automobile for a city several hundred miles distant.

Worn out physically and emotionally, they arrived at their destination long after midnight and attempted unsuccessfully to consummate the marriage. But the young man found himself incapable of doing so. Alarmed and frightened, unnerved and wondering what was wrong, he worried all next day and, as could be expected, remained in the same condition. A habit had been started and a mental block established.

Continuation of this situation for fourteen months left Jerry and his wife desperate and almost hopeless. His physician attempted by hormone treatments to build up his sexual powers, but this was unsuccessful and he was sent to a urologist. After a thorough examination, this physician recognized the situation as psychological and recommended hypnotherapy.

After Jerry had been assured that the condition could easily be overcome, the causes of the trouble were pointed out to him. It was explained how the emotional experiences of the wedding day plus physical fatigue from the long trip had continued the condition through suggestion until a mental block was established. When a deep hypnotic state had been induced, it was suggested that he would be able to consummate the marriage two weeks later at a certain hour on a definite day. Accepting the explanation, he became convinced of his ability and on the morning following the specified time telephoned triumphantly of complete success. A belated honeymoon ensued and six months later the couple reported being happy and normal.

In this case there seemed no need for deep analysis. The difficulty was largely a matter of suggestion. As Jerry was a good hypnotic subject, only seven sittings were needed, each devoted to education and repetitive suggestive assurance of no further trouble.

Another case where it seemed advisable to resort to direct suggestion without detailed analysis was that of Mr. T——, a man aged sixty-seven suffering acute anxiety attacks. The accompanying tension prevented food digestion, or so the patient believed, and he was unable to eat for a number of hours after each onset, one occurring every two or three days. Also present was a fear of impending insanity and a feeling of deep depression. His physical condition was poor, owing to failure to eat, and he had lost twenty-five pounds in weight.

Mr. T—— was a businessman with a small income who had been forced to retire a year previously when his difficulty became acute, thus having too much leisure in which to think of his troubles. Fifteen years earlier he had gone through a similar series of anxiety attacks, but they had finally diminished in intensity and he had been free of them except for infrequent mild feelings of anxiety rather than the severe spasms he now experienced.

With a man of his advanced years and a neurosis of such long standing, neither the referring physician nor LeCron entertained much hope of relief. For these reasons analysis seemed useless, but it was thought that direct suggestion might perhaps reduce the severity of the anxiety. And while hypnotherapy was applied, the physician began to build up Mr. T——'s physical condition.

Only a light degree of hypnosis was ever obtained, but the patient responded to suggestion and after two weeks the symptom lessened in intensity and in frequency. As Mr. T—— was of superior intelligence, bibliotherapy was attempted and he was instructed to read some of the better popular books on neurotic conditions. Under guidance he was able to apply his new knowledge to an understanding of his

own case. Since no environmental conditions or present conflicts seemed to be influencing the situation, it was thought
futile to probe for causes which probably no longer were
dynamic, and treatment was devoted to direct hypnotic suggestion, education and reassurance.

At the end of a month no anxiety had been experienced
for several days and the most recent neurotic reactions had
been light and infrequent. Mr. T—— felt much better and was
gaining weight. His mind was relieved and he was now convinced that he would recover. Treatment was continued for
two more weeks, then a month later a final sitting was held,
making a total of eleven visits. After the first six weeks, all
anxiety had ceased and at the end of a year he seemed permanently relieved.

The influence of Freud on psychoanalysts has been tremendous. When he abandoned the use of hypnotism, his followers did the same; consequently no attention was paid to
the few who voiced its advantages, and they were effectively
hushed by the rise of the psychoanalytic vogue. When any
good analyst could be continuously occupied with a few
patients able to pay fees amounting to thousands of dollars,
brief psychotherapy seemed unimportant. But conscientious
analysts came to realize that some short treatment must be
made available for people of ordinary financial means. This
led to attempts to formulate shorter, simpler and better systems. Meyer and Stekel managed to clip off hundreds of hours
with their methods. Stekel even asserted that psychoanalysis
was useless if more than six months was required. He is another who recognized that the will to get well is the basis of
all psychotherapy, and he believed that there could be no
cure where the will to sickness was stronger than the will to
get well.

First attempts to combine hypnotism with analysis were made at the end of the first World War by Morton Prince, Keller, William Brown, Simmel, and Hadfield. Prince was the first to use hypnosis for exploring hidden complexes, and it was Hadfield [22] who coined the hyphenated word "hypno-analysis." His method was analytic only in that it added abreaction and education to suggestion. Simmel [23] and Schilder and Kauders were among the first to apply hypnotic technique to actual analysis in seeking brevity of treatment.

More thorough development of hypnoanalysis has come only in the very recent past. Leaders in the evolution have been Erickson, L. S. Kubie, Lewis Wolberg, R. H. Lindner, and certain of the Menninger Clinic members. Their reported achievements have been so successful that the merits of hypnotic procedure in psychotherapy can no longer be ignored, and others are now beginning to follow the lead of these pioneers. Greatly contributing to the expansion of hypnoanalysis has been the work of psychiatrists in the armed services during World War II who have sought a brief psychotherapy as a military necessity. From their studies and practice has come also an incipient knowledge of narcosis and narcoanalysis.

Hypnoanalysis at present is well understood by few, but the short treatment time is forcing general adoption. Publication in book form of the findings and experiences of the present leaders in the movement is only now becoming available and is attracting the attention and consideration of more orthodox psychoanalysts. Though much additional investigation remains to be made, the formulation of a more or less standard system of hypnoanalysis should develop from a study of these reports.

Published accounts have been largely from hypnoanalysts who in general follow the Freudian principles, using standard psychoanalytic technique shortened by employment of hypnotic phenomena. Other than to overcome resistances and produce phenomena, therapeutic use of direct suggestion is usually avoided.

Anywhere from about forty to more than one hundred hours of treatment is required with this style of hypnoanalysis. This is progress in the right direction, but the required time is still too long and treatment therefore expensive. However, these hypnoanalysts are sincerely convinced that a complete and permanent cure and alteration of a patient's personality pattern can be achieved only by a detailed, exhaustive exploration.

This belief is undoubtedly correct as to acute chronic cases. Alexander and French and their associates at the Chicago Institute for Psychoanalysis point out that psychoanalytic therapy in the past has been confined mostly to such cases, and they believe that the next logical step is to develop a brief therapy for the simpler cases, designated by them as the acute, the mild chronic, and the incipient neuroses. For these they recommend a psychoanalytic method of flexibility, planned carefully for each individual case. Frequency of interview, choice of chair or couch for the patient during the interview, interruptions of long or short duration in treatment, and the combination of psychotherapy with narcosis or other treatments are mentioned as matters of flexibility, but most important is control and manipulation of the transference relationship in whatever way deemed most desirable by the analyst. Essentially, with a different approach, they follow the path of Stekel and Meyer.

With these less acute cases, long exhaustive probing and interpretation with intensive analysis seem quite unnecessary, and it is possible to make a further saving in time by following a more direct path through hypnoanalysis. Here the role of the analyst is active rather than passive, and material sometimes is almost forced out and resistances are quickly overcome, provided it is warranted in the particular case. Education is rapid; thorough but not too detailed. Interpretations are not pressed on the patient, who is encouraged to interpret for himself under the analyst's guidance. Thus the patient with strengthened ego in a very short time is able to stand alone.

## Hypnoanalytic Procedure

The objectives of every type of analysis are to uncover repressed emotional experiences, conflicts and drives so that there can be emotional discharge and breaking up of faulty reaction patterns, and to develop insight through reeducation so that the significance of the repressed material and the reasons for neurotic behavior are understood. Knowledge and understanding serve to strengthen the patient's ego and to modify his personality so that he can face and resolve past, present or future conflicts and situations. Symptoms should vanish as progress is made. Other matters such as resistance, the transference situation and the termination of treatment are very important but incidental factors in therapy. The basic aim is to enable the neurotic patient to make a satisfactory adjustment to his environment and to develop his capacities in comfort. All modern psychotherapy is aimed at the objectives stated above, though opinions differ as to the best way to attain the desired results.

Hypnoanalytic procedure to gain these objectives varies with the analytic method preferred by the therapist, though only to a slight extent. The hypnotic phenomena utilized depend to a large extent on the patient's development as a hypnotic subject, and on the type of case and its severity. If deep hypnosis is possible, more of the phenomena are then available. How much is used depends on whether the analysis is to be brief or extensive.

The chief difficulty encountered in employing hypnosis lies in developing a trance of sufficient depth to permit the production of phenomena which the operator desires to use therapeutically. This is reported as one of the reasons why Freud turned away from hypnosis. Some phenomena may be brought out in the light or medium states, but only somnambulism permits the development of age regression, recall of repressed memories and complete amnesia.

While better methods of trance induction are needed, some advances in technique have recently been made. Erickson and others have shown the importance of persistent application of sleep suggestions over a period of time, perhaps as long as four hours. Pitzer mentioned this fifty years ago. Erickson frequently trains a patient through several sessions for eight or ten hours or even more until a stuporous trance is obtained, then spends more time developing somnambulism in this deep state so that the patient can walk, talk and be mentally active although in deep hypnosis.

Narcosis under pentothal is an important discovery which often enables the operator to overcome resistance to hypnosis or which may serve as a substitute for the hypnotic state. Verbal induction of hypnosis may be easy thereafter if suggestion to that effect is given during narcosis.

Free association is regarded by most analysts as one of the most important means of uncovering material. The trend in hypnoanalysis is to direct the associations so that they are less free. Association may be employed in the waking state or while the patient is hypnotized. Lindner [24] prefers to use association in the waking state during the first part of a sitting. He resorts to hypnosis when a block develops, finding that resistance may then be overcome and the free association continued while the patient remains in the trance. Lindner found that material released under hypnosis usually appeared in waking free association at the next sitting. By inducing posthypnotic amnesia for the material obtained, he considers it possible to prove the validity of the material. If real, it appears again in the next waking free association period; it is forgotten if it was imagined or fabricated. This would hardly seem to be valid proof, for one can remember from one day to the next a fabrication or an imagination, and there seems to be no reason why it would not appear again.

The hypnotic state does not of itself always overcome resistance to free association. Sometimes it cannot be broken even when strong suggestion is given, or it may quickly return. To thwart resistance, some indirect methods are employed. For instance, the hypnotized patient is told that he will be able to think of a significant word or perhaps jumbled letters which will make up such a word. It is also possible to say that he will see an image or vision applicable to the situation, to appear immediately after the operator has counted up to five.

Of great value in the process of uncovering repressed material are automatic writing and drawing, and crystal or mirror gazing. It is possible to develop ability along these lines in a patient without resort to hypnosis, but when hypnotic suggestion of ability is given, it is much easier. Once the process has been learned while hypnotized, the patient may continue it in a waking state without the presence of the analyst, who can study and interpret such material at leisure after it has been brought to him.

As in dreams, it is usually necessary to find a meaning in automatic writing and drawing or the visions seen in the crystal or mirror, for they seem to follow the same symbolic pattern found in dreams, though often less disguised. When asked for the meaning while hypnotized, many patients are able correctly to interpret any such material, giving the symbolism and significance much as though they were interpreting from one language into another and, curiously, feeling a certainty of the accuracy of the translation.

It is not necessary to restrict hypnotic interpretations of this nature to material produced by the subject himself, for that obtained from another person can also be translated. In fact, a check may be made on the rendition by having two or more subjects give their explanations, which will be found to coincide very closely or exactly. This applies to common meanings, individual symbolism not being detectable.

Wolberg believes it important to suggest amnesia for the interpretations of the patient's own material so that he will have no conscious knowledge of what has appeared, otherwise there may be resistance to the production of more material. Only after the ego is sufficiently strong to tolerate implications inherent in it should he be given this knowledge.

Sometimes it is easier to obtain information from drawing than from writing. Automatic drawing often resembles that of primitives or children, and primitive symbols may be employed.

During crystal gazing, visions of the emotional trauma can be suggested and will then be seen by the patient. Abreaction may thus be brought about effectively because the patient relives the terrifying scene being witnessed, sometimes to the accompaniment of disturbing emotions and actions.

Age regression ranks as most important in the therapeutic use of hypnotic phenomena. Erickson and Kubie [25] have pointed out two types of age regression. It may be a regression where the subject describes a former experience as though witnessing it but with his description in terms of the present, or the experience may actually be relived as though it were recurring. The last is true regression. Then the present time and the subject's entire life after the suggested period are blotted from his mind. The phenomenon is complicated by the operator's necessity of maintaining control. To do this he must transform himself ostensibly into someone known to the patient at the earlier period of time, such as a teacher or relative. This can be accomplished by suggestion, although some subjects automatically make such a transposition without its being mentioned by the operator.

Regression is exceedingly beneficial as a means of obtaining a catharsis for the emotional trauma and also is used to find the trauma the memory of which has been repressed. When hunting the trauma by this technique, the patient is regressed to a period prior to the appearance of his symptoms and then carried forward again in time until the cause appears. After this is revealed, the subject is kept regressed while conflicts are probed and explanations furnished which will give him a new or different viewpoint. Positive suggestion should be used to counteract any negative autosuggestions which the patient may have accepted at the regressed period as a result of the emotional shock.

The technique of securing regression should be explained, as it is not sufficient to suggest simply and directly a return to a certain age or period. A deep trance state is necessary and the subject is then gradually disoriented as to time and place. Erickson and Kubie give a clear description of the process, saying: "The hypnotist suggests first, a state of general confusion as to the exact day, carrying this over step by step to include the week, the month, and the year. Then this is elaborated towards an intensification of a desire to recall certain unspecified things which had occurred in previous years which also are left indeterminate. The process is a slow one and involves jumping from one confusing idea to another until out of the stage of general confusion the patient develops an intense need for some definite and reassuring feeling of certainty about something, whereupon he becomes only too glad to accept definite reassurance and definite commands." Depending on the situation and purpose, regression may be directed to a specific time, often a birthday or a certain date, or the time may be a period left vague and indefinite, perhaps stated as prior to a certain age.

As an example, Betty R——, a forty-two-year-old spinster, had come to us with a neurosis of long standing, one of the symptoms of which was a compulsive necessity to clear her throat every few moments. This was not only extremely annoying and embarrassing, but had compelled her to give up a promising career as a singer and become an office worker— employment which she despised. During hypnoanalysis, an effort was made to locate the cause for this particular symptom. Questioning brought a statement that it had first developed eighteen years earlier, and she was sure she was twenty-four years old at the time.

Placed in a deep trance, she was successfully regressed to that age, but it was found that the throat distress was still present. She was then instructed to regress still further to a time left indefinite but just before the genesis of the trouble, whereupon she stated that she was twenty-two and her throat no longer bothered her. She was then told to reexperience whatever strong emotional event had occurred at that time, whereupon she told of attending a picnic with her fiancé, whom she loved deeply and was to marry within a few days. They picnicked at a lake on which they went canoeing, and she told of the craft tipping over and their struggles in the water. She was unable to swim, but the young man saved her by pulling her to the overturned canoe, to which she clung until rescued by others. Not a good swimmer himself and exhausted by his efforts, he had gone down and was drowned. All was described with great emotional discharge, and finally she seemed to be choking as though swallowing water. After she had become calmer she cried, "I love him so, I can't stand losing him. I just can't swallow it; it sticks in my throat." Then she added, "Why, that's the reason I clear my throat!" She was instructed to remember the whole matter on awakening, was returned to the present and the trance was ended. Subsequently, with further insight and reeducation the symptom disappeared and she found herself better adjusted to life.

At times it is not advisable to permit the patient on awaking to remember the experiences uncovered during regression until he is better prepared for such knowledge. Then amnesia can be suggested in order to prevent recall. As is frequently found necessary in catharsis of war experiences in battle neuroses, the process of abreaction may have to be repeated for full release of anxiety and other emotions. In war neuroses it was noted that abreaction was more easily obtained when the elapsed time after the experience was short, which is undoubtedly true also in civilian cases of neurosis.

Sometimes repressions and anxiety are released only after considerable urging by the operator. If the experience was terrifying, the patient often returns again and again during abreaction to the main scene and may display great agitation. During the climax, the therapist must comfort and reassure the patient and urge him to continue. Following this, if danger was involved it should be pointed out that all danger is past and he is safe. At this point, properly phrased suggestion may be very helpful in strengthening the patient's ego and preparing him for conscious recollection of the trauma.

The study of dreams is an important part of psychoanalysis, but the analyst must wait for their spontaneous appearance. However, in hypnoanalysis they can be induced by suggestion to occur either in normal sleep or during hypnosis. Using normal rather than neurotic subjects, Farber and Fisher [26] made a thorough study of dream formation under hypnosis. It was they who discovered that a person under hypnosis could interpret his own dreams or those of others even if the meaning was not apparent to him when in the waking state. Contrary to Klein's results, they found much sexual symbolism in the dreams produced by their subjects, possibly as a result of operator attitude. If they expected such dreams, there would be a strong tendency on the part of the subjects to produce what the operators desired.

To accustom a subject to the production of dreams, posthypnotic suggestion is made for a dream to appear during normal sleep at a certain hour, and the patient is told he will recall it on awakening. When this has been accomplished, a dream about some definite topic is suggested to the hypnotized subject. As a further step, during the trance he is led to produce some indefinite dream, then to dream in hypnosis about a stated topic, and finally to dream of repressed material and to report the content while still hypnotized. After a patient has learned to dream in this fashion, the operator is able to suggest dreams at will and through them to uncover hidden drives and conflicts and unconscious motivation of various kinds, and to learn why resistances appear. Through such dreams, the analyst can discover the patient's real attitude towards environment, or towards relatives and other people, including the analyst himself. This last may be of aid in handling the transference situation. Dreams also permit the study of the patient's character and personality pattern, his true traits showing under the curtain of symbolism and because of the release of inhibitions during sleep.

A detailed discussion of the various factors in dream induction and interpretation during hypnoanalysis has been presented by Wolberg. He claims that the patient's spontaneous dreams occurring immediately after initiation of treatment often will contain the crux of the whole problem, the central conflict and the basis of the neurosis—a fact which we too have observed. In his opinion, interpretation of dreams should be made during hypnosis and the subject then allowed to accept or reject the accuracy of the translation according to his own decisions.

Dream symbolism is not cut and dried. Every individual develops more or less his own symbolism, although patterns are similar and the same reasoning applies to all. The meaning of symbols must be appraised in the light of an understanding of the particular individual. Symbolism tends to be primitive and seems to follow racial and cultural lines, tinged with the educational and environmental backgrounds.

Too often an analyst by reason of his experience and knowledge undertakes interpretation of a patient's dreams according to his own attitudes and beliefs, arbitrarily assigning meanings to the symbolism. Yet analysts of different schools may interpret the same dream and arrive at different conclusions based on their own beliefs. Analysts usually teach patients to interpret according to the analysts' ideas, and they may not be correct. Hence it is better to allow patients to make their own deductions and interpretations after they have had general instruction as to symbolism and its significance. Under hypnosis, the subject not only finds the latent content and symbolism apparent: he often has a strong impression of certainty as to the accuracy of his interpretations.

Most neurotic patients have various resistances which

must be overcome in the process of analysis, an important one being resistance to cure. Since neurotic symptoms often are painful and unpleasant, there is usually a conscious desire to be cured but unconsciously there is strong resistance to any disturbance of the status quo to which the person has become adjusted, even though he may be very uncomfortable because of his illness. Unless the desire to become well outweighs the wish to remain ill, there can be no cure, as we have previously indicated. Therefore this resistance must be overcome or psychotherapy fails. It may prevent a patient from yielding to hypnosis and accepting suggestion, so the first task of the hypnoanalyst is to accustom the patient to hypnosis before beginning the analysis, which might cause resistance to be manifested. Then he must proceed to eliminate or modify that attitude.

Another resistance which acts to prevent induction of hypnosis arises from the neurotic fears of the prospective subject. Even though he may accept the thought of being cured, his neurosis has a background of anxiety and uncertainty and he may be too apprehensive to yield to hypnosis until this resistance is overcome. Sometimes such a resistance cannot be considered abnormal or neurotic, for misinformation and lack of knowledge as to hypnotism may render a normal person too full of apprehension to be hypnotized.

Another form of resistance involves the uncovering of repressed material. This is one of the chief reasons for the long time involved in standard psychoanalysis, many hours being necessarily wasted because of mental blocks. Emotions of anxiety, tension or even fear may be exhibited when some repression nears the surface.

Alarmed as resistances weaken and not yet properly adjusted to face revealed conflicts and memories, sometimes the patient becomes negative towards the analyst—the negative transference. Resentment and even hostility may appear. The hypnotic situation enables the hypnoanalyst to handle negative (or positive) transference to the best advantage in the way deemed most advisable. The natural rapport under hypnosis makes control much easier. The patient can be left free to respond emotionally in either a positive or a negative way, or transference may even be entirely inhibited. Because of the underlying rapport with the hypnotist, if it is decided to allow a transference neurosis to develop, the patient will tend to accept more readily the explanations made to resolve the neurosis.

Under hypnosis an assault against resistance may be sharp and dramatic, tending to overwhelm the patient's neurotic defenses, but the speed and nature of their destruction always depends on the situation and the individual's personality and ability to adjust. Too strong attempts to break the barrier of resistance may arouse antagonism, and it may be best to proceed slowly until insight is gained. Suggestion of amnesia after awakening is of aid in bringing out hidden information, as then the patient may feel able to uncover it while in the trance, and after discussion with the analyst may find his ego strong enough to tolerate the knowledge in the waking state.

Ordinarily resistances are readily weakened because the subconscious is nearer the surface under hypnosis, a fact which can be utilized to advantage by the analyst. All of the usual forms of resistance, all of the patient's neurotic urges and conflicts and behavior are unaffected by hypnosis of itself, but utilization of hypnotic phenomena and the hypnotic situation permits a solution and insight with resulting relief in far quicker time.

One criticism of hypnotherapy has been in regard to the

transference situation. It has been claimed that too much dependence on the hypnotist develops and the patient becomes unable to work out his own salvation, leaning entirely on the hypnotist. This idea undoubtedly stems from the false beliefs that a hypnotist has the subject "in his power" and dominates his will so that it is weakened and during hypnosis he then becomes an automaton. Such criticism maintains that the patient undergoing analysis must play an active role, whereas in hypnosis he is passive. Wolberg points out the fallacy of these arguments. Instead, hypnoanalysis implies tremendous activity on the patient's part once somnambulism has been produced. Laboratory tests and experience show that hypnosis can never weaken the will, and power of the operator over the subject is only a delegated matter which can be withdrawn if there is any reason for noncompliance and refusal of cooperation.

In standard psychoanalysis, transference is considered an essential part of the treatment and a transference neurosis inevitable. Alexander and French believe that it is within the power of the therapist to determine to what extent it shall develop and that it can be avoided or utilized at the discretion of the analyst. In some cases it may be desirable and in others it may be a complication with little positive value.

Hypnotic rapport automatically establishes positive transference unless neurotic factors prevent. The whole relationship between the patient and the hypnotist becomes influenced by a combination of hypnotic, neurotic and natural tendencies, depending on the particular case. The subject may regard the hypnotist as a person possessed of great power who will protect him and make him well. There may be a substitution of the hypnotist for a parent, or merely recognition of the hypnotist as someone to whom he has come for help. Neurotic feelings of dependence, insecurity, need for affection and love, as well as resentment and hostility will enter into the relationship.

The hypnotic situation permits the analyst to direct transference into the most desirable channels, or aids in preventing its development if it is not wanted. This manipulation can be useful in eliminating some of the dangers encountered in the transference situation. Some degree of transference may be of value in bringing out neurotic patterns and in giving the patient insight into his reactions. The testing of insight through trial situations may also be furthered, and the hypnotic situation assists in their regulation.

As an example of a case where it seemed best to avoid any transference other than a natural rapport, and one which also shows the brevity of treatment sometimes possible with hypnoanalysis, one of Bordeaux's cases is cited. An intelligent young man who had no previous record of emotional disturbances had become involved in the common love-triangle situation. He had married a girl but quickly regretted it, and matters were complicated by the fact that he was now father of a small boy of whom he was very fond. Having fallen in love with another woman, his conflict was to decide between her and his wife, who would retain custody of the son. After much internal debate, he followed his desires and chose the other woman. Stormy scenes and floods of tears resulted when his wife was informed of his decision, but he obtained a divorce and married the other girl.

Having a very guilty conscience over his shabby treatment of wife and child, he soon found that he had developed a phobia. Great anxiety was felt whenever a cloudy sky was to be seen, and a real storm forced him to stay home in fear which became actual terror if there was thunder. To escape severe thunderstorms he moved to California but found the winter rains almost as unpleasant when they continued for two or three days.

Hypnoanalysis brought out the memory of being taken into the cellar of their home by his mother whenever a thunderstorm had occurred during his childhood. This was the main contributing cause of the neurosis, while the stormy scenes with the wife, with resulting guilt and conflict, were the precipitating factor. When an explanation of the symbolism was accepted, the symptom promptly disappeared. Brief education and reassurance followed. Relief was attained in only five sessions and thereafter the patient was able to enjoy the California rains. A year later he reported remaining completely free of difficulty.

# CHAPTER XIII

# A System of Brief Hypnoanalysis

ALL TYPES of psychotherapy having now been considered, some conclusions can be reached. As indicated, each system has certain advantages and each can claim some positive results. The neuroses, among the most prevalent of all diseases afflicting civilized man, may often be overcome no matter whether the method used is persuasion, suggestion, psychoanalysis, hypnoanalysis, or perhaps faith alone. Probably only in shock treatment is there a physical as well as a psychological effect.

On the other hand, failures are common to all methods. The neuroses are universally regarded as difficult to cure. No psychotherapist acknowledges the percentage of sterile results although it is admittedly large in every system. There is much greater knowledge of etiology than of successful therapy.

With our present understanding of the elusive neuroses and an appreciation of the need for a more efficient therapy, if a method can be evolved which does not require a great deal of time in most cases and which brings good results, then it could be generally adopted. In our opinion, specific features from the various systems can be selected and combined to form a satisfactory method. In the following pages we describe a procedure formulated by taking the most suitable and helpful elements from several systems and combining them to make a reasonable, logical plan. Basically it is psychoanalysis, though not of the orthodox type, with the addition of some points taken from other schools of psychotherapy and the supplemental application of hypnotism. It embodies nothing new, merely being a logical arrangement of known facts, but it emphasizes some which have been ignored in modern psychotherapy. It aims essentially at brevity, but brevity depends on the particular case, and perhaps thorough study and analysis of the patient's entire personality will be required, involving up to a hundred hours of treatment. But principally it is directed at the less acute cases which sometimes can be successfully treated in only a few sessions.

The aim of hypnoanalysis should be to secure complete and permanent results as quickly as possible. A careful study of the patient's personality and case history will give the therapist some idea as to the rate at which he can proceed. As he makes progress, susceptibility to hypnosis, resistances displayed, and the patient's ability to accept education and to develop a new viewpoint and ego strength will determine the length of treatment. The uncovering of repressed material is, of course, indeterminate in time. A few cases may be satisfactorily terminated in five or six sessions, but in mild cases ten to thirty are more often required and many more may be necessary when the condition is severe and of long standing.

According to our belief in the possibility of cure (in the sense in which we use the word) whenever the patient becomes convinced that he is cured, as in faith healing, a neurosis may be relieved in one session, though such brevity certainly is not advisable unless the circumstances are exceptional, and relapse is likely unless there is analysis and education.

Bordeaux once treated a stutterer in such a brief way, through necessity. This was a man thirty-eight years old who had been afflicted since early childhood. Living in a distant city, he was to return home at once, and time permitted only one treatment. Fortunately he proved to be a somnambulist and quickly entered a deep hypnosis. Repetitious and emphatic suggestion was given that he need not stutter while in the trance, and he was then directed to talk while hypnotized. After speaking without hesitation, his attention was called to the ease with which he spoke and he was told there was no reason to stutter when awake, for he was relieved of the condition and never would stutter again. Awakened and completely convinced because he had been able to speak perfectly while hypnotized, he had no further difficulty. A year later he wrote to confirm his permanent cure. Causes of this man's speech trouble are still unknown.

Good hypnoanalysis is plastic in execution. No set procedure should be followed, all depending on the individual case and the situations developed. Alexander and French have emphasized the value of devising a definite plan for treatment which constitutes the strategy of attack. This is planned as soon as possible and is based largely on the analyst's observations during the first interview, perhaps modified by a study of the written case history, which should be presented at the second session. There need not be adherence to the original plan if subsequent developments indicate a change, but it saves time to make such a plan at once. Actual tactics to be followed in carrying out the general strategy depend upon developments in the analysis, though some may be determined in connection with the original design.

Before proceeding with analytic work, which may arouse resistance to hypnosis, the hypnoanalyst must teach the patient to become a good hypnotic subject in whom a deep somnambulistic trance can be induced. The benefits and operation of hypnotism are explained and misconceptions about hypnosis are removed by a preliminary talk.

During the early sessions, while studying the case history and the personality of the patient and formulating a plan for the analysis to follow, the main effort is towards establishing deep hypnosis. At the same time, strong suggestions of eventual cure should be made. Modification and disappearance of symptoms as progress is made should also be suggested. Their relative unimportance because they are only incidental should be stressed. At this time it is wise to caution against impatience for cure, and it may be pointed out how symptoms sometimes flare up and temporarily become worse as a result of undertaking treatment. Possibly it may be better to reserve explanation of this fact until it occurs, for there is often an exactly opposite effect.

In this period it is desirable to develop confidence on the part of the patient and to instill a capacity for acceptance of whatever comes forth during analysis. The first steps towards education are begun while discussing the patient's particular problems.

At the introduction of analysis it usually is necessary to break down the barriers of reticence towards intimate matters and hypnotic suggestion can aid in the process. During hypnosis the patient can be made appreciative of the need to view himself properly and to discuss his problems frankly and adequately. This may be made easier for him by manipulation of amnesia, for he then understands that he will not have to deal with repressed conflicts and memories at the conscious level until able to face them with strengthened ego. In this way, even the most modest woman soon finds herself able to make disclosures of her sex life. Discussion and confession often bring a great feeling of relief.

Psychoanalytic theory regards causative factors in a neurosis as possessing a dynamic force which produces the symptoms, the energy arising from the repression of memories and conflicts. Some psychotherapists such as Fink, who are much in minority, believe that causes sometimes activate symptoms which through repetition tend to become either habits or conditioned reflexes. Also, they believe that symptoms may possibly generate as a result of suggestion. The authors find themselves in accordance. This does not mean that the neurosis itself arises from suggestion or is a habit or conditioned reflex. The neurotic pattern must be present and causes may be a complex matter, but some symptoms do seem to originate or continue in this way.

As an example, Mr. N—— came to LeCron to be rid of some neurotic difficulties. The main symptom was a continually dry mouth with an ever-present bad taste in it. After examination, his physician had informed him that there was no physical cause for the trouble. It was functional only.

Mr. N—— was a very successful fifty-five-year-old businessman. His history showed no previous neurotic troubles, he had no apparent problems, and he seemed well adjusted. No deep insight was needed to find the precipitating cause of the symptom. Although himself innocent, he had become involved in a case of blackmail and bribery which ended in court. Called as a witness, he was afraid that he would be asked a question which he intended to answer truthfully, and his business would then have been ruined. For two weeks he waited to be called or was on the witness stand and was under great emotional strain throughout the period. Figuratively, as he had commented at the time, the whole matter left a "bad taste in his mouth." By the time the situation ended with the question still unasked, an actual bad taste had appeared, wholly symbolic and apparently a result of suggestion. The condition had now persisted for three years.

Mr. N——'s figurative oral bad taste was impressed on a mind influenced by a combination of fear, disgust and anger, all strong emotions. The common figurative expression suggested an actual bad taste, which then appeared. Maintained for a time, it developed into a habit. Suggestion thus may generate a symptom which is kept alive by habit after repeated occurrence.

It has been an axiom of standard psychoanalysis that the actual causes of a neurosis must be learned so that the energies generated by the repressed conflict and memories can be discharged by the patient as a part of cure. Undoubtedly a knowledge of causative factors is valuable, for it aids both patient and analyst to understand the situation. When they are known, these factors may be worked through and the patient given insight and taught to readjust. If the cause, such as an environmental matter, is still active, there will either be a relapse or no cure will be effected unless the cause is uncovered. But causes may extend back into childhood and be completely inactive though still motivating behavior. If dynamic energy is still being generated, this would explain the presence of symptoms arising out of such old causes, and it would be necessary to remove them through knowledge of the causes. However, if they are considered as being still exhibited because they have become habits or conditioned reflexes, the case is different and it is not so important to know the causes, though it would still be desirable.

This would seem to be substantiated by cures made in faith healing, where causes remain unknown and entirely disregarded. The same is true of cures wrought by the old-school medical hypnotists by direct suggestion. There is a tendency to ignore such cures or question them as temporary only, and many relapses do occur because there is no insight and the underlying neurotic trends have not been affected. But such cures cannot be shrugged off, and many are permanent, if we confine the definition of "cure" as relief from distress and ability to exist comfortably while carrying on an occupation. Brenman and Gill mention the effectiveness and frequent permanence of the old-style hypnotic cures. Alexander and French accept the actuality of faith cures and believe that they may result from "benign traumata" which "occur occasionally in the form of intensive emotional experiences during treatment or by chance in ordinary life," with permanent changes of the ego resulting. Janet's study of the cures at Lourdes is particularly impressive. In all such cases it would indicate that no dynamic force activates the symptoms (after they have been established), for such a force would inevitably make them reappear, or perhaps the "benign traumata" permanently discharge the energy.

It therefore seems logical to believe that some visible symptoms may be generated by an outside influence or situation or by an emotion or thought. If through repetition they have become habits or conditioned reflexes, direct hypnotic suggestion may be of material aid in dislodging them and breaking up the pattern.

During psychotherapy the patient's nervous condition is often overlooked or disregarded or considered as something which will disappear with other symptoms as treatment progresses. Many neurotics are more or less nervous; some are under extreme nervous tension. Nervousness is a study in itself and is the subject of many books and articles. It is a frequent accompaniment of anxiety. Jacobson,[27] Fink, Pierce and others have devised systems of relaxation exercises, some of them extremely complicated, to teach control of nervousness. They are based on the principle that physical tension in the muscles prevents discharge of nervous energy and so relaxation relieves the feeling of nervousness. But hypnosis automatically brings a physical relaxation which is far greater than can be voluntarily achieved. After a sitting, the therapist who uses hypnosis in treating nervous patients often hears the statement, "I seem to have lost all my nervous tension." Mitigation of nervousness is highly beneficial, and many patients look forward to their trance sessions because of the relief felt thereafter. The effect may be increased by suggesting that the patient's nervousness will disappear while he sleeps and that he will awaken refreshed and invigorated, free from tension.

When coming to a practitioner, the neurotic patient seeks relief and wants it quickly though his condition may be of long standing. The way is paved for acceptance of belief in cure if symptoms can be eliminated or diminished, and nothing is more conducive to this than to reduce the nervousness which may exaggerate or even generate some symptoms. As nervous tension lessens and symptoms begin to abate, the patient feels that better and more rapid progress can be made in analysis and treatment.

One of the great advantages in hypnotic psychotherapy is that hypnosis is invariably found a pleasant matter. It is a new and interesting experience to be hypnotized, and the subject quickly discovers enjoyment in it, particularly in the release from nervous tension. Frequently he mentions looking forward to his periods of hypnotic treatment.

The neurotic person always is a victim of a vicious circle of thought, emotions and action. He has become intensely introspective, usually spending most of the time thinking about himself and his troubles, both neurotic and economic, and feeling sorry for himself. He may be unable to work and thus gains more time for brooding. The more he thinks about his illness the more the symptoms are stimulated and intensified, and the more exaggerated his neurotic trends become the worse he feels. The worse he feels, the more he worries and thinks about it. He enters into a vicious circle difficult to overcome. As a result he becomes more and more nervous and may have physical reactions such as digestive upsets or any of a host of new physical symptoms.

Horney has mentioned these vicious circles as being one of the most important processes in neuroses and the main reason why severe neuroses are bound to become worse, even though external conditions are unchanged. She cites other examples of their operation: anxiety causing excessive need for affection and love; a sense of having been rebuffed and frustrated if the need is not met, which is followed by intense hostility; then hostility must be repressed, owing to fear of losing affection, and this provokes rage, increased anxiety and need for reassurance. The circle continues with ever-increasing anxiety.

One of the important phases of psychoanalysis is to uncover these circles and to change their direction of flow. Insight and education bring this about, but it may be extremely difficult to stop and reverse them even when they are recognized. Hypnotic suggestion can aid materially in accomplishing this. Sometimes autosuggestion and autohypnosis may be used to supplement the therapist's suggestion, their main value being in enabling the patient to participate and to practice the advice of the analyst in directing thoughts into proper channels.

In some cases autohypnosis can be helpful in treating a neurosis. It will aid in overcoming nervousness and during reeducation may aid in building ego and in developing self-confidence. But it must be used discreetly, for no patient is qualified without technical guidance to be his own therapist. Those who suffer from hysteria are not qualified to learn it, and it should be taught only to some few intelligent neurotics who do not have acute chronic disturbances.

Many psychoanalysts deem it unwise for the patient to

have much knowledge of psychoanalytic theory until an analysis has progressed for some time, believing that such knowledge might influence the patient's revelations and mislead the analyst. But in lighter cases, we believe that the sooner the patient obtains a correct understanding of his conditions, the quicker a cure can be effected. Of course the personality and intellect of the patient must be taken into consideration, and too much knowledge may lead to resistances and to criticism of the analyst's methods.

To aid a patient in understanding his condition and also to effect a saving in time, some of the good popular books on nervousness and neurotic conditions may be recommended for reading. (Such bibliotherapy also should include good books on general subjects.) Here again there must be discretion, for a suggestible person reading about neurotic disturbances might apply too much of the information to himself, or it might do harm by lulling him or convincing him that he is being helped when such is not the case. But bibliotherapy can be of value if carefully handled and if accompanied by discussion and interpretation with the analyst.

In our consideration of brief hypnoanalysis, we have mentioned some matters not concerned with either hypnosis or psychoanalysis but which can be incorporated supplementally to advantage in the treatment of many cases. And if medicine can also be employed, as is sometimes possible, then by all means it should be used. The main thing is to bring relief to the patient no matter what the means. Essentially the method of psychotherapy being outlined is hypnoanalysis, but nothing which can be of service should be overlooked or neglected.

Basically, hypnoanalytic treatment is modified psychoanalysis with inclusion of hypnotism for brevity. All the hypnotic phenomena described in the previous chapter are vital to the brief method being presented here, but their application need not be discussed again. To obtain the lifting of repressions and the recall of buried memories resort can be made to age regression, dream induction and analysis, automatic writing and drawing, crystal and mirror gazing, and direct inquiry under hypnosis. Resistances are overcome, the transference dealt with as desired, and the hypnotic situation and hypnosis itself directed and employed according to plan and to situations as they arise.

In general, a patient should arrive at insight and knowledge by his own understanding developed through educational processes. He must learn to comprehend his instincts, drives, urges, his complexes and conflicts. He should understand why his symptoms have appeared and why he behaves as he does. Reeducation is continued throughout the analysis with new habits of thought and new viewpoints developed. Insight and education teach him to resolve his conflicts, to ease his guilt feelings and to face reality. In the process his "vicious circles" are broken, anxiety is relieved and self-confidence is gradually gained as ego strength is built.

Everyone responds to honest praise and the analyst must point out to the patient his good points in character and personality. Judicious compliments are helpful. During this "build-up" of ego, the fact must be stressed that the patient will cure himself and that cure lies entirely within himself, though not through mere wishing. (Rank even believes that cure may be volitional.) The knowledge and experience of the therapist are at the service of the patient to aid him cure himself while the analyst guides him along the proper path. To make an analogy, proper hypnoanalysis is a tandem bicycle whose rear seat is occupied by the strenuously pedaling patient, while the therapist rides in front to steer and to help pedal.

Just how far personality analysis should proceed is always a problem for the analyst. In the most serious cases probing may be deep and long continued, but in those neuroses which are lighter a complete understanding of every detail is unnecessary. Few normal, well-adjusted people have more than a glimmering of insight into their personality and behavior. Frequently treatment may be ended with expectancy of the development of further insight in the course of normal living. When the road has been properly paved, ego strength and adjustment will continue to improve. This is frequently observed after a lapse of time, when a check of progress is made.

Throughout hypnoanalysis there is not only resort to the phenomena which have been described but suggestion is continually directed at promoting insight and increasing ego strength. The hypnotic instigation of conflicts has been mentioned as one way of showing the mechanism of emotions and behavior as a result of conflicts. Resistances and the transference are hypnotically controlled, and progress may be checked by test situations hypnotically produced.

Frequently the analyst finds that he must not only deal with the patient but endeavor to revise the mental attitude of his family. Family and home environment can defeat all psychotherapy, and perhaps the situation is such that a cure is impossible, for generative factors in the neurosis may be active and not subject to change. This may be a matter of finances or of improper family life. The problem may involve marital relations, which brings up the question: Is the therapist warranted in suggesting divorce? He might then face a damage suit if his patient's spouse learns that such advice has been given. Such problems can be decided only in each individual case. Every therapist must make his own decisions.

Concluding the treatment is not usually difficult with

hypnoanalysis, particularly if there has been brief treatment. Dependence on the analyst has been controlled and the patient has been taught to stand on his own feet. In standard analysis, he has been closely associated with the analyst over a period of months or even years and sometimes is panic-stricken at the thought of severing the connection. Termination is recognized as a period of danger of relapse. With brief hypnoanalysis, there is no reason for further treatment when self-confidence has been stimulated through insight and bolstered by hypnotic suggestion and when symptoms have disappeared and the patient, with new-found ego strength, has learned to face reality. Then he feels no need to continue. Convinced of his cure, he is ready to go his own way.

# CHAPTER XIV

# Psychosomatic Hypnotherapy

ONLY WITHIN the past decade has psychosomatic medicine been recognized as an important branch of medical science. The reason for its evolution has been the better comprehension by medical men of the interrelationship of body and mind, and that as one affects the other so they must be dealt with together. Many people, including some physicians, mistakenly believe that the term "psychosomatic" is merely a synonym for "neurotic." Actually it refers to a combination of medical and psychological recognition of those human ailments which arise from emotional as well as organic causes.

Diagnosticians now estimate that at least one-third and probably more of all who seek medical aid suffer only from functional disturbances. About 10 to 15 per cent of the ailing are thought to have a purely organic disease. The remaining 50 per cent (an approximate estimate) suffer from a complication of physical and mental conditions. This last is the psychosomatic field, concerned with both psychological and physiological manifestations and interrelationships occurring in the same disease process.

Psychiatrists are fully occupied with the treatment of functional illnesses, principally the psychoses, and are far too few in number for that purpose alone. Since the medical profession outside of the psychiatrists has had little or no psychological training, the sphere of psychosomatics has scarcely been touched as yet. Under present conditions in medicine, a patient usually is treated for the organic aspects of his disease. Of necessity a busy physician disregards or neglects the emotional phase, though he may realize that it is an important contributing factor in the condition for which he prescribes. Literally, there is almost no one to undertake such therapy, for at the present time only a handful of physicians are psychosomatic specialists.

This is no fault of the medical profession, for the psychological aspects of organic diseases have been so recently recognized that time has not been available to train physicians for the work. Unfortunately, some medical schools largely ignore this new field, concentrating student education on physical therapy. Some do not even mention the word "psychosomatic" in their catalogues, although the labels on courses of study do not necessarily cover all the instruction given.

Eventually hypnotherapy will probably play an important role in psychosomatics. It offers a brief way to treat organic diseases which have an emotional factor, and brevity is essential. Even the shortest forms of psychoanalysis are beyond the financial means of a large percentage of the sick.

Present knowledge of psychosomatics makes it difficult for diagnosticians to distinguish between some forms of diseases. For instance, a digestive upset may be entirely physiological, arising from food poisoning, infections or other causes. It may be the chief symptom of a neurosis, or it may be partly organic with a neurotic aspect as well, mild or acute. Neurotic and nervous symptoms may accompany organic disease and be either causes or effects. Jelliffe [28] remarks that purely neurotic symptoms tend to become exaggerated after sufficient duration until they may become actually organic, usually after an approximate age of forty is reached.

Psychosomatic illness is further complicated by the problem of susceptibility to disease, which is only vaguely understood although we do know various factors involved, such as lowered resistance when the body is fatigued. Furthermore, emotions and mental conflicts and worry act to lower resistance. This applies even to infectious diseases such as the common cold, influenza and tuberculosis, as well as to allergies and internal conditions and many other diseases.

Environment, childhood training, emotions, mental conflicts, repressions and all the elements entering into neurotic disturbances may be concerned in psychosomatic disease. The heart, the skin, the digestive organs, the glandular system and the respiratory tract all may reflect conflict and become the seat of neurotic symptoms. This is true of any part of the body which is susceptible to emotional effects. The relationship of emotions to bodily changes has been well described by Dunbar.[29]

In general, hypnotherapy for psychosomatic disease should follow hypnoanalytic lines. Each case must be examined in the light of its severity, duration, probable causation, symptoms and the personality of the patient, as well as any other pertinent factors. A severe neurosis may be discovered or the emotional factors may be mildly disturbing and rather easily uncovered. Treatment may involve a long, detailed examination of the entire personality, but frequently the approach may be somewhat more direct than in the hypnoanalytic methods discussed in the previous chapter.

Psychosomatic illness ordinarily requires medical treatment as well as psychological, and sometimes direct hypnotic suggestion can be used supplementally in dealing with the organic phase of the disease.

In the following pages the application of hypnotherapy to some psychosomatic and other diseases and conditions will be considered. Classification is somewhat haphazard, and ar-

bitrary, major complex manifestations or minor simple dis-
functions are discussed. Some subjects are complicated, and
entire volumes (both popular and medical) have been written about some such as insomnia, alcoholism, stuttering, etc.
Brevity in our account is of course necessary.

*Insomnia.* The enormous sale of sleeping pills in this
country indicates the huge number of people troubled with
this condition. Such sedative pills are manufactured by the
billions, their sale being entirely unregulated in many states.

Insomnia ranges in degree from an occasional episode
due to worry, overeating or change in sleeping habits to the
insomniac condition—a neurosis with insomnia as the chief
symptom displayed. Some who may suffer to a marked extent
are merely victims of a bad habit and perhaps autosuggestion.

But insomnia may have an organic genesis as well as a
psychologic. There may be a lesion of the sleep-producing
centers of the brain. Inflammatory or toxic conditions of the
body may be responsible. Boils or any painful condition may
result in wakefulness, and extreme fatigue may have the same
effect.

The pattern of sleep is largely a matter of habit. When
habit patterns are upset, sleep becomes difficult, as is often
seen when one makes a trip or sleeps in a strange bed. A pre-
occupied or worried mind, and sometimes nervousness, tends
to keep one awake and disturbed emotions produce the same
result.

The insomniac or severe case often declares that he is
unable to sleep an hour during the night, sometimes not at all,
though he may look healthy and appear physically well. As a
matter of fact, nature takes care that the needed amount of
sleep is obtained, requirements varying greatly in different
individuals. Even when not asleep, the insomnia sufferer rests
during the night and the body recuperates. Usually there is

more sleep than is realized and the statements of such patients must be discounted.

The true insomniac is often extremely difficult to hypnotize. Mention of the word "sleep" during attempts at induction of hypnosis may bring out strong subconscious resistances. With such persons it may be necessary to rephrase suggestions and to omit the word "sleep" or "drowsiness." Words like "tired," "relaxed" and phrases like "you are feeling more and more comfortable" must be substituted. The word "sleep" is only a convenient term, and its omission will not affect induction of hypnosis.

When insomnia results from a neurosis, hypnotherapy is conducted as for any other neurosis. The condition may be difficult to relieve, owing to strong resistances. The insomniac may have a fear of sleep or of being unconscious. Subconsciously he does not want to sleep. Like the hysteric, he is perhaps subconsciously well satisfied with his condition as it elicits sympathy and attention which may be part of his neurotic needs. When an insomnia sufferer cannot be hypnotized, it may be advisable to resort to narcosis; however, this may lead to increased dependence on barbiturates if the patient has been using them for relief.

Milder cases of insomnia often yield readily to hypnotic treatment. Causes should be learned and dealt with but bad sleeping habits may be replaced through hypnotic suggestion with a pattern of sound normal sleep. Direct posthypnotic suggestion may be given of sound sleep to come at a certain time or whenever the patient goes to bed and is ready for sleep. Depending on circumstances and the sufferer's personality, autohypnosis may be useful for continued treatment. The subject is then taught to hypnotize himself and to pass at will from hypnosis into deep normal sleep. This is often found very effective.

*Stuttering.* There are technical distinctions between the terms "stuttering" and "stammering," but there is a tendency by speech pathologists to abandon the latter word and group the conditions under the heading of stuttering. Speech disorders of this nature may have an organic basis, and a number of theories have been advanced as to causation in those cases which are functional.

In 80 per cent of all cases the disorders appear before the age of six. The incidence in boys is eight or nine times greater than in girls. Estimates show that approximately 2 per cent of school children stutter, though many outgrow the condition and it may gradually disappear during the early twenties, probably because of better reality adjustment.

Stuttering often is a neurosis, perhaps of compulsive type, the speech difficulty being the main neurotic symptom manifested. It is common for stuttering to appear as a result of an emotional trauma such as was described in the case of Roy T——, cited as illustrative of such shocks. Stuttering may be comparable to a facial tic or a contracture, the muscles of the throat, larynx, face and even of the diaphragm and breathing apparatus being involved. A number of different neurotic drives and conflicts are found in this type of stuttering, and we have observed cases arising from frustrated rage and hostility of various kinds, one case resulting from sibling rivalry. Conversion may be implicated, and Adler believed that a feeling of inferiority which produces anxiety and uncertainty is manifested by stuttering.

If stuttering is determined in a particular case to be a neurosis, the basic procedure of hypnoanalysis for treatment should be followed. It also is advisable to use direct suggestion aimed at the symptom to give reassurance and aid in ego development. When a stutterer is deeply hypnotized he often finds that he can speak freely without any trace of stutter—

to his great relief. This fact can contribute greatly to removal of the symptom, for it encourages him to believe that he can be cured and helps him overcome self-consciousness. It tends also to weaken or break the habit pattern of stuttering.

Cure of the condition is usually a difficult matter because of the many factors involved, and our limited knowledge. In some cases the condition has become a deep-seated habit, and one which is hard to break. As a rule it is easier to remedy if the patient is young; it is exceedingly difficult to secure results after the age of thirty.

*Alcoholism*. Though known to be a common condition, the extent of alcoholism is seldom realized. The U. S. Public Health Service estimates that there are nearly two million intemperate drinkers in this country, six hundred thousand of whom are chronic alcoholics.

Acute alcoholism is not only prevalent; it is a serious condition. Its sufferers vary from periodic drinkers to those who never draw a sober breath and reach for a bottle as soon as their eyes open from sleep, and it may even result in a psychosis. Excessive or chronic drinking may be the main symptom of a neurosis, the condition characterized by a desire to escape from reality, perhaps from an environmental situation, or even from oneself.

Therapy for alcoholism must aim at the organic condition as well as the psychologic, each supplementing the other. Hypnotherapy should follow the usual procedure of hypnoanalysis, but it has further possibilities in treatment.

No matter how much he may wish to abstain, at the start of treatment the alcoholic feels strongly the urge to drink. He misses the "lift" supposedly provided by alcohol (though it is actually a "letdown") and release of inhibitions, and the desire to drink may sometimes be overwhelming. Direct hypnotic suggestion is helpful in removing this feeling and in curbing or eliminating desire during the early part of the treatment—the crucial period. If the patient is able to escape this desire, it is far easier for him to carry out his resolve to stop drinking, and easier for the therapist to proceed with treatment. Those who have vainly sought a cure but have only found themselves again at the bottle, and who have later received hypnotherapy, often remark on the efficacy of hypnotic suggestion in removing desire—to their pleased surprise. Sometimes it is possible to make such a suggestion immediately effective; in other cases suggestion to give up liquor may meet with strong resistance, and it may be necessary to modify it and only say that desire will grow less and less and will soon vanish because the patient is now taking proper steps for cure.

Physicians sometimes treat alcoholism by setting up a conditioned reflex in a patient which causes him to be nauseated every time he imbibes. This is brought about by injection of a mixture of certain drugs followed by administration of any drink he desires. The drug causes violent nausea, and repetition of the process over a period of time establishes a conditioned reflex which may be kept alive indefinitely. Thereafter, the patient's stomach revolts every time he tries to drink. With a good hypnotic subject, posthypnotic suggestion may be substituted for the drugs and the same effect attained.

An alcoholic is very suggestible and easily hypnotized unless neurotic resistances are encountered or his neurotic needs prevent—and provided he is sober at the time. Frequently the alcoholic comes for his first treatment while suffering from a "hangover" and is then nervous and shaky, in no condition to concentrate or to respond properly to hypnosis. If he can remain sober, a later attempt at induction should be successful.

Alcoholism is difficult of treatment and relapse after apparent cure is frequent. However, Alcoholics Anonymous claims success in approximately half of the cases treated by the society. Medical men have learned to respect this method. The AA group refuses to extend aid to anyone who has not reached a point where he is willing to make a sincere effort to stop drinking, and will accept only those who realize their condition and have a strong desire to be cured.

Without this attitude on the part of the drinker, there can be no success no matter what system of therapy is employed. The desire to stop drinking must be present, and there must be a realization that no alcoholic can drink socially. Invariably he wishes to be able to drink moderately, but half measures are worthless. The patient must stop completely and be willing to face a hard struggle to overcome his difficulty. With those who fulfill these requirements, hypnotherapy succeeds in a high percentage of cases if the patient is hypnotizable. To be certain of good results, treatment should continue for a year, usually with one session a month during the last part of the period.

One of the basic principles in the Alcoholics Anonymous treatment is the development of a substitute for drinking. This amounts to sublimation and is a part of the patient's readjustment. The drinker faces quite a change of environment when he undertakes cure and probably will find himself extremely bored. It is important to avoid boredom, and if health permits, full occupation of the patient's time is essential.

Another important part of the AA treatment is the aid and reassurance provided by association with those who have faced the same situation now confronting the patient. AA members speak the patient's language and know how he feels and how to help him deal with his problems because they have been alcoholics themselves. They urge him to start each day with the determination to go through the next twenty-four hours without a drink, which does not seem too long a time, and endeavor to carry this idea forward. Soon he can look back on a number of dry days, and each day his task becomes easier. The AA method definitely is psychotherapy with education and adjustment and a new viewpoint taught.

In the authors' practice, the combination of hypnoanalysis and the methods of the AA have been found extremely beneficial. We always try to interest our alcoholic clients in the society, urging them to attend meetings regularly and to seek the aid of members in conjunction with hypnotherapy.

Treatment for *drug addiction* is almost exactly the same as for alcoholism. However, it is never advisable to handle addicts without the personal attention of a physician. The reaction of a drug addict when cut off from his supply differs entirely from that of an alcoholic. For years the so-called "reduction" method was believed the best treatment for drug addiction. Today, the medical profession in general believes in cutting off the drug completely and abruptly. This is the "cold turkey" procedure devised by Lichtenstein at the Tombs prison in New York City. It can be carried out properly only in a sanitarium where the patient can be watched and treated for complications, for the reactions may be violent or even convulsive.

Direct hypnotic suggestion can be of material aid in curing drug addiction but is not dependable, for the craving is physical and it may not be overcome by suggestions to inhibit desire. Hypnoanalysis should be undertaken and is likely to be a long-drawn-out proposition, for drug addiction is usually a deep-seated acute neurosis, especially if the use of drugs has become chronic.

Although the *tobacco habit* is seldom a disease, it deserves mention because hypnotic suggestion can remove the desire for tobacco and cause its taste to become repugnant or nauseating. Sometimes excessive smoking, particularly the chain variety, is a neurotic symptom. Where it is evidenced in a neurosis, the cause should be sought during hypnoanalysis.

*Headaches* arise from many different causes. Those of mild type, such as fatigue or eyestrain, often yield readily to direct hypnotic suggestion. Unless the cause is apparent, it must always be remembered that the condition may be a symptom of something else, a danger signal not to be disregarded and not to be arbitrarily removed just to secure relief.

Migraine headaches, have many different causes, and little of a positive nature is known about them. They may be due to allergy, they may have an emotional aspect and some are found to be the main symptom of a neurosis. Migraine appears two or three times more frequently in women than in men and is more often seen in smaller women of good physique and above average intelligence. Men sufferers are usually large, strong individuals, also above average in intelligence and with great ambition. They are perfectionists, often artistic, and it is said that the headache follows emotional upsets and that psychoanalysis often finds frustrated rage as a factor.

Medical treatment of migraine depends on the type of headache, including use of oxygen inhalation and injections of ergotamine tartrate or histamine.

Hypnoanalysis in the ordinary form permits brief psychotherapy, and it may locate the cause and so make possible its removal. Direct hypnotic suggestion sometimes will remove the headache, though it would be unlikely to have any effect during a sharp attack, even if the sufferer could be hypnotized.

A physician (M.D.) who was afflicted with migraine (histamine-sensitive) came to LeCron as a last resort after having tried to find relief through all the usual methods, but to no avail. The condition dated back to adolescence and was experienced as acute attacks which came on suddenly and continued for months as a constant dull ache on one side of the head with occasional "blitz" headaches lasting perhaps only a few minutes or sometimes for two hours. These might be felt several times a day. The present onset had begun less than a month before, and previous ones had endured for several months.

Dr. T—— was himself a psychoanalyst and during his training had undergone analysis by a leading European psychiatrist. Likely causes of the headaches were known to him, but the condition persisted in spite of his knowledge of himself and of psychotherapy. He had become convinced that direct hypnotic suggestion could eliminate the headache, and this was the method followed. During the first four sessions it was impossible to produce hypnosis, probably because of the pain and discomfort, but suggestion brought modification of the headache after only one session. By the fifth, all pain had left and there was only slight discomfort remaining. During this sitting, the doctor was rather surprised to find himself in hypnosis. Suggestive treatment and reassurance were continued for a short time, and Dr. T—— by then apparently had made mental adjustments which eliminated his subconscious need for the headache. A year later there had been no recurrence.

*Skin diseases, allergies, asthma, etc.* These terms cover a multitude of ailments which may be organic but sometimes are psychogenic—neurotic symptoms which appear through conversion. Many dermatologists now recognize the emotional causes of some forms of skin disorders such as eczema, psoriasis, acne, allergic rashes and lesions, etc. Asthma, hay fever and eczema seem to have a close psychogenic relationship. Kalz [30] mentions a patient whose "itching feet" were found to be due to frustration. She desired to go out socially, but her home-loving husband refused to stir from the family fireside.

Thus a symbolic symptom developed from her personality need.

In a case referred to Bordeaux the patient was a woman in her mid-forties who had a peculiar burning rash covering some three square inches of the skin on the outer wrist of the right hand. The condition had persisted over a period of about seventeen months without responding to the medication of the referring physician.

Under hypnoanalysis only a light trance could be produced at first, and there were strong evidences of marked resistances. By the seventh session a deep state had been attained and resort was made to age regression to locate causes. Step by step over a period of about two hours she was regressed to the age of six. At that age it was found that she had broken the right arm for the fourth time. During convalescence, the attending physician had remarked to the child's father that he believed she would always have a skin blemish at the point of fracture. For many years that suggestion lay dormant in the woman's subconscious mind. About eighteen months before referral she had been burned by hot grease at the spot where the rash appeared and was afraid the burn would never heal, the rash being produced to confirm her neurotic fear and satisfy her neurotic need.

The analysis brought out her neurotic drives and conflicts, and with insight and explanation she was able to make adjustments. Within ten days the symptom had been eliminated, and her recovery seemed permanent when two years had elapsed with no recurrence.

In studying bronchial asthma, Alexander and French [31] and their associates often found present a repressed fear of estrangement from the mother (or a mother substitute), the fear based on uncertainty as to her reactions to the patient's thoughts and feelings, which might prove offensive to her. An asthma attack is likely to occur if the mother is not found tolerant when a confession is made, or an attack may come if confession is withheld. Confession is a primary need in therapy. With hypnoanalysis, these repressed thoughts can be brought out and the neurotic fear relieved. The rapport factor makes it easier to obtain confession and then through insight to diminish the underlying insecurity and dependence felt by the patient. Brief therapy in cases of neurotic asthma is often possible through hypnoanalysis.

*Digestive disorders.* The effect of emotional reactions on the various glands and organs is now widely recognized. Stomach and digestive activity can be strongly affected by emotions or by suggestion (either hetero or auto). At the Mayo Clinic the work of W. C. Alvarez [32-34] in this field has been of the utmost importance. An internist, he recognized the emotional aspects in many digestive disorders, particularly the emotional background in many cases of peptic ulcer, colitis, and indigestion. For instance, boredom has at times been found to cause constipation; excitement may bring on diarrhea. Alvarez noted that wrangling and irritability displayed at mealtime upset the entire digestive process. He found that sudden strong emotions may cause a long-healed ulcer to flare up and perforate within a few hours, or a new one may form, in a person subject to ulcer. Owing to the emotion, gastric juice acidity increases while alkaline and neutralizing secretions diminish. Alvarez advised extra feeding at short intervals to prevent ulcer formation after such strong emotional episodes experienced by anyone with a tendency for ulcers. Another of his recommendations for treatment of digestive disorders was to correct and eliminate insomnia if it is present.

Diet and medical treatment, perhaps even surgery, are required in digestive disturbances if they are severe. Even though emotional and neurotic relationships are recognized, too often treatment is only by medication, but unless psychotherapy is instituted to remove the causes there is likely to be recurrence of the disturbance. Hypnotherapy therefore should be supplemental to medical treatment. With hypnoanalysis the causes may be ascertained and eliminated, and direct suggestion should be aimed at the physical condition. Hypnosis is particularly indicated because suggestion can directly influence the affected organs. Neurotic symptoms often take the form of digestive disorders, and an acute neurosis may be present to be dealt with. A detailed personality analysis would then be indicated.

*Muscular aches and pains.* In neurotic conditions some of the symptoms most commonly exhibited are nagging backaches and other muscular aches and pains often accompanied by fatigue and lack of energy. Dr. Edward Weiss [35] investigated this condition in forty patients, all but five of whom were women and of whom only four were unmarried. These were neurotic cases, but the same symptoms may be present in fibrositis or in undulant fever, errors in diagnosis thus being possible unless neurotic causes are considered.

In the cases Weiss studied, he found the cause to lie in unconscious, smoldering resentment, frequently aroused by marital difficulties. Muscles serve as means of defense and offense. Internal tension is relieved by muscular action, but if there is no action the patient feels aches or pains in the muscles. Weiss compares them to "growing pains" because of the patient's background of emotional immaturity.

*Sex problems and disturbances* take many different forms, such as frigidity, impotence, nymphomania, homosexuality and many others, and they may be somatic, emotional, or acutely neurotic. Simple conditions may be only a result of ignorance and lack of sexual knowledge which can be corrected with advice and perhaps the reading of informative books.

The incidence of these conditions seldom is realized even by physicians because of reticence on the part of sufferers, who feel deep humiliation and sometimes guilt (particularly in homosexuality). Psychiatrists and psychotherapists know them to be very common. Freud believed that sexual urges in one form or another were the basis of almost every neurosis, although this idea is now discounted considerably by many psychoanalysts. Depending entirely on causation, medical treatment is usually supplemental to psychological.

Less acute disturbances may be remedied easily, but deep-seated ones are found very difficult of cure. In perversions and homosexuality the individual seldom has any wish to change and is satisfied to stay as he is. Where there is sincere desire for cure, analysis may be successful, hypnoanalysis offering the usual brevity and flexibility in treatment. In general, therapy is difficult in patients who have passed the age of thirty, though there are many exceptions.

*Hypnosis in gynecology and obstetrics.* Medical hypnotists of the past have noted that various menstrual disturbances are often amenable to hypnotic treatment. Menstrual pains that are not a symptom of disease have sometimes been observed to be only a product of suggestion. Healthy women of primitive races have been said to feel no such pain, though it is also claimed that the pain is there but not evidenced because of cultural differences in self-expression. Whether true or not, when the civilized girl reaches puberty, she learns from mother, sisters or friends to expect discomfort and pain and to consider the monthly period as the "curse" of women. As a result of such suggestion, she usually feels the mentioned symptoms.

If a female is a good hypnotic subject, suggestion will

remove some types of menstrual pain, though diagnosis should be made to determine whether or not this is desirable. Menorrhagia or excessive blood flow during menstruation has frequently been reported as hypnotically controllable. Mention has also been made of hypnotic regulation of the length of period when it is abnormal, though these matters undoubtedly are dependent on causation.

As is supposedly true of pain during menstruation, pain in childbirth is partly due to suggestion and expectancy. Civilized women have been taught to expect pain at this time and are convinced that labor must be painful, so of course it is. As every dentist knows, anticipation increases pain, partly through muscular tension, and consequently the prospective mother feels great pain during delivery unless she is anaesthetized, because she has been told that the event will be a terrific ordeal. In primitive races no such belief is held, and primitive women bear children with much less pain.

Pain in childbirth sometimes can be prevented through hypnotic anaesthesia (the more common term is still being used instead of the technical "analgesia"). Before the recent war its use was frequently reported in Germany and Austria, and it was commonly practiced in hospitals in the larger Russian cities. In the United States hypnotism's ill repute has caused obstetricians to refrain from employing it, though in one Chicago hospital it has been the anaesthetic in many maternity cases; a San Francisco obstetrician has often resorted to it; and other isolated instances are now and then recorded.

The method has a real disadvantage in that only a small percentage of expectant mothers are good enough hypnotic subjects for the induction of complete anaesthesia. With many more, pain can be lessened. The number with whom it would be efficacious could be greatly increased if time were taken to teach them to become good subjects. The time required to produce hypnotic anaesthesia and to show the woman how to apply it herself is, of course, another drawback.

There is no need for the hypnotist to be present at delivery. Properly applied, the subject should be able to hypnotize herself, or else posthypnotic suggestion is given for her to enter the trance when the physician says the proper time has arrived. Of course it would be best if the obstetrician were the hypnotist.

Aside from feeling no pain, there are other beneficial aspects to such anaesthesia during childbirth. Absence of shock after delivery—possible cause of bad aftereffects—has been noted, and there can be full conscious cooperation and participation in the birth by the mother. This is said to be psychologically desirable. Physicians who have had experience with hypnotic childbirth seem to be unanimous in considering it highly satisfactory in every way.

A matter of interest to obstetricians forced to hurry to the hospital at all hours of the night are assertions by some old-time writers of the possibility of hypnotic control of the hour of delivery and the length of time in labor. Though doctors might welcome the idea, it must be regarded as a very doubtful matter since so many factors are involved. There may be a possibility of influencing the duration of labor because of the more active participation of the mother.

Many women suffer from nausea during part of their pregnancy—the so-called "morning sickness." Again depending on cause, it has been found possible to eliminate the condition through hypnotic suggestion. Moll and others have attested to the hypnotic stimulation of milk in mothers who nursed their children, when there was insufficient mammary gland secretion or secretion was prevented through emotional causes.

In connection with hypnotic anaesthesia for childbirth, writers of long ago such as Bernheim, Moll, Bramwell and many others told of the very rapid healing of damaged tissue through suggestion. These were physicians who should have been able to evaluate their results properly. So far as we know, there has been no controlled scientific investigation of this interesting subject. The abrupt healing of wounds and lesions also has been observed in connection with various faith cures.

Cellular growth is a concern of the autonomic nervous system, and it is barely possible that hypnotic stimulation and control might be effectual. The implications are fascinating. While the matter must be considered quite unproved, it is worthy of investigation. Kalz's experiments on warts tend to confirm the findings of the old-time hypnotic practitioners, for suggestion apparently caused the granules of warts to be replaced by good tissue.

*Mental hygiene in children.* Since children are extremely suggestible and are almost invariably good hypnotic subjects, resort to hypnotism in their behalf offers great possibilities. Unfortunately, parents, distrustful of hypnotism and fearful of its "dangers," seldom are willing to permit their offspring to be hypnotized. Child psychologists would find their work greatly simplified in many cases if they could employ hypnosis.

Neurotic difficulties so often have their roots in childhood that it is logical to undertake prevention then, either by mental hygiene or by psychoanalysis in severe cases—work to which Anna Freud and others have devoted attention. The hypnotizability and suggestibility of children would point to suggestion and hypnoanalysis as offering very brief, effective methods of treatment. While not child psychologists, the authors sometimes have children referred to them and are often successful in aiding them provided parental cooperation is achieved. In such cases the parents possibly need as much attention as does the child. "Bad habits" such as nail-biting, and other conditions such as temper tantrums, enuresis and stuttering are products of emotion, as a rule, and at times we have been able to correct them in a remarkably short while.

Space does not permit individual consideration of many other psychosomatic conditions to which hypnotherapy can be successfully applied. However, treatment would follow the general formula of hypnoanalysis plus supplemental use of direct suggestion if indicated in the particular case. Among the conditions which might be named at random are neuritis, arthritis, neuralgia and related conditions, hypertension, control of body weight, which sometimes has an emotional and neurotic background, and those eye conditions in which the Bates method of exercise is found beneficial. Many other diseases, even infectious ones, may have an emotional relationship and undoubtedly medical science will locate emotions behind some where they are not now suspected. This should become more evident as additional knowledge is gained, particularly of glandular action and disorders.

# CHAPTER XV

# Research in Hypnotism

DESPITE MORE than a hundred years of experience with hypnotism, investigation has uncovered only a small amount of definite knowledge of hypnosis, and hypnotic phenomena are little understood. Hypnotism has been in scientific disfavor throughout its history, hence research is still in its infancy and much remains to be accomplished before there can be full comprehension of the possibilities inherent in the science. Most research has been in the realm of psychology rather than in a study of practical applications—an effort to find its basis rather than its values. Those who have written of their experiences have too often confused the issues by over-enthusiasm, reporting as facts matters which should be regarded as conjectural until proved beyond doubt.

Although Hull's experiments at Yale, published in book form in 1933, gave some impetus to investigation, a lack of interest on the part of most psychologists still caused a lag in research. Hull made an important contribution in demonstrating controlled experimental procedures and pointing out the need for scientific study. With the present revival of interest in medical circles through new appreciation of the advantages of hypnoanalysis, those physicians who undertake hypnotherapy will demand more knowledge. With the work of Erickson and a few others an era of extensive research has dawned, the first phase of which is the investigation of possibilities in the treatment of functional disease and a clarification of methods leading to standardized practices and procedures.

A requirement now unrecognized should be standardization of reporting methods for all hypnotic investigation. Informed readers who wish to interpret or evaluate the results of reported hypnotic research according to their own experience and knowledge now find much of the available literature of little value because the experimenter fails to state the exact wording of the suggestions given subjects and frequently does not indicate his own attitude, both being matters of the utmost importance. While written reports cannot show the inflections and intonations of the operator's words, which may have a highly important bearing, it is essential to know what words were used.

Another vital point seldom mentioned in researchers' reports is the attitude of the subject towards the experiment Psychotherapists know the strong resistances encountered in neurotic people. Resistances are also evidenced by normal individuals. The hypnotist often finds a suggestion rejected for no apparent reason. Some subconscious conflict, perhaps very minor, or some personality trait may be the answer. Any such conflict must be brought into consciousness and settled before the suggestion will be effective. Whenever a posthypnotic suggestion is not carried out by a good subject, resistance of some sort is involved. When experimenters during an investigation find some subjects who perform in a positive way while others are negative, the total result might be materially altered if an attempt were made to ascertain directly from the resisting subjects why they failed to carry out the suggestions performed by others. At the conclusion of every experiment, inquiry under hypnosis should be made as to the subject's personal attitude towards the experiment. Only when this is known and resistances are considered can there be any proper evaluation of some kinds of experiments.

In most hypnotic research, subjects are expected to remain completely somnolent except when called on to perform the task under consideration; a lethargic condition is maintained otherwise. It would aid results in most cases if lethargy were dispelled and the subject were treated as a normal human being rather than a doped guinea-pig. Much better cooperation would be had from an alert though hypnotized subject, and all somnambulistic subjects can be taught to remain alert. One who is able to enjoy and be interested in an experiment to which he is lending himself most certainly will carry out his part more eagerly and positively than one treated as an automaton.

Even many hypnotists who should know better are in the habit of allowing the subject to remain lethargic, considering him a robot. In general, much information can be gleaned from a subject simply by asking him direct questions instead of making surmises based on his behavior. If interrogated, perhaps he can offer a complete explanation. In this connection, when a suggestion is made during hypnosis, it is frequently feasible to ask the subject if he has any objection to carrying it out, and it is much more likely to be accepted if the subject agrees or promises to complete the requested action, which then becomes cooperative rather than forced.

In some types of tests it is important to know whether the subject remained in hypnosis or drifted into normal sleep. When the attitude of sleep is retained, such an occurrence is not at all unusual. It has happened in experiments conducted by us, and sometimes most unexpectedly. One way out of the difficulty is to abandon the maintenance of lassitude. Another is the knee-jerk test described by Bass, which should be a control in many tests and also should be a matter of record.

A study of the literature leads us to believe that much of the experimental work heretofore accomplished has been wasted effort, owing to lack of information on some of the factors mentioned, or because of omission of others.

While knowledge is badly needed on many aspects of hypnosis, only a few can be listed here. One broad field is the study of personality and human behavior, which can be greatly facilitated through use of hypnosis. Freud first called attention to the need for knowledge of the subconscious and learned much about it from his studies, but only a start has been made. Freud's work was with neurotic people, which led him to err in believing that many neurotic sexual drives are common to normal people, as Horney has remarked. Most of the study of the subconscious has concerned the abnormal rather than the normal. As the subconscious is much nearer the surface in hypnosis, it is then easier to reach and investigate.

A phase where much has been accomplished is the application of hypnosis to psychoanalysis in the treatment of functional disease. Here investigation has proved the advantages of the use of hypnosis, and the result is a rapidly growing interest among psychotherapists. Research is thus followed by practical application of what is learned.

It is of great importance to find out exactly what can be accomplished with hypnotism physiologically as well as mentally. Many statements have been made, but most remain unproved and entirely conjectural.

The matter of producing blistering of the skin through hypnotic suggestion is one which has been argued pro and con. The "cons" maintain that experimenters claiming positive results did not apply proper controls. Pattie [36] undertook to summarize the reports of a number of such experiments where control was apparently proper and a blister did appear despite observation continuously maintained.

Briefly, these experiments consist of suggesting to a subject that a cold object placed against the skin will burn him and cause a blister to form. The area touched is then covered over, sealed, and the subject is watched to prevent artificial stimulation of the area so as to produce a blister which his desire to please the operator and show results might cause him to attempt. The test is considered successful if a blister subsequently develops under these controlled conditions.

Pattie claimed that he was unable to believe these positive reports even though controls were admittedly adequate, because he was unable to find a logical physiological explanation of how a blister possibly could form as a result of suggestion. Erickson also considers that controls could not have been sufficient and in experiments has never been able to produce such a blister. Skepticism is warranted, but it must be remembered that operator attitude is always a factor which may enter.

The latest inquiry into blistering was conducted by the Russian psychologist Kartamishev, as reported by Kalz. Dr. Kalz personally did not witness the experiments but he talked to physicians who did attend the experiments. These men considered the controls such that there could be no doubt of the reliability of the tests, whose results were positive. Kartamishev's reputation is excellent. He is a trained and accurate observer and the head of a Soviet state experimental clinic. The matter of blisters must still be considered unproved until large-scale tests decide.

There has been almost no scientific delving into the practical aspect of the use of hypnotic suggestion in the treatment of organic disease. Claims of favorable results have frequently been voiced, though some sound preposterous. In the early 1900s, Quackenbos [37] asserted that he cured several cases of diabetes mellitus long before insulin was discovered, describing each case in detail and telling in medical terms of the results. Liebeault claimed success with cases of lead poisoning, anemia and pulmonary tuberculosis. Others cited results in Parkinson's disease, organic paralyses, in softening a sclerosis, and in remedying other conditions. But we can only wonder if the diagnosis of these cases was not in error.

Ever since the days of Braid, a few reputable physicians have used hypnotic suggestion therapeutically with firm conviction as to its practical value. But psychologists and medical men are trained in science, and scientific training develops skepticism and conservatism. The great majority have refused to entertain the thought that suggestion can be a matter of science. With them as with the public, it retains a tinge of the mystical, the supernormal and occult. When combined with hypnotism, the tinge becomes a taint. The skeptical scientist asks, "How can mere words heal an organically diseased body?" The question is pertinent, and at first thought the idea seems absurd. It does seem impossible for words to kill bacteria or destroy a virus or to cause a change in tissue. The medical man scoffs at the possibility and yet there is a possibility.

Let us hasten to say that these matters are only presented as worthy of investigation. Though we may be accused of overoptimism, we intend only to be open-minded—and curious. We have no idea what results experiment would show. With some, in our opinion the results would be entirely negative, but others might prove positive. We make no claims ourselves, but we believe that research is warranted.

Let us review some previous statements as to suggestion with special consideration of its medical employment. The human body has many natural ways of combating disease, biotic methods of overcoming the ailments with which we are afflicted. Some of these means are known and their functioning is understood. Fever and the action of white blood corpuscles are recognized weapons in the body's war against illness. We have only a slight knowledge of the actions of anti-bodies in the blood stream, and of glandular and other secretions and action. Undoubtedly the human body acts in other ways to resist and throw off disease, and to immunize itself. In the case of physical injury, the damage is repaired by increased cellular action and growth as flesh is healed or broken bones are mended.

It is known that suggestion can inhibit or excite activity in the organs and probably any gland or other part of the body which can be affected by emotion. Ideas are recognized as being able to cause, through emotion, physical changes in the body. Emotion and suggestion operate in exactly the same way to cause physical reactions. Thus words can have a physical effect either as suggestion or by stimulating emotion. Research has been too restricted to know the limitations here, but there is a possibility of words thus being used to stimulate the production of white corpuscles (or of red) and antibodies, to change body temperature or blood pressure, to increase cellular growth or to inhibit it, and experiment could easily decide the point. The question is—can it be done? The only answer at present is "very doubtful, but barely possible."

As has been mentioned, the dermatologist Dr. Frederick Kalz has written of experiments in the use of suggestion on skin ailments. Many old superstitious beliefs as to the removal of warts were examined, and our old friend "suggestion" was found at work again. Warts disappeared with these methods and were also removed by direct hypnotic suggestion. This was control of cellular activity and growth (if we grant that the experiments were properly controlled).

In these wart investigations an even stranger effect was noted, but its implications were apparently overlooked. Some warts are of an infectious, virus type. After such warts were treated by suggestion, microscopic examination of the tissue showed that the infection was eliminated as the wart healed. Perhaps hypnotic suggestion of increase in the natural processes of the body in fighting infection would have a positive result.

Proof or disproof of the effects of hypnotic suggestion on organic disease could easily be demonstrated. Towards such a matter our attitude certainly should be skeptical and critical. But in the face of scores of statements by medical men that hypnotism in their experience has shown some positive results in organic disease, and with similar evidence of faith-healing cures, research is indicated even if it be with lifted eyebrow. All this is pure speculation, but there has been enough smoke to suggest a fire.

The need for study to produce better methods of inducing hypnosis has been mentioned. So far as we know, only Erickson has done anything along this line recently. He has shown the necessity of producing a very deep trance to use hypnotic phenomena to the best advantage, and he has described how to produce it by giving proper suggestion over relatively long periods of time. Having prepared the way for the subject to enter such a trance, by suggesting deep sleep, he has found it beneficial to leave the room for perhaps a half hour while the subject sleeps undisturbed. During this time the subject goes through a mental process of orientation and adaptation to the deep trance.

This matter is of such real importance that we quote from the article "A study of clinical and experimental findings on hypnotic deafness" by Erickson:

"Essentially, the procedure consisted of the induction of a deep trance, followed by a deep hypnotic stupor and succeeded in turn by a profound somnambulistic state. Thus, after the first selection had been made to secure subjects capable of deep trances, attention was directed to the induction of stuporous trance states. A slow systematic technique of graduated suggestions was employed. On the average, two hours of systematic suggestion for the susceptible subject were given before he was considered to have reached a sufficiently stuporous state, which resembled closely a profound catatonic stupor.

"The next step in training was the teaching of the subjects to become somnambulistic without lessening the degree of their hypnosis. Usually, the procedure with a deeply hypnotized subject is to suggest that he open his eyes and act as if he were awake. Long experience on the part of the experimenter and his colleagues has shown, however, that in somnambulistic states thus crudely suggested, critical observation can detect a definite mixture of normal waking and hypnotic behavior leading to unsatisfactory findings and to a more or less ready disorganization of the somnambulism as a state in itself.

"To avoid such difficulties and uncertainties, a special technique of suggestion was devised by which the subject in the stuporous trance could slowly and gradually adjust himself to the demands of the somnambulistic trance. Usually an hour or more was spent in systematic suggestion, building up the somnambulistic state so that all behavior manifested was actually in response to the immediate hypnotic situation with no need on the part of the subject to bring into the situation his usual responses to a normal waking situation. Essentially, this training was directed to a complete inhibition of all spontaneous activity while giving entire freedom for all responsible activity. The final step in the preliminary training was the repetition of the entire process over and over again at irregular intervals during a period of a week or more until it was possible to secure the stuporous trance and the somnambulistic state within 10 minutes."

Transcendence of normal physical abilities under hypnosis has previously been mentioned as a moot question. The authors are convinced that augmented physical strength is possible with hypnotic stimulation, for it has often been observed at times of great peril or when one is under great stress. Hadfield's [38] tests of a number of subjects for strength of hand grip with a dynamometer under controlled conditions revealed that 101 pounds was the average grip in the waking state. In gymnasiums few men are found who are strong enough to squeeze the instrument above 150 pounds, yet Hadfield's control group averaged 150 pounds with hypnotic suggestion of increased strength. This is a truly remarkable showing.

Critics claim that such a test does not prove normal ability transcended because the person tested in the waking state may not squeeze as hard as possible. They also point out the display of strength under fear or stress, but the latter is not normal and the hypnotized subject is under no such emotions. It seems that he does transcend the normal capacity. More investigation of this matter in different ways would be interesting.

Some other areas where study should be further undertaken are the narcotic state as compared to hypnosis, the whole field of suggestion and its laws, whether suggestion given during normal sleep is effective, and answers should be sought as to questions about hypersensitivity. In particular, more investigation is needed of the trance state itself.

The science of medicine has made tremendous strides in the past two decades—probably more than in the accumulated total of all the previous years of medical history. Today, doctors eagerly look for new methods, follow their medical journals closely lest they find themselves out of date, and begin to employ new drugs and therapeutic measures almost before investigators can confirm their findings. Hypnoanalysis has suddenly received recognition by psychiatrists after a dormant period of almost thirty years, and the Menninger Clinic has recently received funds for hypnotic research in functional conditions—in itself an astounding and hopeful event.

Almost every physician we know has mentioned to us regret that his medical training omitted the study of general and abnormal psychology. Up until recently few medical schools have required any course in psychology for graduation, though medical educators are well aware of the deficiency and some schools have now made psychology a premedic requirement. Even today one of the largest medical schools in California offers a postgraduate course in psychiatry without requiring a course in psychology other than the abnormal psychology taught incidental to the psychiatric course. A medical psychologist can thus be licensed who has never studied psychology!

From internship, most physicians enter private practice with little or no knowledge of the mental or emotional phases of disease. As a result, they are at a loss when neurotic patients visit them.

Some medical men express the belief that only a physician should treat disease. Ideally, treatment of disease of functional nature and psychosomatic disease should be by medical psychologists, but the only practitioners with this qualification are psychiatrists and some psychotherapists. Since there are fewer than four thousand psychiatrists and not many competent psychotherapists with medical degrees in the United States, about 95 per cent of the mentally sick must look elsewhere. According to the U. S. Public Health Service there are about eight million neurotic United States citizens today, and more than half the hospital beds in America are occupied by mental patients, the great majority of whom are psychotic—for the neurotic is seldom in need of hospitalization. There are not enough medical psychologists today to treat even the psychotics properly. To whom shall all the others who are mentally ailing turn for relief?

This is a fact which cannot be minimized, and medical science is faced with a grave situation. The general practitioner freely admits a lack of knowledge for treatment of neurotics and preferably wants nothing to do with neurotic patients. Nor does he often have knowledge as to the psychological side of psychosomatic disease, now recognized as including a very large percentage of all sickness. The general physician's advice to the neurotic person is to "consult a psychiatrist," which would be excellent advice if there were thirty or forty thousand psychiatrists. As it is, psychiatry is only for the wealthy. Consequently the neurotic often ends up in the hands of the medical camp-followers, some of whom are licensed by law to practice. Christian Science, other sects of various kinds, evangelists, healers of all descriptions and a crew of miscellaneous charlatans and quacks wait to gather in the sufferer from neurotic troubles. Some, such as Christian Science, are sincere and legitimate and do much good as well as some harm. Most resemble wolves in full cry after their prey. Politicians do not care to antagonize religious groups, and in most states a small fee permits the founding or incorporation of a "church" with full freedom to become a religious "healer."

The condition of the neurotic is one for which there is no immediate solution, though it can be solved eventually if medical students are taught psychology. Some measures can be taken which would be of material aid. A newly created six-man National Advisory Mental Health Council is now planning such measures with a government appropriation of $10,000,000 to back a war on mental illness. Research is one part of the program and a mental health institute for training (and research) is to be built at Bethesda, Maryland.

Training should also be provided to produce large numbers of clinical psychologists. Today the clinical psychologist is in a most disadvantageous position. The medical profession rightly and correctly seeks state medical laws which will protect the public from the charlatan and themselves from encroachment in their field by those with no training. Principally because of the religious loophole, these laws are not too successful, but they often are so broad that the psychologist with training is barred from practicing psychology. There has been recent recognition of the clinical psychologist, however, notably by the Veterans Administration and even by the American Psychiatric Association. In many states no attempt is made to prevent legitimate psychologists from practicing psychotherapy provided treatment is not called "treatment" and is psychological only. This is as it should be. The clinical psychologist certainly should not be concerned with diagnosis and properly should serve only to assist physicians and to give psychological treatment. Essentially psychoanalysis is the study of personality and abnormally evidenced behavior. It is a proper field for the clinical psychologist provided a physician is in charge of each case and attends to its medical aspects, and the psychologist should be able to practice psychotherapy under such conditions without being subject to a charge of practicing medicine without license. Recognition of this by the medical profession would be a progressive step to relieve the situation for the neurotic patient.

# REFERENCES

## PART ONE

1 Bulletins of the Menninger Clinic, Topeka, Kans.
2 Freud, S.: *Collected Papers*. London, Hogarth (Vol. 2) .
3 Hull, Clark: *Hypnosis and Suggestibility*. New York, Appleton-Century, 1933.
4 Wells, W. R.: "Experiments in the hypnotic production of crime." Journal of Psychology, *11*:63, 1941.
5 Estabrooks, G. H.: *Hypnotism*. New York, Dutton, 1943.
6 Erickson, M. H.: "Possible detrimental effects of experimental hypnosis." Journal of Abnormal & Social Psychology, *27*:321, 1932.
7 Rowland, L. W.: "Will hypnotized persons try to harm themselves or others?" Journal of Abnormal & Social Psychology, *34*:114, 1939.
8 Satow, Louis: *Hypnotism and Suggestion*, New York, Dodd Mead, 1923.
9 Goldsmith, M.: *Franz Anton Mesmer*. New York, Doubleday Doran, 1934.
10 Binet, A., and Féré, C.: *Animal Magnetism*. New York, Appleton, 1888.
11 Braid, James: *Neurypnology*. London, Geo. Redway, 1899.
12 Moll, A.: *Hypnotism*. New York, Chas. Scribner's Sons, 1898.
13 Esdaile, James: *Mesmerism in India*.
14 Bernheim, H.: *Suggestive Therapeutics*. New York, Putnam, 1889.
15 Pitzer, George C.: *Suggestion*. (Published by author.) 1901.
16 Erickson, M. H.: "The applications of hypnosis to psychiatry." Medical Record, *150*:60, 1939.
17 —— and Erickson, E. M.: "Concerning the nature and character of post-hypnotic behavior." Journal of General Psychology, *24*:95, 1941.
18 Grinker, R., and Spiegel, J.: *War Neuroses*. Philadelphia, Blakiston, 1945.
19 Brenman, M., and Gill, M.: "Hypnotherapy." Josiah Macy, Jr., Foundation Bulletin, 1944.
20 Horsley, J. S.: *Narco-analysis*. London, Oxford University Press, 1943.
21 Schilder, P., and Kauders, O.: *Hypnosis*. New York, Nervous and Mental Disease Publishing Company, 1927.
22 Kubie, L. S.: "Manual of emergency treatment for acute war neuroses." War Medicine, *46*:582, 1943.
23 —— and Margolin, S.: "The therapeutic role of drugs in the process of repression, dissociation and synthesis." Psychosomatic Medicine, *7*:147, 1945.
24 Wetterstrand, O.: *Hypnotism and Its Application to Practical Medicine*. New York, Putnam, 1897.
25 Behanon, K. T.: *Yoga, A Scientific Evaluation*. New York, Macmillan, 1937.

# REFERENCES

26 Forel, A.: *Hypnotism and Psychotherapy*. Allied Book, 1907.

27 Davis, L. W., and Husband, R. W.: "Hypnotic suggestibility in relation to personality traits." Journal of Abnormal and Social Psychology, *26*:175, 1931.

28 Friedlander, J. W., and Sarbin, T. R.: "Depth of hypnosis." Journal of Abnormal and Social Psychology, *33*:453, 1938.

29 Erickson, M. H.: "A study of clinical and experimental findings on hypnotic deafness." Journal of General Psychology, *19*:127, 1938.

30 Bramwell, James: *Hypnotism*. London, Rider & Son, 1913.

31 Messerschmidt, R.: From Hull.

32 McDougall, W.: *Outline of Abnormal Psychology*. New York, Scribner, 1926.

33 Sidis, Boris: *The Psychology of Suggestion*. New York, Appleton, 1921.

34 Baudouin, Charles: *Suggestion and Auto Suggestion*. New York, Dodd Mead, 1922.

35 Coué, É.: *How to Practice Suggestion and Auto-Suggestion*. American Library Service, 1923.

36 Pierce, F.: *Mobilizing the Mid-brain*. New York, Dutton, 1924.

37 Erickson, M. H.: "An experimental investigation of the possible anti-social use of hypnosis." Psychiatry, *2*:391, 1939.

38 Nicholson, N. C.: "Notes on muscular work during hypnosis." Johns Hopkins Hospital Bulletin, *31*:89, 1920.

39 Winn, Ralph: *Scientific Hypnotism*. Christopher, 1939.

40 Pitzer, George C.: *Therapeutic Suggestion Applied*. (Published by the author.) 1899.

41 Young, P. C.: "Is rapport an essential characteristic of hypnosis?" Journal of Abnormal and Social Psychology, *22*:130, 1927.

42 Bechterev, W.: *General Principles of Human Reflexology*. New York, International Publishers, 1928.

43 Erickson, M. H.: "The induction of color blindness by a technique of hypnotic suggestion." Journal of General Psychology, *20*:61, 1939.

44 —— and Erickson, E. M.: "The hypnotic induction of hallucinatory color vision followed by pseudo negative after-images." Journal of Experimental Psychology, *22*:581, 1938.

44a Sampimon, R. L. H., and Woodruff, M. F. A.: "Observations concerning the use of hypnosis as a substitute for anaesthesia." Medical Journal of Australia, *33*:392, 1946. (Quoted from Psychosomatic Medicine, vol. 8, no. 5, 1946.)

45 Rhine, J. B.: *Extra Sensory Perception*. New York, Holt, 1940.

46 Rivers, W. H. R.: *Instinct and the Unconscious*. Cambridge University Press, 1922.

47 Wingfield, H. E.: *An Introduction to the Study of Hypnotism*. London, Baillière, Tindall & Cox, 1920.

48 Wolberg, L.: *Hypnoanalysis*. New York, Grune & Stratton, 1945.

49 Erickson, M. H.: "An experimental investigation of the hypnotic subject's apparent ability to become unaware of stimuli." Journal of General Psychology, *31*:191, 1944.

50 Klein, D. B.: "Experimental production of dreams during sleep." University of Texas Bulletin, 1930.

51 Fink, D.: *Release from Nervous Tension*. New York, Simon & Schuster, 1943.

52 White, R. W.: "A preface to the theory of hypnotism." Journal of Abnormal and Social Psychology, *36:*477, 1941.

53 Dorcus, R. M., and Shaffer, G. W.: *Textbook of Abnormal Psychology*. Baltimore, Williams & Wilkins, 1945.

54 Wible, C. L., and Jenness, A.: "Respiration and heart action in sleep and hypnosis." Journal of General Psychology, *16:*197, 1937.

55 ——: "Electrocardiograms during sleep and hypnosis." Journal of General Psychology, *1:*235, 1936.

56 Bass, M. J.: "Differences of the hypnotic trance from normal sleep." Journal of Experimental Psychology, *14:*382, 1931.

57 Brown, W.: *Suggestion and Mental Analysis*. New York, Doran, 1922.

58 Ferenczi, S.: *Theory and Technique of Psychoanalysis*. New York, Boni & Liveright, 1927.

59 Janet, Pierre: *Psychological Healing*. New York, Macmillan, 1925.

60 Prince, M.: *The Unconscious*. New York, Macmillan, 1921.

61 Pavlov, I. P.: *Conditioned Reflexes*. London, Oxford University Press, 1927.

62 Sadler, W.: *The Mind at Mischief*. New York, Funk & Wagnalls, 1929.

63 Mühl, A. M.: "Automatic writing in determining conflict and early childhood repressions." Journal of Abnormal Psychology, *18:*1, 1923.

## PART TWO

1 Conklin, E. S.: *Principles of Abnormal Psychology*. New York, Holt, 1935.

2 Janet, P.: *Major Symptoms of Hysteria*. New York, Macmillan, 1920.

3 Sidis, B.: *Nervous Ills, Their Cause and Cure*. Badger, 1922.

4 Horney, K.: *The Neurotic Personality of Our Time*. New York, Norton, 1937.

5 Babinski, J.: "My conceptions of hysteria and hypnotism." Alienist and Neurologist, *19:*1, 1908.

6 Luria, A. R.: *The Nature of Human Conflicts*. New York, Liveright, 1932.

7 Erickson, M. H.: "The method employed to formulate a complex story for the induction of an experimental neurosis in a hypnotic subject." Journal of General Psychology, *31:*67, 1944.

8 ——: "A study of an experimental neurosis hypnotically induced in a case of ejaculatio praecox." British Journal of Medical Psychology, *15:*34, 1935.

9 Kraepelin, E.: *Clinical Psychiatry*. New York, Macmillan, 1902.

10 DuBois, P.: *The Psychic Treatment of Nervous Disorders*. New York, Funk & Wagnalls, 1907.

11 Alexander, F., and French, T. M.: *Psychoanalytic Therapy*. New York, Ronald Press, 1946.

12 Freud, S.: *A General Introduction to Psychoanalysis*. New York, Boni & Liveright, 1922.

13 —— *The Interpretation of Dreams*. New York, Macmillan, 1913.

14 Jung, C. G.: *Psychology of the Unconscious*. London, Kegan Paul, 1922.

15 Adler, A.: *Problems of Neurosis*. New York, Cosmopolitan, 1930.

16 Rank, O.: *Will Therapy and Truth and Reality*. New York, Knopf, 1945.

REFERENCES

[17] Stekel, W.: *Psychoanalysis and Suggestion Therapy*. London, Kegan Paul, 1923.

[18] Meyer, A.: from Dorcus and Shaffer: *Textbook of Abnormal Psychology*.

[19] Mayo, Elton: "Frightened people." Harvard Alumni Bulletin, vol. 13, no. 2.

[20] Sadler, W. S.: *Worry and Nervousness*. Chicago, McClurg, 1915.

[21] Carrel, Alexis: *Man the Unknown*. New York, Harper, 1935.

[22] Hadfield, J. A., E. Miller, ed.: in *The Neuroses in War*. New York, Macmillan, 1940.

[23] Simmel, E., Ernest Jones, ed.: in *Psycho-analysis and the War Neuroses*. International Psycho-analytic Press, 1921.

[24] Lindner, R. M.: *Rebel without a Cause*. New York, Grune & Stratton, 1944.

[25] Erickson, M. H., and Kubie, L. S.: "The successful treatment of a case of acute hysterical depression by a return under hypnosis to a critical phase of childhood." Psycho-analytic Quarterly, *10*:592, 1941.

[26] Farber, L. H., and Fisher, C.: "An experimental approach to dream psychology through the use of hypnosis." Psycho-analytic Quarterly, *12*:202, 1943.

[27] Jacobson, E.: *You Must Relax*. New York, Whittlesey House, 1942.

[28] Jelliffe, S., Sandor Lorand, ed.: in *Psychoanalysis Today*. New York, Covici Friede, 1933.

[29] Dunbar, H. F.: *Emotions and Bodily Changes*. New York, Columbia University Press, 1938.

[30] Kalz, F.: "Psychological factors in skin diseases." Canadian Medical Association Journal, *53*:247, 1945.

[31] Alexander, F. French, T. M., et al.: *Psychogenic Factors in Bronchial Asthma*. Psychosomatic Medicine Monographs, 1941.

[32] Alvarez, W. C.: "Treatment of nervous indigestion." Journal of the American Medical Association, *89*:440, 1927.

[33] ——: "Ways in which emotion can affect the digestive tract." Journal of the American Medical Association, *92*:1230, 1929.

[34] ——: "How to avoid flare-ups of peptic ulcer." Journal of the American Medical Association, *125*:903.

[35] Weiss, E.: From a paper read to the American Society for Research in Psychosomatic Problems.

[36] Pattie, F. A.: "The production of blisters by hypnotic suggestion." Journal of Abnormal and Social Psychology, *36*:62, 1941.

[37] Quackenbos, J. D.: *Hypnotic Therapeutics in Theory and Practice*. New York, Harper, 1908.

[38] Hadfield, J. A.: *The Psychology of Power*. New York, Macmillan, 1924.

# Index

## A PERSONAL WORD FROM MELVIN POWERS
## PUBLISHER, WILSHIRE BOOK COMPANY

Dear Friend:

My goal is to publish interesting, informative, and inspirational books. You can help me accomplish this by answering the following questions, either by phone or by mail. Or, if convenient for you, I would welcome the opportunity to visit with you in my office and hear your comments in person.

Did you enjoy reading this book? Why?

Would you enjoy reading another similar book?

What idea in the book impressed you the most?

If applicable to your situation, have you incorporated this idea in your daily life?

Is there a chapter that could serve as a theme for an entire book? Please explain.

If you have an idea for a book, I would welcome discussing it with you. If you already have one in progress, write or call me concerning possible publication. I can be reached at (213) 875-1711 or (213) 983-1105.

Sincerely yours,

MELVIN POWERS

*12015 Sherman Road*
*North Hollywood, California 91605*

# MELVIN POWERS SELF-IMPROVEMENT LIBRARY

## ASTROLOGY

| | |
|---|---|
| _____ ASTROLOGY: HOW TO CHART YOUR HOROSCOPE *Max Heindel* | 3.00 |
| _____ ASTROLOGY: YOUR PERSONAL SUN-SIGN GUIDE *Beatrice Ryder* | 3.00 |
| _____ ASTROLOGY FOR EVERYDAY LIVING *Janet Harris* | 2.00 |
| _____ ASTROLOGY MADE EASY *Astarte* | 3.00 |
| _____ ASTROLOGY MADE PRACTICAL *Alexandra Kayhle* | 3.00 |
| _____ ASTROLOGY, ROMANCE, YOU AND THE STARS *Anthony Norvell* | 4.00 |
| _____ MY WORLD OF ASTROLOGY *Sydney Omarr* | 5.00 |
| _____ THOUGHT DIAL *Sidney Omarr* | 4.00 |
| _____ WHAT THE STARS REVEAL ABOUT THE MEN IN YOUR LIFE *Thelma White* | 3.00 |

## BRIDGE

| | |
|---|---|
| _____ BRIDGE BIDDING MADE EASY *Edwin B. Kantar* | 7.00 |
| _____ BRIDGE CONVENTIONS *Edwin B. Kantar* | 7.00 |
| _____ BRIDGE HUMOR *Edwin B. Kantar* | 5.00 |
| _____ COMPETITIVE BIDDING IN MODERN BRIDGE *Edgar Kaplan* | 4.00 |
| _____ DEFENSIVE BRIDGE PLAY COMPLETE *Edwin B. Kantar* | 10.00 |
| _____ GAMESMAN BRIDGE—Play Better with Kantar *Edwin B. Kantar* | 5.00 |
| _____ HOW TO IMPROVE YOUR BRIDGE *Alfred Sheinwold* | 5.00 |
| _____ IMPROVING YOUR BIDDING SKILLS *Edwin B. Kantar* | 4.00 |
| _____ INTRODUCTION TO DECLARER'S PLAY *Edwin B. Kantar* | 5.00 |
| _____ INTRODUCTION TO DEFENDER'S PLAY *Edwin B. Kantar* | 3.00 |
| _____ KANTAR FOR THE DEFENSE *Edwin B. Kantar* | 5.00 |
| _____ SHORT CUT TO WINNING BRIDGE *Alfred Sheinwold* | 3.00 |
| _____ TEST YOUR BRIDGE PLAY *Edwin B. Kantar* | 5.00 |
| _____ VOLUME 2—TEST YOUR BRIDGE PLAY *Edwin B. Kantar* | 5.00 |
| _____ WINNING DECLARER PLAY *Dorothy Hayden Truscott* | 4.00 |

## BUSINESS, STUDY & REFERENCE

| | |
|---|---|
| _____ CONVERSATION MADE EASY *Elliot Russell* | 3.00 |
| _____ EXAM SECRET *Dennis B. Jackson* | 3.00 |
| _____ FIX-IT BOOK *Arthur Symons* | 2.00 |
| _____ HOW TO DEVELOP A BETTER SPEAKING VOICE *M. Hellier* | 3.00 |
| _____ HOW TO MAKE A FORTUNE IN REAL ESTATE *Albert Winnikoff* | 4.00 |
| _____ INCREASE YOUR LEARNING POWER *Geoffrey A. Dudley* | 3.00 |
| _____ PRACTICAL GUIDE TO BETTER CONCENTRATION *Melvin Powers* | 3.00 |
| _____ PRACTICAL GUIDE TO PUBLIC SPEAKING *Maurice Forley* | 5.00 |
| _____ 7 DAYS TO FASTER READING *William S. Schaill* | 3.00 |
| _____ SONGWRITERS' RHYMING DICTIONARY *Jane Shaw Whitfield* | 5.00 |
| _____ SPELLING MADE EASY *Lester D. Basch & Dr. Milton Finkelstein* | 3.00 |
| _____ STUDENT'S GUIDE TO BETTER GRADES *J. A. Rickard* | 3.00 |
| _____ TEST YOURSELF—Find Your Hidden Talent *Jack Shafer* | 3.00 |
| _____ YOUR WILL & WHAT TO DO ABOUT IT *Attorney Samuel G. Kling* | 4.00 |

## CALLIGRAPHY

| | |
|---|---|
| _____ ADVANCED CALLIGRAPHY *Katherine Jeffares* | 7.00 |
| _____ CALLIGRAPHER'S REFERENCE BOOK *Anne Leptich & Jacque Evans* | 7.00 |
| _____ CALLIGRAPHY—The Art of Beautiful Writing *Katherine Jeffares* | 7.00 |
| _____ CALLIGRAPHY FOR FUN & PROFIT *Anne Leptich & Jacque Evans* | 7.00 |
| _____ CALLIGRAPHY MADE EASY *Tina Serafini* | 7.00 |

## CHESS & CHECKERS

| | |
|---|---|
| _____ BEGINNER'S GUIDE TO WINNING CHESS *Fred Reinfeld* | 4.00 |
| _____ CHECKERS MADE EASY *Tom Wiswell* | 2.00 |
| _____ CHESS IN TEN EASY LESSONS *Larry Evans* | 3.00 |
| _____ CHESS MADE EASY *Milton L. Hanauer* | 3.00 |
| _____ CHESS PROBLEMS FOR BEGINNERS *edited by Fred Reinfeld* | 2.00 |
| _____ CHESS SECRETS REVEALED *Fred Reinfeld* | 2.00 |
| _____ CHESS STRATEGY—An Expert's Guide *Fred Reinfeld* | 2.00 |
| _____ CHESS TACTICS FOR BEGINNERS *edited by Fred Reinfeld* | 3.00 |
| _____ CHESS THEORY & PRACTICE *Morry & Mitchell* | 2.00 |
| _____ HOW TO WIN AT CHECKERS *Fred Reinfeld* | 3.00 |
| _____ 1001 BRILLIANT WAYS TO CHECKMATE *Fred Reinfeld* | 4.00 |

| | | |
|---|---|---|
| ____ 1001 WINNING CHESS SACRIFICES & COMBINATIONS *Fred Reinfeld* | | 4.00 |
| ____ SOVIET CHESS *Edited by R. G. Wade* | | 3.00 |

## COOKERY & HERBS

| | | |
|---|---|---|
| ____ CULPEPER'S HERBAL REMEDIES *Dr. Nicholas Culpeper* | | 3.00 |
| ____ FAST GOURMET COOKBOOK *Poppy Cannon* | | 2.50 |
| ____ GINSENG The Myth & The Truth *Joseph P. Hou* | | 3.00 |
| ____ HEALING POWER OF HERBS *May Bethel* | | 4.00 |
| ____ HEALING POWER OF NATURAL FOODS *May Bethel* | | 3.00 |
| ____ HERB HANDBOOK *Dawn MacLeod* | | 3.00 |
| ____ HERBS FOR COOKING AND HEALING *Dr. Donald Law* | | 2.00 |
| ____ HERBS FOR HEALTH—How to Grow & Use Them *Louise Evans Doole* | | 3.00 |
| ____ HOME GARDEN COOKBOOK—Delicious Natural Food Recipes *Ken Kraft* | | 3.00 |
| ____ MEDICAL HERBALIST *edited by Dr. J. R. Yemm* | | 3.00 |
| ____ NATURAL FOOD COOKBOOK *Dr. Harry C. Bond* | | 3.00 |
| ____ NATURE'S MEDICINES *Richard Lucas* | | 3.00 |
| ____ VEGETABLE GARDENING FOR BEGINNERS *Hugh Wiberg* | | 2.00 |
| ____ VEGETABLES FOR TODAY'S GARDENS *R. Milton Carleton* | | 2.00 |
| ____ VEGETARIAN COOKERY *Janet Walker* | | 4.00 |
| ____ VEGETARIAN COOKING MADE EASY & DELECTABLE *Veronica Vezza* | | 3.00 |
| ____ VEGETARIAN DELIGHTS—A Happy Cookbook for Health *K. R. Mehta* | | 2.00 |
| ____ VEGETARIAN GOURMET COOKBOOK *Joyce McKinnel* | | 3.00 |

## GAMBLING & POKER

| | | |
|---|---|---|
| ____ ADVANCED POKER STRATEGY & WINNING PLAY *A. D. Livingston* | | 5.00 |
| ____ HOW NOT TO LOSE AT POKER *Jeffrey Lloyd Castle* | | 3.00 |
| ____ HOW TO WIN AT DICE GAMES *Skip Frey* | | 3.00 |
| ____ HOW TO WIN AT POKER *Terence Reese & Anthony T. Watkins* | | 3.00 |
| ____ SECRETS OF WINNING POKER *George S. Coffin* | | 3.00 |
| ____ WINNING AT CRAPS *Dr. Lloyd T. Commins* | | 3.00 |
| ____ WINNING AT GIN *Chester Wander & Cy Rice* | | 3.00 |
| ____ WINNING AT POKER—An Expert's Guide *John Archer* | | 3.00 |
| ____ WINNING AT 21—An Expert's Guide *John Archer* | | 5.00 |
| ____ WINNING POKER SYSTEMS *Norman Zadeh* | | 3.00 |

## HEALTH

| | | |
|---|---|---|
| ____ BEE POLLEN *Lynda Lyngheim & Jack Scagnetti* | | 3.00 |
| ____ DR. LINDNER'S SPECIAL WEIGHT CONTROL METHOD *P. G. Lindner, M.D.* | | 2.00 |
| ____ HELP YOURSELF TO BETTER SIGHT *Margaret Darst Corbett* | | 3.00 |
| ____ HOW TO IMPROVE YOUR VISION *Dr. Robert A. Kraskin* | | 3.00 |
| ____ HOW YOU CAN STOP SMOKING PERMANENTLY *Ernest Caldwell* | | 3.00 |
| ____ MIND OVER PLATTER *Peter G. Lindner, M.D.* | | 3.00 |
| ____ NATURE'S WAY TO NUTRITION & VIBRANT HEALTH *Robert J. Scrutton* | | 3.00 |
| ____ NEW CARBOHYDRATE DIET COUNTER *Patti Lopez-Pereira* | | 2.00 |
| ____ QUICK & EASY EXERCISES FOR FACIAL BEAUTY *Judy Smith-deal* | | 2.00 |
| ____ QUICK & EASY EXERCISES FOR FIGURE BEAUTY *Judy Smith-deal* | | 2.00 |
| ____ REFLEXOLOGY *Dr. Maybelle Segal* | | 3.00 |
| ____ REFLEXOLOGY FOR GOOD HEALTH *Anna Kaye & Don C. Matchan* | | 3.00 |
| ____ YOU CAN LEARN TO RELAX *Dr. Samuel Gutwirth* | | 3.00 |
| ____ YOUR ALLERGY—What To Do About It *Allan Knight, M.D.* | | 3.00 |

## HOBBIES

| | | |
|---|---|---|
| ____ BEACHCOMBING FOR BEGINNERS *Norman Hickin* | | 2.00 |
| ____ BLACKSTONE'S MODERN CARD TRICKS *Harry Blackstone* | | 3.00 |
| ____ BLACKSTONE'S SECRETS OF MAGIC *Harry Blackstone* | | 3.00 |
| ____ COIN COLLECTING FOR BEGINNERS *Burton Hobson & Fred Reinfeld* | | 3.00 |
| ____ ENTERTAINING WITH ESP *Tony 'Doc' Shiels* | | 2.00 |
| ____ 400 FASCINATING MAGIC TRICKS YOU CAN DO *Howard Thurston* | | 4.00 |
| ____ HOW I TURN JUNK INTO FUN AND PROFIT *Sari* | | 3.00 |
| ____ HOW TO WRITE A HIT SONG & SELL IT *Tommy Boyce* | | 7.00 |
| ____ JUGGLING MADE EASY *Rudolf Dittrich* | | 3.00 |
| ____ MAGIC FOR ALL AGES *Walter Gibson* | | 4.00 |
| ____ MAGIC MADE EASY *Byron Wels* | | 2.00 |
| ____ STAMP COLLECTING FOR BEGINNERS *Burton Hobson* | | 3.00 |

## HORSE PLAYERS' WINNING GUIDES

| | | |
|---|---|---|
| ____ BETTING HORSES TO WIN *Les Conklin* | | 3.00 |

| | | |
|---|---|---|
| ____ | ENCYCLOPEDIA OF MODERN SEX & LOVE TECHNIQUES *Macandrew* | 5.00 |
| ____ | GUIDE TO SUCCESSFUL MARRIAGE *Drs. Albert Ellis & Robert Harper* | 5.00 |
| ____ | HOW TO RAISE AN EMOTIONALLY HEALTHY, HAPPY CHILD *A. Ellis* | 4.00 |
| ____ | SEX WITHOUT GUILT *Albert Ellis, Ph.D.* | 5.00 |
| ____ | SEXUALLY ADEQUATE MALE *Frank S. Caprio, M.D.* | 3.00 |
| ____ | SEXUALLY FULFILLED MAN *Dr. Rachel Copelan* | 5.00 |

## MELVIN POWERS' MAIL ORDER LIBRARY

| | | |
|---|---|---|
| ____ | HOW TO GET RICH IN MAIL ORDER *Melvin Powers* | 10.00 |
| ____ | HOW TO WRITE A GOOD ADVERTISEMENT *Victor O. Schwab* | 15.00 |
| ____ | MAIL ORDER MADE EASY *J. Frank Brumbaugh* | 10.00 |
| ____ | U.S. MAIL ORDER SHOPPER'S GUIDE *Susan Spitzer* | 10.00 |

## METAPHYSICS & OCCULT

| | | |
|---|---|---|
| ____ | BOOK OF TALISMANS, AMULETS & ZODIACAL GEMS *William Pavitt* | 5.00 |
| ____ | CONCENTRATION—A Guide to Mental Mastery *Mouni Sadhu* | 4.00 |
| ____ | CRITIQUES OF GOD *Edited by Peter Angeles* | 7.00 |
| ____ | EXTRA-TERRESTRIAL INTELLIGENCE—The First Encounter | 6.00 |
| ____ | FORTUNE TELLING WITH CARDS *P. Foli* | 3.00 |
| ____ | HANDWRITING ANALYSIS MADE EASY *John Marley* | 4.00 |
| ____ | HANDWRITING TELLS *Nadya Olyanova* | 5.00 |
| ____ | HOW TO INTERPRET DREAMS, OMENS & FORTUNE TELLING SIGNS *Gettings* | 3.00 |
| ____ | HOW TO UNDERSTAND YOUR DREAMS *Geoffrey A. Dudley* | 3.00 |
| ____ | ILLUSTRATED YOGA *William Zorn* | 3.00 |
| ____ | IN DAYS OF GREAT PEACE *Mouni Sadhu* | 3.00 |
| ____ | LSD—THE AGE OF MIND *Bernard Roseman* | 2.00 |
| ____ | MAGICIAN—His Training and Work *W. E. Butler* | 3.00 |
| ____ | MEDITATION *Mouni Sadhu* | 5.00 |
| ____ | MODERN NUMEROLOGY *Morris C. Goodman* | 3.00 |
| ____ | NUMEROLOGY—ITS FACTS AND SECRETS *Ariel Yvon Taylor* | 3.00 |
| ____ | NUMEROLOGY MADE EASY *W. Mykian* | 3.00 |
| ____ | PALMISTRY MADE EASY *Fred Gettings* | 3.00 |
| ____ | PALMISTRY MADE PRACTICAL *Elizabeth Daniels Squire* | 4.00 |
| ____ | PALMISTRY SECRETS REVEALED *Henry Frith* | 3.00 |
| ____ | PROPHECY IN OUR TIME *Martin Ebon* | 2.50 |
| ____ | PSYCHOLOGY OF HANDWRITING *Nadya Olyanova* | 5.00 |
| ____ | SUPERSTITION—Are You Superstitious? *Eric Maple* | 2.00 |
| ____ | TAROT *Mouni Sadhu* | 6.00 |
| ____ | TAROT OF THE BOHEMIANS *Papus* | 5.00 |
| ____ | WAYS TO SELF-REALIZATION *Mouni Sadhu* | 3.00 |
| ____ | WHAT YOUR HANDWRITING REVEALS *Albert E. Hughes* | 3.00 |
| ____ | WITCHCRAFT, MAGIC & OCCULTISM—A Fascinating History *W. B. Crow* | 5.00 |
| ____ | WITCHCRAFT—THE SIXTH SENSE *Justine Glass* | 5.00 |
| ____ | WORLD OF PSYCHIC RESEARCH *Hereward Carrington* | 2.00 |

## SELF-HELP & INSPIRATIONAL

| | | |
|---|---|---|
| ____ | DAILY POWER FOR JOYFUL LIVING *Dr. Donald Curtis* | 5.00 |
| ____ | DYNAMIC THINKING *Melvin Powers* | 2.00 |
| ____ | EXUBERANCE—Your Guide to Happiness & Fulfillment *Dr. Paul Kurtz* | 3.00 |
| ____ | GREATEST POWER IN THE UNIVERSE *U. S. Andersen* | 5.00 |
| ____ | GROW RICH WHILE YOU SLEEP *Ben Sweetland* | 3.00 |
| ____ | GROWTH THROUGH REASON *Albert Ellis, Ph.D.* | 4.00 |
| ____ | GUIDE TO DEVELOPING YOUR POTENTIAL *Herbert A. Otto, Ph.D.* | 3.00 |
| ____ | GUIDE TO PERSONAL HAPPINESS *Albert Ellis, Ph.D. & Irving Becker, Ed. D.* | 5.00 |
| ____ | HELPING YOURSELF WITH APPLIED PSYCHOLOGY *R. Henderson* | 2.00 |
| ____ | HELPING YOURSELF WITH PSYCHIATRY *Frank S. Caprio, M.D.* | 2.00 |
| ____ | HOW TO ATTRACT GOOD LUCK *A. H. Z. Carr* | 4.00 |
| ____ | HOW TO DEVELOP A WINNING PERSONALITY *Martin Panzer* | 5.00 |
| ____ | HOW TO DEVELOP AN EXCEPTIONAL MEMORY *Young & Gibson* | 4.00 |
| ____ | HOW TO LIVE WITH A NEUROTIC *Albert Ellis, Ph. D.* | 5.00 |
| ____ | HOW TO OVERCOME YOUR FEARS *M. P. Leahy, M.D.* | 3.00 |
| ____ | HOW YOU CAN HAVE CONFIDENCE AND POWER *Les Giblin* | 5.00 |
| ____ | HUMAN PROBLEMS & HOW TO SOLVE THEM *Dr. Donald Curtis* | 5.00 |
| ____ | I CAN *Ben Sweetland* | 5.00 |
| ____ | I WILL *Ben Sweetland* | 3.00 |
| ____ | LEFT-HANDED PEOPLE *Michael Barsley* | 4.00 |

| | |
|---|---|
| _____ MAGIC IN YOUR MIND *U. S. Andersen* | 5.00 |
| _____ MAGIC OF THINKING BIG *Dr. David J. Schwartz* | 3.00 |
| _____ MAGIC POWER OF YOUR MIND *Walter M. Germain* | 5.00 |
| _____ MENTAL POWER THROUGH SLEEP SUGGESTION *Melvin Powers* | 3.00 |
| _____ NEW GUIDE TO RATIONAL LIVING *Albert Ellis, Ph.D. & R. Harper, Ph.D.* | 3.00 |
| _____ PSYCHO-CYBERNETICS *Maxwell Maltz, M.D.* | 4.00 |
| _____ SCIENCE OF MIND IN DAILY LIVING *Dr. Donald Curtis* | 5.00 |
| _____ SECRET OF SECRETS *U. S. Andersen* | 5.00 |
| _____ SECRET POWER OF THE PYRAMIDS *U. S. Andersen* | 5.00 |
| _____ STUTTERING AND WHAT YOU CAN DO ABOUT IT *W. Johnson, Ph.D.* | 2.50 |
| _____ SUCCESS-CYBERNETICS *U. S. Andersen* | 5.00 |
| _____ 10 DAYS TO A GREAT NEW LIFE *William E. Edwards* | 3.00 |
| _____ THINK AND GROW RICH *Napoleon Hill* | 4.00 |
| _____ THINK YOUR WAY TO SUCCESS *Dr. Lew Losoncy* | 5.00 |
| _____ THREE MAGIC WORDS *U. S. Andersen* | 5.00 |
| _____ TREASURY OF COMFORT *edited by Rabbi Sidney Greenberg* | 5.00 |
| _____ TREASURY OF THE ART OF LIVING *Sidney S. Greenberg* | 5.00 |
| _____ YOU ARE NOT THE TARGET *Laura Huxley* | 5.00 |
| _____ YOUR SUBCONSCIOUS POWER *Charles M. Simmons* | 5.00 |
| _____ YOUR THOUGHTS CAN CHANGE YOUR LIFE *Dr. Donald Curtis* | 5.00 |

## SPORTS

| | |
|---|---|
| _____ BICYCLING FOR FUN AND GOOD HEALTH *Kenneth E. Luther* | 2.00 |
| _____ BILLIARDS—Pocket • Carom • Three Cushion *Clive Cottingham, Jr.* | 3.00 |
| _____ CAMPING-OUT 101 Ideas & Activities *Bruno Knobel* | 2.00 |
| _____ COMPLETE GUIDE TO FISHING *Vlad Evanoff* | 2.00 |
| _____ HOW TO IMPROVE YOUR RACQUETBALL *Lubarsky Kaufman & Scagnetti* | 3.00 |
| _____ HOW TO WIN AT POCKET BILLIARDS *Edward D. Knuchell* | 4.00 |
| _____ JOY OF WALKING *Jack Scagnetti* | 3.00 |
| _____ LEARNING & TEACHING SOCCER SKILLS *Eric Worthington* | 3.00 |
| _____ MOTORCYCLING FOR BEGINNERS *I. G. Edmonds* | 3.00 |
| _____ RACQUETBALL FOR WOMEN *Toni Hudson, Jack Scagnetti & Vince Rondone* | 3.00 |
| _____ RACQUETBALL MADE EASY *Steve Lubarsky, Rod Delson & Jack Scagnetti* | 4.00 |
| _____ SECRET OF BOWLING STRIKES *Dawson Taylor* | 3.00 |
| _____ SECRET OF PERFECT PUTTING *Horton Smith & Dawson Taylor* | 3.00 |
| _____ SOCCER—The Game & How to Play It *Gary Rosenthal* | 3.00 |
| _____ STARTING SOCCER *Edward F. Dolan, Jr.* | 3.00 |
| _____ TABLE TENNIS MADE EASY *Johnny Leach* | 2.00 |

## TENNIS LOVERS' LIBRARY

| | |
|---|---|
| _____ BEGINNER'S GUIDE TO WINNING TENNIS *Helen Hull Jacobs* | 2.00 |
| _____ HOW TO BEAT BETTER TENNIS PLAYERS *Loring Fiske* | 4.00 |
| _____ HOW TO IMPROVE YOUR TENNIS—Style, Strategy & Analysis *C. Wilson* | 2.00 |
| _____ INSIDE TENNIS—Techniques of Winning *Jim Leighton* | 3.00 |
| _____ PLAY TENNIS WITH ROSEWALL *Ken Rosewall* | 2.00 |
| _____ PSYCH YOURSELF TO BETTER TENNIS *Dr. Walter A. Luszki* | 2.00 |
| _____ SUCCESSFUL TENNIS *Neale Fraser* | 3.00 |
| _____ TENNIS FOR BEGINNERS, *Dr. H. A. Murray* | 2.00 |
| _____ TENNIS MADE EASY *Joel Brecheen* | 3.00 |
| _____ WEEKEND TENNIS—How to Have Fun & Win at the Same Time *Bill Talbert* | 3.00 |
| _____ WINNING WITH PERCENTAGE TENNIS—Smart Strategy *Jack Lowe* | 2.00 |

## WILSHIRE PET LIBRARY

| | |
|---|---|
| _____ DOG OBEDIENCE TRAINING *Gust Kessopulos* | 5.00 |
| _____ DOG TRAINING MADE EASY & FUN *John W. Kellogg* | 4.00 |
| _____ HOW TO BRING UP YOUR PET DOG *Kurt Unkelbach* | 2.00 |
| _____ HOW TO RAISE & TRAIN YOUR PUPPY *Jeff Griffen* | 3.00 |
| _____ PIGEONS: HOW TO RAISE & TRAIN THEM *William H. Allen, Jr.* | 2.00 |

*The books listed above can be obtained from your book dealer or directly from Melvin Powers. When ordering, please remit 50¢ per book postage & handling. Send for our free illustrated catalog of self-improvement books.*

# Melvin Powers
12015 Sherman Road, No. Hollywood, California 91605

## WILSHIRE HORSE LOVERS' LIBRARY

| | | |
|---|---|---|
| 181-6 | _____ AMATEUR HORSE BREEDER *A. C. Leighton Hardman* | 4.00 |
| 237-5 | _____ AMERICAN QUARTER HORSE IN PICTURES *Margaret Cabell Self* | 3.00 |
| 182-4 | _____ APPALOOSA HORSE *Donna & Bill Richardson* | 5.00 |
| 183-2 | _____ ARABIAN HORSE *Reginald S. Summerhays* | 3.00 |
| 273-1 | _____ ART OF WESTERN RIDING *Suzanne Norton Jones* | 3.00 |
| 184-0 | _____ AT THE HORSE SHOW *Margaret Cabell Self* | 3.00 |
| 186-7 | _____ BACK-YARD HORSE *Peggy Jett Pittinger* | 4.00 |
| 219-7 | _____ BASIC DRESSAGE *Jean Froissard* | 2.00 |
| 284-7 | _____ BEGINNER'S GUIDE TO HORSEBACK RIDING *Sheila Wall* | 2.00 |
| 271-5 | _____ BEGINNER'S GUIDE TO THE WESTERN HORSE *Natlee Kenoyer* | 2.00 |
| 231-6 | _____ BITS—THEIR HISTORY, USE AND MISUSE *Louis Taylor* | 5.00 |
| 272-3 | _____ BREAKING & TRAINING THE DRIVING HORSE *Doris Ganton* | 3.00 |
| 334-7 | _____ BREAKING YOUR HORSE'S BAD HABITS *W. Dayton Sumner* | 5.00 |
| 235-9 | _____ COMPLETE TRAINING OF HORSE AND RIDER *Colonel Alois Podhajsky* | 5.00 |
| 281-2 | _____ DISORDERS OF THE HORSE & WHAT TO DO ABOUT THEM *E. Hanauer* | 3.00 |
| 028-3 | _____ DOG TRAINING MADE EASY & FUN *John W. Kellogg* | 4.00 |
| 187-5 | _____ DRESSAGE—A Study of the Finer Points in Riding *Henry Wynmalen* | 5.00 |
| 393-2 | _____ DRIVE ON *Doris Ganton* | 7.00 |
| 242-1 | _____ DRIVING HORSES *Sallie Walrond* | 3.00 |
| 316-9 | _____ ENDURANCE RIDING *Ann Hyland* | 2.00 |
| 188-3 | _____ EQUITATION *Jean Froissard* | 5.00 |
| 189-1 | _____ FIRST AID FOR HORSES *Dr. Charles H. Denning, Jr.* | 3.00 |
| 190-5 | _____ FUN OF RAISING A COLT *Rubye & Frank Griffith* | 3.00 |
| 191-3 | _____ FUN ON HORSEBACK *Margaret Caball Self* | 4.00 |
| 329-0 | _____ GYMKHANA GAMES *Natlee Kenoyer* | 2.00 |
| 302-9 | _____ HORSE DISEASES—Causes, Symptoms & Treatment *Dr. H. G. Belschner* | 5.00 |
| 192-1 | _____ HORSE OWNER'S CONCISE GUIDE *Elsie V. Hanauer* | 2.00 |
| 193-X | _____ HORSE SELECTION & CARE FOR BEGINNERS *George H. Conn* | 5.00 |
| 229-4 | _____ HORSEBACK RIDING FOR BEGINNERS *Louis Taylor* | 4.00 |
| 194-8 | _____ HORSEBACK RIDING MADE EASY & FUN *Sue Henderson Coen* | 5.00 |
| 195-6 | _____ HORSES—Their Selection, Care & Handling *Margaret Cabell Self* | 4.00 |
| 279-0 | _____ HOW TO BUY A BETTER HORSE & SELL THE HORSE YOU OWN | 3.00 |
| 280-4 | _____ HOW TO ENJOY YOUR QUARTER HORSE *Willard H. Porter* | 3.00 |
| 253-7 | _____ HUNTER IN PICTURES *Margaret Cabell Self* | 2.00 |
| 241-3 | _____ ILLUSTRATED BOOK OF THE HORSE *S. Sidney* (8½″ × 11″) | 10.00 |
| 210-3 | _____ ILLUSTRATED HORSE MANAGEMENT—400 Illustrations *Dr. E. Mayhew* | 6.00 |
| 240-5 | _____ ILLUSTRATED HORSE TRAINING *Captain M. H. Hayes* | 5.00 |
| 196-4 | _____ ILLUSTRATED HORSEBACK RIDING FOR BEGINNERS *Jeanne Mellin* | 3.00 |
| 197-2 | _____ JUMPING—Learning & Teaching *Jean Froissard* | 4.00 |
| 294-4 | _____ KNOW ALL ABOUT HORSES *Harry Disston* | 3.00 |
| 308-8 | _____ LAME HORSE Cause, Symptoms & Treatment *Dr. James R. Rooney* | 5.00 |
| 202-2 | _____ LAW & YOUR HORSE *Edward H. Greene* | 5.00 |
| 198-0 | _____ LIPIZZANERS & THE SPANISH RIDING SCHOOL *W. Reuter* (4¼″ × 6″) | 5.00 |
| 359-2 | _____ MANUAL OF HORSEMANSHIP *Harold Black* | 5.00 |
| 274-X | _____ MOVIE HORSES—The Fascinating Techniques of Training *Anthony Amaral* | 2.00 |
| 199-9 | _____ POLICE HORSES *Judith Campbell* | 2.00 |
| 239-1 | _____ PRACTICAL GUIDE TO HORSESHOEING | 5.00 |
| 292-8 | _____ PRACTICAL GUIDE TO OWNING YOUR OWN HORSE *Steven D. Price* | 3.00 |
| 247-2 | _____ PRACTICAL HORSE PSYCHOLOGY *Moyra Williams* | 4.00 |
| 200-6 | _____ PROBLEM HORSES Guide for Curing Serious Behavior Habits *Summerhays* | 3.00 |
| 333-9 | _____ REINSMAN OF THE WEST—BRIDLES & BITS *Ed Connell* | 5.00 |
| 225-1 | _____ RESCHOOLING THE THOROUGHBRED *Peggy Jett Pittinger* | 3.00 |
| 252-9 | _____ RIDE WESTERN *Louis Taylor* | 5.00 |
| 201-4 | _____ SCHOOLING YOUR YOUNG HORSE *George Wheatley* | 3.00 |
| 258-8 | _____ STABLE MANAGEMENT FOR THE OWNER-GROOM *George Wheatley* | 4.00 |
| 297-9 | _____ STALLION MANAGEMENT—A Guide for Stud Owners *A. C. Hardman* | 5.00 |
| 227-8 | _____ TEACHING YOUR HORSE TO JUMP *W. J. Froud* | 2.00 |
| 335-5 | _____ TRAINING YOUR HORSE TO SHOW *Neale Haley* | 5.00 |
| 255-3 | _____ TREATING COMMON DISEASES OF YOUR HORSE *Dr. George H. Conn* | 5.00 |
| 230-8 | _____ TREATING HORSE AILMENTS *G. W. Serth* | 2.00 |
| 360-6 | _____ YOU AND YOUR PONY *Pepper Mainwaring Healey* (8½″ × 11″) | 6.00 |
| 251-0 | _____ YOUR FIRST HORSE *George C. Saunders, M.D.* | 3.00 |
| 331-2 | _____ YOUR PONY BOOK *Hermann Wiederhold* | 2.00 |

*The books listed above can be obtained from your book dealer or directly from
Melvin Powers. When ordering, please remit 50¢ per book postage & handling.
Send for our free illustrated catalog of self-improvement books.*

# Melvin Powers
12015 Sherman Road, No. Hollywood, California 91605

*Notes*